If you have ever prayed, "Thy kingdom come, . . ." then *Living in the Overlap* is *must* reading for you. Sharing his own journey, yet in a strong biblical framework, Steve invites us all to enter, understand, and grow in the Kingdom of God . . . here and now! Thanks, Steve.

—**Terry Meeuwsen**
Co-host, *The 700 Club*

The good news of God's kingdom—the simple yet central key to our Christian faith—is set forth with clarity and joy in Schaefer's timely book. For those of us seeking to be reminded and revived by the blessed truth of God's purposes, *Living in the Overlap* is a welcome cup of cool, fresh water.

—**Dr. Terry Lindvall**
C. S. Lewis Professor of Communication and Christian Thought
Virginia Wesleyan College

With wonderful clarity and insight, Schaefer examines key issues in the Christian life: healing, temptation, evangelism, loving others, staying focused, and more. . . . Ample Scripture, careful explanations and helpful illustrations make this book painfully convicting, yet delightful to read. Pastors and disciples will welcome this book.

—**David Mundt**
CBA Retailers + Resources magazine

LIVING
IN THE
OVERLAP

HOW JESUS' KINGDOM PROCLAMATION CAN TRANSFORM YOUR WORLD

LIVING
IN THE
OVERLAP

STEVE SCHAEFER

WinePress **WP** Publishing™

WinePress Publishing (PO Box 428, Enumclaw, WA 98022) functions only as book publisher. As such, the ultimate design, content, editorial accuracy, and views expressed or implied in this work are those of the author.

All Scripture quotations in chapters one through ten, unless otherwise noted, are taken from the *Holy Bible, New International Version*®, NIV®. (North American Edition) Copyright © 1973, 1978, 1984 by Biblica, Inc.™ Used by permission of Zondervan. All rights reserved worldwide. All Scripture quotations in chapter eleven are the author's paraphrases unless otherwise noted. WWW. ZONDERVAN.COM

Scripture quotations marked NASB are taken from the *New American Standard Bible,* © 1960, 1963, 1968, 1971, 1972, 1973, 1975, 1977, 1995 by The Lockman Foundation. Used by permission.

Scripture quotations marked THE MESSAGE are taken from *The Message Bible* © 1993 by Eugene N. Peterson, NavPress, PO Box 35001, Colorado Springs, CO 80935, 4th printing in USA 1994. Published in association with the literary agency—Alive Comm. PO Box 49068, Colorado Springs, CO 80949. Used by permission.

The author gratefully acknowledges permission to quote from the following:

The Message of Matthew (BST) by Michael Green. Copyright © 2000 by Michael Green. Used by permission of InterVarsity Press, P. O. Box 1400, Downers Grove, IL 60515. www.ivpress.com and Inter-Varsity Press, Norton Street, Nottingham NG7 3HR, England. All Rights Reserved. Used by permission.

"Joy," by S. S. Smalley, "Exodus," by P. E. Enns, and "Jesus Christ" by I. H. Marshall, *New Dictionary of Biblical Theology,* ed. T. Desmond Alexander, Brian S. Rosner, D. A. Carson, Graeme Goldsworthy, InterVarsity Press, 2000. All Rights Reserved. Used by permission.

"The Return of Christ," by Richard N. Longenecker, and "Living Between Two Ages," by James Robert Ross, *A Guide to Biblical Prophecy,* ed. Carl E. Armerding and W. Ward Gasque, Wipf and Stock, 1977, 1989. All Rights Reserved. Used by permission.

3 Crucial Questions about Spiritual Warfare, Clinton E. Arnold, Baker Academic, a division of Baker Publishing Group, 1997. All Rights Reserved. Used by permission.

"Theology Implications of Radical Discipleship," attributed to David Claydon and published in *Let the Earth Hear His Voice,* the 1974 Lausanne Congress, pages 1294–95. All Rights Reserved. Used by permission.

The Disease of the Health and Wealth Gospels, Gordon D. Fee, Regent College Publishing, 1985, 2006. All Rights Reserved. Used by permission.

"An Evangelism Manifesto," *1977 General Synod Minutes,* Reformed Church Press, 475 Riverside Drive, New York, NY, 10115, USA, All Rights Reserved. Used by permission.

ISBN 13: 978-1-57921-968-0
ISBN 10: 1-57921-968-3
Library of Congress Catalog Card Number: 2008927897

Printed in China.

APC-FT041901

CONTENTS

To Mom and Dad

ACKNOWLEDGMENTS

The French philosopher Blaise Pascal discouraged authors from using the phrase "my book." Other people generally make such significant contributions to the author's work, he said, that the phrase "our book" is preferable. Writing this book has convinced me that he had a point.

I am greatly indebted to the following people who provided valuable feedback on various drafts of the manuscript (or portions of it): the late Dr. Charles L. Holman, Dr. Dennis E. Hensley, Dr. John Rea, Dr. Heath A. Thomas, Dr. Gary S. Greig, Virginia J. Muir, Bob Hostetler, Nancy I. Sanders, Rev. James Blaine, Dr. Terry Lindvall, Ken Bender, Jamisson Fowler, Carol Henry Geddes, Kim Hicks, Mac McTernen, Teri Phoenix, Dr. Glenn Phoenix, Kris Schaefer, Dave Schaefer, Rosalie Brown, David Brown, Shelia Carter, Don Nixon, and Jody Hanford. Their perceptive suggestions improved the book considerably and saved it from many weaknesses in style and content. There were times when I did not choose to make suggested alterations, and many subsequent changes have since taken place over many years, so that any remaining weaknesses are purely my own fault!

I also want to thank Athena Dean, Adam Cothes, George Dillaway, Craig Bubeck, and the WinePress team for shepherding the book through the publication process.

Likewise, my thanks to those authors and publishers who have allowed me to quote from their publications. One need only browse through the Endnotes section to see how much this book owes to the insights of others. Periodically, in that same section, I have recommended certain works that have helped me understand various topics.

There's a larger sense in which I must acknowledge the contributions of many more people. This book deals with discoveries made along a spiritual journey; therefore, in a real way, those family members and friends who have helped me in this journey have also participated in this book. Some helped introduce me to the Bible when I was a child; others helped introduce me to Jesus when I was a teenager; still others have subsequently supported me in my Christian walk. Some friends do not share my Christian beliefs, but have consistently demonstrated that people who differ on foundational beliefs can express their differences with deep affection and respect. To all these family members and friends—especially those who have allowed me to tell their stories within these pages, and those who have supported this project with their prayers—I give my thanks.

Deepest thanks, however, go to my parents, Marion and Glenn Schaefer, whose love and support have been a source of strength not only during the writing of the manuscript, but throughout my life. To them I gratefully dedicate our book.

PART ONE:
WHAT IS THE OVERLAP?

> There are plenty of prophets and kings who would have given their right arm to see what you are seeing but never got so much as a glimpse, to hear what you are hearing but never got so much as a whisper.
> —Luke 10:24, THE MESSAGE

Jesus spoke these words to his inner circle. However, I have a hunch that those venerable old prophets and kings would be jealous of you and me, too.

Why? Because we live during the time of the overlap.

And what is the overlap? Part One deals with that question. I've become convinced that one of the keys to living an effective Christian life is to understand the overlap. It brings a much-needed balance and focus to our lifestyles, our ministries, and our understanding of Scripture.

To become familiar with the overlap, we must take two unusual trips: one through the world of the Old Testament prophets and their predictions, and the second through the world of Jesus and the New Testament writers, who reveal the surprising fulfillment of those predictions. I've found these two trips to be well worth taking. I trust you'll feel the same.

CHAPTER ONE

THE OVERLAP—
OLD TESTAMENT
PREDICTIONS

The only thing more shocking than the message was the messenger himself. Jaws dropped and blood boiled as the maverick rabbi spouted his incendiary pronouncements:

> I tell you the truth, the tax collectors and the prostitutes are entering the kingdom of God ahead of you.
> —Matthew 21:31b

> If I drive out demons by the finger of God, then the kingdom of God has come to you.
> —Luke 11:20

> I tell you the truth, no one can see the kingdom of God unless he is born again.
> —John 3:3

The young Galilean seemed to function as a self-proclaimed expert on all matters related to the kingdom of God: what it was like, why he commanded the pivotal role in it, how to enter it, who would miss out on it. In fact, every aspect of Jesus' life and ministry—his miracles, his

1

parables, his exorcisms, his sermons, even his meals and one-on-one conversations—came together with laser-like focus to accomplish a single goal: to inaugurate and announce the long-awaited kingdom of God.

As theologian Carl F. H. Henry acknowledges,

> No subject was more frequently on the lips of Jesus Christ than the kingdom. He proclaimed kingdom truth with a constant, exuberant joy. It appears as the central theme of His preaching. To delete His kingdom references, parabolic and nonparabolic, would be to excise most of His words. The concept "kingdom of God" or "kingdom of heaven" is heard repeatedly from His lips and it colors all of His works.[1]

What exactly was Jesus' kingdom message? I confess that, although I grew up in the church, I spent years being largely clueless concerning what Jesus taught about the kingdom of God. And I had no idea what the overlap was or how it related to the kingdom. It wasn't until I took a New Testament theology class my junior year of college that the pieces started coming together.

The course sparked a lifelong fascination with the Bible's teaching about the kingdom and the overlap. My subsequent theological studies in graduate school added fuel to the fire as I explored the practical implications of these themes. And as I talked with friends from various denominational backgrounds, I discovered that many Christians admitted to a certain haziness when it came to their understanding of these realities. This is unfortunate, because these themes are at the core of Jesus' teaching.

The Kingdom Jesus Proclaimed

Before we can understand the overlap and its relationship to the kingdom of God, we must understand two things about the kingdom Jesus proclaimed. First, the word "kingdom" as used by Jesus does not refer primarily to a geographical territory but to God's sovereign rule. As New Testament scholar Craig L. Blomberg explains,

The Greek word for "kingdom" is *basileia*, translating an underlying Hebrew *malkuth*. In both languages, "kingdom" refers more to a power than to a place, more to a reign than to a realm. "Kingship" might better render the concept in English or, as Ben Witherington likes to translate it, "the dominion of God."[2]

Second, the kingdom preached by Jesus was the end-time kingdom predicted by the Old Testament prophets. Theologians often describe it as *eschatological*.

ESCHATOLOGY

The Greek word *eschatos* means "last." Therefore, if something is eschatological, it is something that, according to Scripture, pertains to "last things," or the end times.

There is a general sense in which Scripture declares God to be king of the earth, as its creator and sustainer.[3] There is another sense in which Scripture reveals that God was the king of the nation of Israel, a king who was to rule through human kings (though the Old Testament depicts a tragic history in which most of the human kings fell short of fulfilling this expectation).[4]

But there is yet another sense in which Scripture discusses God's kingship.[5] The Old Testament prophets predicted that in a future age God's ultimate kingship would manifest itself in what came to be called *the kingdom of God* (or its synonym, *kingdom of heaven*),[6] eradicating all evil and restoring the world to an Eden-like paradise.

> The Old Testament prophets predicted that in a future age God's ultimate kingship would manifest itself in what came to be called *the kingdom of God*, eradicating all evil and restoring the world to an Eden-like paradise.

3

By Jesus' day, Jewish teachers had come to divide history into two ages, the present age and the age to come, a view affirmed by Jesus.[7] The present age was dominated by the Evil One. In it, God's enemies triumphed. It was an age of death, disease, sin, and conflict.

THE AGE TO COME ≠ NEW AGE

The Bible's teaching about the age to come has nothing to do with current "New Age" teachings. The "New Age" movement distorts the truth by linking biblical terms with heretical concepts. Many well-meaning people have been led astray by this dangerous and deceptive movement.

However, God's people looked forward to the age to come when this end-time kingdom would arrive. This was the kingdom proclaimed by Jesus. [8] The age to come was so closely identified with this eschatological kingdom of God that the two terms became virtual synonyms.

As Diagram #1 shows, the age to come would be ushered in by the eschatological day of the Lord (sometimes called "the day" or "that day" by the prophets).

Diagram #1

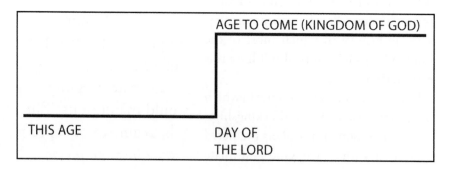

The prophets describe the day of the Lord with fearsome imagery.[9] It would be a time of sudden destruction and judgment. The sun and moon would go dark. The earth would shake, the heavens would tremble, and God's enemies would be judged by fire and the sword.

The day of the Lord was expected to come as suddenly as a thunderbolt. It was not envisioned as a twenty-four-hour day but as a cataclysmic period of limited duration, giving way to the kingdom of God.

The Kingdom Dartboard

What will life be like in this eschatological kingdom? A survey of the Old Testament prophets reveals eighteen key characteristics represented in a diagram I call The Kingdom Dartboard (See Diagram #2).

Kingdom Characteristic:
Messiah Will Rule

"In love a throne will be established," predicted Isaiah the prophet, "in faithfulness a man will sit on it—one from the house of David—one who in judging seeks justice and speeds the cause of righteousness" (Isaiah 16:5). This is one of many prophecies concerning the *Messiah* (Hebrew for "Anointed One"), who would not only be a descendant of David but whose reign would surpass David's.[10]

Micah predicted that he would be born in David's hometown of Bethlehem. Ezekiel predicted that the Messiah (so closely identified with his ancestor that Ezekiel calls him David) would tend the nation like a shepherd.

HISTORICAL BACKGROUND—THE KINGS AND THEIR KINGDOMS

David was Israel's second king. He followed Saul, the statuesque spear-chucker whose reign and life had ended in disgrace. David, the former shepherd boy, had expanded Israel's territory and unified the nation. He was "a man after God's own heart"[11] who shepherded the nation into its golden period of prosperity.

David's son and successor Solomon initially seemed poised to leave an even greater legacy than his father. Over a twenty year period he built the magnificent Jerusalem temple and his own sumptuous palace, both from boatloads of gold and forests of cedars, not to mention the sweat of thirty-thousand conscripted laborers. But his weakness for women (seven hundred wives and three hundred concubines!) who turned his heart to their foreign gods, plus his heavy taxation and conscription policies, led to the split of the kingdom after his death.

The ten northern tribes revolted and broke away, leaving Solomon's son Rehoboam ruling over a remnant of only two southern tribes. The Northern kingdom retained the name Israel and was eventually crushed by bloodthirsty Assyria in 722 B.C. The Babylonians vanquished the Southern kingdom of Judah in 586 B.C. They reduced Jerusalem to rubble and hauled off thousands of its residents into exile. Persia defeated Babylonia, allowing the exiles to return and rebuild. They rebuilt Jerusalem and for centuries awaited the coming of the messianic king.

Kingdom Characteristics:
Justice and Righteousness ❖ *Wicked Destroyed* ❖ *Love*

In contrast to many of Israel and Judah's kings, the Messiah would rule with *justice and righteousness*.[12] In fact these two traits, so often paired like twins in prophetic speeches, would characterize everyone in the Messiah's kingdom as well. In contrast to the injustice (like oppressing the poor) and unrighteousness (like following false gods) that plagued Israel and Judah before their respective falls, the future kingdom of God would be a kingdom where justice lived in the desert and righteousness lived in the fertile field, blanketing the entire nation.

The coming of this kingdom would mean the *destruction of the wicked*,[13] God's enemies, at the day of the Lord, leaving only those who would submit to God's kingship and that of his Anointed One.

God's motivation for establishing this kingdom was his *love*,[14] and it would be a kingdom where the people would love God and each other. In this kingdom God's love was not just reserved for his chosen people of Israel, but for all people.

HISTORICAL BACKGROUND—GOD'S LOVE AND HIS COVENANTS

God's love was the driving force behind the whole Old Testament story. Sin had entered the world with the first couple in Eden, rupturing the relationship between the creator and his people, resulting in physical and spiritual death. God then launched a plan to remedy this tragedy, a plan that involved a series of covenants with his chosen people.

He chose Abraham to be the father of a great nation and made a covenant with him, giving him and his descendants the land of Canaan, promising that his descendants would be numberless and that the world would be blessed through him.[15]

Seeking relief from famine, Abraham's descendants settled in Egypt, eventually multiplying into twelve mammoth tribes. Egypt's king, or Pharaoh, enslaved them and forced them into backbreaking labor on his favorite building projects. God chose Moses to lead them out of captivity by making a way through the sea. Like a pair of elevator doors the waters miraculously separated, creating a dry path out of Egypt for Moses and the masses, then slammed together to entomb the pursuing soldiers. After their liberation (known as the Exodus from Egypt) God made a covenant with Moses and the tribes, pledging that they would be a kingdom of priests and a holy nation.[16] He gave them the Torah (or law), which they as the covenant nation were to obey.

> God's love was the driving force behind the whole Old Testament story.

After eventually conquering and settling the promised land and living through a chaotic period of being governed by regional judges, the twelve tribes decided they wanted to be unified under a king. God granted their wish and Saul became king. After Saul's death, God made a covenant with David, pledging that David's descendant would reign over an eternal kingdom.[17]

Each of these covenants advanced God's plan to deal once and for all with the tragedy of sin and to bless the world. But as the kingdom split and as Israel and Judah crumbled, it was obvious that the people and their kings had not lived up to the required Torah obedience.

Kingdom Characteristics:
New Covenant ❖ *Intimacy with God*

During the turbulent period spanning the divided kingdom, the Babylonian exile, the return, and the early days of resettlement, God sent his prophets to call the people back to holy living. Some of these prophets revealed that a *new covenant* was on the way.[18] It would be the charter of the eschatological kingdom of God, the culmination of his loving plan.

In a celebrated oracle, the prophet Jeremiah revealed some key aspects of this new covenant:

> "The time is coming," declares the LORD, "when I will make a new covenant with the house of Israel and with the house of Judah. It will not be like the covenant I made with their forefathers when I took them by the hand to lead them out of Egypt, because they broke my covenant, though I was a husband to them," declares the LORD. "This is the covenant I will make with the house of Israel after that time," declares the LORD. "I will put my law in their minds and write it on their hearts. I will be their God and they will be my people. No longer will a man teach his neighbor, or a man his brother, saying 'Know the LORD,' because they will all know me, from the least of them to the greatest," declares the LORD. "For I will forgive their wickedness and will remember their sins no more."
>
> —Jeremiah 31:31–34

In the kingdom, all God's people would know him. The Hebrew verb that means "to know" in English signifies the kind of intimacy that a faithful husband and wife enjoy. Thus the new covenant pledged *intimacy with God,* which would transform the way the average person would relate to him.[19] In Old Testament times the average Israelite's relationship with God was largely "secondhand." God generally dealt with Israel as a nation rather than dealing directly with each individual. He related to the Israelites through intermediaries.

He would speak to prophets who would then represent him by relaying his message to the nation. Conversely, the people would go to priests, who would represent them to God by offering sacrifices. The people could not go directly into God's presence. In fact, only the high priest could enter the holiest part of the temple, the Holy of Holies, where God was present, and that was only on one day each year, the Day of Atonement.[20] The people's relationship to God was something like the average American's relationship to the President of the United States. Most of us cannot just saunter into the Oval Office whenever we wish to have a chat. In the same way, the average Israelite could never enter the Lord's throne room, the Holy of Holies, to approach God. He or she had to rely on the designated intermediary.

> The average Israelite could never enter the Lord's throne room, the Holy of Holies, to approach God.

However, under the new covenant, that would change. As biblical scholar O. Palmer Robertson reveals:

> But under the new covenant, no mediator would be necessary for the communication of the will of God to his people. From the smallest to the greatest, all would know the Lord, im-mediately [sic]*. . . . The immediate knowledge of God by each and every participant of the covenant gives expression to the idea of the essence of the covenant relationship which runs throughout Scripture. What is the point of the covenant? It is to establish a oneness between God and his people. That oneness which was interrupted by the entrance of sin must be reconstituted through the covenant of redemption. "I shall be your God and you shall be my people," functioning as the central unifying theme of the covenant, underscores the role of oneness of the essence of the goal of the covenant.[21]

Kingdom Characteristics:
Forgiveness of Sins ❖ Newness

God would also *forgive their sins* and remember them no more.[22] The phrase "remember their sins no more" is significant. It doesn't merely refer to a lack of recalling sins. When Scripture says that God remembered something, it

---

* Robertson's rendering of the hyphenated "im-mediately" is intentional, referring to being "without a mediator."

implies that he needed to take further action to make things right. Therefore, as theologian William J. Dumbrell points out:

> God thus "remembered" Noah and caused the waters to abate (Genesis 8:1). God also "remembered" Hannah (1 Samuel 1:19), and the promise of a son became an actuality. . . . In Jeremiah 31:34, for God not to remember means that no action in the new age will need to be taken against sin. The forgiveness of which this verse speaks is so comprehensive that sin has finally been dealt with in the experience of the nation and individual believer. [23]

The new covenant that brings about this comprehensive forgiveness is representative of a wholesale *newness* that would characterize the eschatological kingdom.[24]

"I am doing a new thing," God told Isaiah. He would give his people a new heart and a new spirit. Zion would have a new name. Creation itself would be renewed when God would create new heavens and a new earth.

Kingdom Characteristic: *Spirit Poured Out*

Furthermore, in this new age *God's Spirit would be poured out* on all kinds of people regardless of gender, age, or station in life.[25] In Old Testament times most people had not experienced the empowering of the Holy Spirit. As biblical studies professor James M. Hamilton, Jr. says,

> The Old Testament teaches that God was *with* His people by dwelling *among* them in the temple rather than *in* them as under the new covenant. . . . The concern in the Old Testament is with God's presence with the nation, not with individual covenant members possessing the Spirit. . . . On the contrary, each time the Old Testament describes someone as having the Spirit, it does so precisely to mark that person out from other old covenant believers.[26]

The Holy Spirit—God himself, the third person of the Trinity— would sometimes come upon certain select individuals to empower them for certain tasks. But, usually, this empowering was temporary. For example, Saul was empowered to lead the men of Israel and Judah into battle, but later the Spirit left him.[27] And most people would never experience such empowering at all, even temporarily.

We see this demonstrated when Moses assembled seventy of the elders in the tent outside the camp. The Spirit came upon them and they began prophesying. However, two elders, Eldad and Medad, had remained in the camp. The Spirit came upon them, and they also began to prophesy. Joshua thought this reflected a threat to Moses' leadership, and he begged Moses to stop them.

> The Holy Spirit would sometimes come upon certain select individuals to empower them for certain tasks. But, usually, this empowering was temporary.

Moses responded, "Are you jealous for my sake? I wish that all the LORD's people were prophets and that the LORD would put his Spirit on them!"[28] He could only wish for a day when all God's people would be empowered by the Spirit. But he was never to see that day.

Kingdom Characteristics:
All Nations Included ❖ *God's Presence* ❖ *God's Glory Revealed*

What Moses wished to see would be experienced by ordinary people when the kingdom of God arrived. And this kingdom would not just include physical descendants of Abraham. One of the most startling predictions was that *all nations would be included* in the messianic kingdom. [29] During a time when Gentile nations such as Assyria and Babylonia were threatening Israel and Judah, this was a shocking assertion. But Isaiah predicted that in this eschatological kingdom all nations would stream to the mountain of the Lord and that the temple would be a house of prayer for all nations.

God would be present[30] with his people forever in this temple, and *God's glory would be revealed*[31] to all humankind.

Kingdom Characteristics:
Peace (Shalom) ❖ Physical Wholeness ❖ Safety and Security

The kingdom of God would be a kingdom of *peace.*[32] Nations would not go to war, but would beat their swords into plowshares. The wolf and lamb would feed together in this eschatological kingdom ruled by the Messiah, who would also be known as the Prince of Peace (according to Isaiah) and who (according to Micah) would be peace personified.

And the peace of this kingdom would not just mean the absence of conflict. The Hebrew word for "peace" (*shalom*) signifies wholeness and harmony in every aspect of one's being. Therefore, the kingdom would be characterized by *physical wholeness,* where the eyes of the blind would see, the ears of the deaf would be unstopped, the lame would leap like deer, and the mute would shout for joy.[33]

> The Hebrew word for "peace" (*shalom*) signifies wholeness and harmony in every aspect of one's being.

The kingdom of peace would be a kingdom of absolute *safety and security* in which the infant could play near the cobra's hole and where no lion or ferocious beast would live.[34]

Kingdom Characteristic:
Death Destroyed

Some prophets even offered tantalizing hints that the *shalom* of the kingdom might actually extend to people after death. The prevailing belief was that when life on earth is over, people went to *sheol,* the shadowy place of the dead.

But some prophets began whispering about a future resurrection. In certain cases this was obviously a metaphorical way to view the future restoration of Israel. Nevertheless, some enigmatic oracles seemed to indicate more than that. They fanned hopes that at least some individuals could enjoy some sort of resurrection when the kingdom arrived, that in some way *death would be destroyed.*[35]

"He will swallow up death forever," predicted Isaiah (25:8), who also prophesied, "Your dead will live; their bodies will rise" (26:19). "Multitudes who sleep in the dust of the earth will awake: some to everlasting life, others to shame and everlasting contempt," predicted Daniel (12:2). Were these metaphors that stood for another reality, such as a new beginning for the nation of Israel? Or, did they hint at a literal resurrection of individuals? If the latter, who would be raised? Only certain people who had died at a certain place and time under certain conditions? Or, would there be a general resurrection? Such questions would be raised and debated generations later, though they generally went unexplored during the time of the prophets.

Kingdom Characteristics:
Abundant Provision ❖ *Joy*

But though the afterlife remained ambiguous, other aspects of the *shalom* of the eschatological kingdom were more palpable. The renewed Eden-like creation would yield *abundant provision*, in which the crops would grow so fast the reaper would be overtaken by the one plowing, and the planter by the one treading grapes. New wine would flow from the mountains, and the hills would drip with milk. On Mount Zion, God himself would prepare a feast of wine and meat.[36]

"They will come and shout for joy on the heights of Zion; they will rejoice in the bounty of the Lord," Jeremiah predicted (31:12). The result of the kingdom blessings would be dizzying *joy*.[37] "Gladness and joy will overtake them" (Isaiah 35:10; 51:11). Joy would not just be an emotion felt by the inhabitants of the kingdom; it is personified as a pursuer conquering its quarry like a cop flattening a fleeing bank robber with a flying tackle.

As Old Testament scholar John N. Oswalt says,

> This is the apex of the eschatological vision: a day when the people of God can be set free from their own sins and the sins of others, when they can come home to their God and be fully restored to his image, when a lifelong struggle to avoid grief and pain will be ended in their being overwhelmed by gladness and joy.[38]

Waiting for Fulfillment

This then was the hope of those who returned from exile to rebuild their nation, the people who around this time began to be known as Jews. The expectation was that soon after the return of the exiles from Babylon the kingdom of God would be inaugurated, resulting in a world in which every one of these predicted characteristics would become reality.

But years passed . . . then decades . . . then centuries. The Greeks replaced the Persians as the dominant world power. Then the Romans replaced the Greeks, ruling the Jews with an iron fist.

Four hundred years after the final prophet, Malachi, had spoken,[39] God's people still longed for the arrival of the eschatological kingdom. Had God forgotten? Had the prophets been wrong? They labored to keep the hope alive.

Then one day in David's town, Bethlehem, a baby's cry pierced the air. The messianic king had arrived and the long-awaited kingdom of God would dawn. But it would dawn with a surprising twist, in a way no one had anticipated. . . .

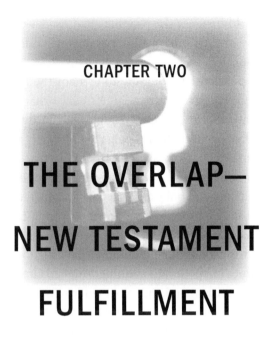

CHAPTER TWO

THE OVERLAP—
NEW TESTAMENT
FULFILLMENT

I baptize you with water. But one more powerful than I will
come, the thongs of whose sandals I am not worthy to untie.
He will baptize you with the Holy Spirit and with fire.

—Luke 3:16

These words rang out in the desert, proclaimed by a prophet named
John who was baptizing repentant multitudes in the Jordan River.
But he was not one of the Old Testament prophets making a long-term
prediction about the coming kingdom of God. Instead, he announced
that the kingdom was just around the corner, to be inaugurated by one
of his contemporaries.[1]

Fire was known to be symbolic of God's judgment, the kind of judgment that the day of the Lord would bring. The Holy Spirit was to be
a blessing of the eschatological kingdom. Could John be right? After
decades of Roman subjugation, after centuries of dashed hopes, would
the Messiah actually appear in their day to cast off their shackles and
establish the long-anticipated kingdom?

Then the man of whom John had spoken appeared—Jesus. And he
was indeed announcing the kingdom. People naturally expected him to

echo the same bold imagery the prophets had used—either the violent images of the day of the Lord, or the extravagantly Eden-like images of the kingdom itself.

Imagine their puzzlement when he told them the kingdom is like a tiny mustard seed that grows into a large tree, or that it is like a pinch of yeast mixed into a large clump of dough.[2] It's hard to envision more benign or mundane images than these. How could a majestic reign—ushered in by earthquakes and slaughter—be like a seed or yeast?

The confusion only deepened with his seemingly contradictory proclamations. Sometimes he spoke as if the kingdom were to arrive in the future. (He told his disciples to pray for it to come, for example, and he told them that some people within earshot would not taste death before they saw the Son of Man coming in his kingdom.)[3]

But at other times he spoke as if the kingdom had already arrived. (For instance he said that his exorcisms were evidence that the kingdom had come, and he said that tax collectors and prostitutes were now entering it.)[4] How could these apparently incongruous assertions be reconciled with each other and with the predictions of God's prophets?

The Overlap

The key is to recognize that Jesus was revealing a new truth about the kingdom, a truth not foretold by the prophets. He was revealing that it would arrive in two separate stages.[5] His first coming brought the first stage; his second coming will bring the second. Thus there is a sense in which the kingdom will one day arrive in all its fullness following the day of the Lord, just as everyone was expecting.

> Jesus was revealing a new truth about the kingdom, a truth not foretold by the prophets. He was revealing that it would arrive in two separate stages.

But there is another sense in which the kingdom has already arrived. It may seem like an almost invisible beginning, like a puny seed lying unnoticed in the dirt, but it will one day be present in a way that is impossible to overlook, like a gigantic tree. Therefore, though our

16

diagram of the two ages is correct as far as it goes, it does not go far enough. We need to make an important adjustment.

As Diagram #3 reveals, although the present age continues until Christ's second coming,[6] the age to come and the corresponding kingdom of God began with Christ's first coming. Therefore, the two ages exist simultaneously between the first and second comings of Christ. They overlap.

Diagram #3

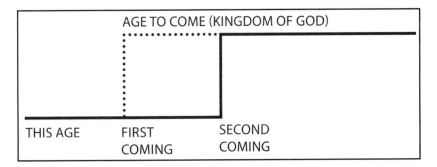

The implications of this overlap are monumental. It means that right now in this present age we can begin to experience some blessings of the age to come (at least to some degree), even though we won't fully experience all the kingdom blessings until Christ comes again and the present age ends.[7]

The Gospel of John emphasizes this in a way that is easy to miss in most English translations of the Bible. Although this Gospel mentions the kingdom, it does not use the term as extensively as the other three Gospels do. Instead, it stresses the theme of "eternal life." I had long assumed that eternal life refers mainly to life that goes on forever with God. But though this idea is present, it is not the primary meaning. The Greek word for "eternal" (*aiōnios*) comes from the Greek word for "age" (*aiōn*). Eternal life, then, is literally "the life of the age." Thus New Testament scholar Raymond E. Brown points out that "for John 'eternal life' is the life of the Age to Come given here and now. . . . The fourth evangelist, who reports little concerning the kingdom, seems to have taken an expression associated with the kingdom, namely 'life' or

> Eternal life, therefore, is life in which blessings of the age to come can be enjoyed here and now.

'eternal life,' and have made it a main theme of the Gospel."[8]

Biblical scholar R. V. G. Tasker points out that "although the idea of duration is not absent from the word *aiōnios*, it is the different *quality* of life that it stresses. . . . 'Eternal life' is life characteristic of that final age, which Christ inaugurated."[9] Eternal life, therefore, is life in which blessings of the age to come can be enjoyed here and now.

The overlap of the ages may not be a major topic of conversation among most churchgoers. But it is a seminal and frequent topic among biblical scholars.[10]

The Kingdom: "Already" and "Not Yet"

As such scholars reveal, the overlap of the ages has created a situation where the kingdom of God can be described as both "already" and "not yet." Theologians sometimes express this by saying that the kingdom was "inaugurated" at Jesus' first coming (making some kingdom blessings available now) and will be "consummated" at his second coming (when all the kingdom blessings will be poured out in all their fullness).[11]

A couple of analogies might help clarify our already/not-yet status in the overlap. Theologian Oscar Cullmann compares our situation to that of an army that has won the decisive battle in a war.[12] The war may still rage, but it is only a matter of time until the enemy surrenders (Victory Day). We saw a comparable situation during World War II. After the Allies invaded France on D-Day, their victory was assured; yet the Nazis could still attack until they were finally forced to surrender. After D-Day there was an "already" and "not yet" aspect to the Allied victory. In the same way, we live in a time when the Evil One has lost the pivotal battle, yet still has power to strike. Because of Jesus' death, resurrection, and ascension, the Evil One's ultimate destruction and God's ultimate victory are assured, but they are still in the future.

Or using another analogy, imagine that after dating for a while, on the spur of the moment a couple decides to elope. They immediately find a minister and some witnesses and get married. A second couple, also dating for a while, gets engaged. For many months they live in a transitional state in which they are more than just dating, yet less than married. Though they are not yet husband and wife, they enjoy certain practices and blessings of marriage. They may receive some wedding gifts, merge their bank accounts, even buy a house. But it's only because of a future event—the wedding—that they experience these things. In a sense some of the blessings of that future event have spilled backward in time to become present realities.

> Just as the many spokes of a bicycle wheel diverge from the same central hub, the many elements of Jesus' ministry actually diverge from the same central theme of kingdom proclamation.

It is against this background that we can understand Jesus' ministry. I used to see Jesus' ministry as largely consisting of a hodgepodge of unrelated benevolent actions. But, just as the many spokes of a bicycle wheel diverge from the same central hub, the many elements of Jesus' ministry actually diverge from the same central theme of kingdom proclamation.

Kingdom Characteristic: Abundant Provision

Some of Jesus' most memorable miracles involved food and drink. Giant jugs of water turned into giant jugs of wine, a fruitless night in a fishing boat suddenly resulted in a net-busting load of fish, a small basket of bread rolls and fishes multiplied to feed thousands.[13] But these were not merely charitable magic tricks designed to spare his companions a trip to the local winery or falafel stand.

As Craig Blomberg explains, they were object lessons about the *abundant provision* of the kingdom:

Jesus' marvellous deeds are thus more than acts of mercy, and more than pointers to his divine origin, for as already noted, his enemies could allege that the supernatural source of his power was the devil rather than God. Instead they are primarily signs and indications of the fact that the Messianic age for which the Jews had so long been waiting, the time of the new covenant and the era of the kingdom of God inaugurated on earth, had now arrived in the person and ministry of Jesus. . . . Jesus provides food in abundance and masters the wind and the waves since God's kingdom was to bring an overflowing harvest and complete protection from danger.[14]

Thus these miracles were both previews of what the kingdom of abundance would look like when it arrived in all its fullness and evidence that in some sense it had already arrived. And, according to Jesus and the New Testament writers, the abundance of the kingdom goes beyond food and drink.

The life itself is abundant, Jesus said,[15] and the New Testament writers seem to fall all over themselves struggling to squeeze into words just how abundant it is:

From the fullness of his grace we have all received one blessing after another.

—John 1:16

No eye has seen, no ear has heard, no mind has conceived what God has prepared for those who love him.

—1 Corinthians 2:9

Praise be to the God and Father of our Lord Jesus Christ, who has blessed us in the heavenly realms with every spiritual blessing in Christ. . . . In him we have redemption through his blood, the forgiveness of sins, in accordance with the riches of God's grace that he lavished on us with all wisdom and understanding.

—Ephesians 1:3, 7–8

In this age we are not yet free from famine, drought, or poverty. But, already, we are tasting the abundance of an age so lavish its heavenly city is pictured as having gates crafted of jumbo pearls and a main boulevard paved with pure gold.[16]

Kingdom Characteristic:
Physical Wholeness

Jesus' healing miracles were no less impressive than his other miracles. But, again, they were more than mere benevolent acts. This is clear in Jesus' response to John the Baptist's disciples.

Jesus was not meeting John's expectations of bringing the judgment and glorious political kingdom people were anticipating. Moreover, John, who was in prison, presumably expected that if Jesus was indeed the Messiah, Jesus would get him released. So John sent his disciples to ask Jesus if he was the Messiah or if they should expect someone else. Jesus instructed John's followers to tell him, "The blind receive sight, the lame walk, those who have leprosy are cured, the deaf hear, the dead are raised, and the good news is preached to the poor" (Matthew 11:5).

This was a reference to Isaiah's prediction about the kingdom: "Then will the eyes of the blind be opened and the ears of the deaf unstopped. Then will the lame leap like a deer, and the mute tongue shout for joy" (Isaiah 35:5–6a). [17] As New Testament scholar Graham H. Twelftree affirms, Jesus' point is unmistakable: "But it is not that Jesus is simply appealing to the miraculous to prove his status; he is helping John to see that the kingdom had come."[18]

Although we do not yet live in a world free from sickness and disease, Jesus' healings demonstrate that the kingdom of *physical wholeness* has already broken into this world, giving us a preview of what the consummated kingdom will be like.[19]

Kingdom Characteristics:
Wicked Destroyed ❖ Safety and Security

Jesus' exorcisms also give this kind of preview. The Old Testament prophets had predicted that the coming of the kingdom would mean the *destruction of the wicked*. Though at the time God's human enemies were envisioned, as the centuries passed God's people realized that the destruction of the wicked must ultimately mean the destruction of the

Evil One himself.[20] By Jesus' day people expected the coming of the kingdom to mean that Satan and his angels would be destroyed, with the result that *safety and security* would naturally follow.[21]

"If I drive out demons by the Spirit of God, then the kingdom of God has come upon you," announced Jesus (Matthew 12:28), revealing the beginning of a military campaign against the Evil One that would culminate in a victory on the cross, even if the final results of that victory are still yet to be seen at the end of the age when the Evil One and his angels will be cast into the fiery lake.

As theologian Peter T. O'Brien says in discussing Paul's letter to the Ephesians, "Christ's triumph over the powers has 'already' occurred (1:21), so believers no longer live in fear of them. But the fruits of that victory have 'not yet' been fully realized, so Christians must be aware of the conflict and be equipped with divine power to stand against them."[22]

Kingdom Characteristics:
Forgiveness of Sins ❖ *New Covenant*

The victory of the cross also results in the wholesale *forgiveness of sins*[23] promised by the *new covenant*,[24] inaugurated by Jesus' blood. During Jesus' ministry this forgiveness was prefigured by his meals with "sinners," meals that scandalized the religious establishment, as N. T. Wright explains:

> It was not just that he as an individual was associating with disreputable people; that would not have been a great offense. It was because he was doing so *as a prophet of the kingdom* and was indeed making these meals and their free-for-all welcome a central feature of his program. The meals spoke powerfully about Jesus' vision of the kingdom; what they said was subversive of other kingdom-agendas. Jesus' welcome symbolized God's radical acceptance and forgiveness. . . . Jesus' offer of forgiveness, then, was in itself a way of saying that the kingdom was dawning in and through his work.[25]

Jesus' sacrificial death dealt with sin once and for all, making any further sacrifices unnecessary. When the kingdom is consummated, the results of sin will be reversed, resulting in the fullness of the new creation. But already the guilt and penalty of sin have been dealt with because of that sacrifice.

Kingdom Characteristic:
Justice and Righteousness

This forgiveness of sins exemplified the *justice and righteousness* that would be a hallmark of the kingdom.[26] Justice was satisfied because the penalty for sin had been paid. But, paradoxically, in the process sinners could truly be declared righteous.

In his discussion of Romans 3, C. Marvin Pate explains the difference between the Christian view of righteousness and that of some ancient rabbis:

> According to the rabbis, two impulses reside in humans: the good impulse (*yetzer hatob*) and the bad impulse (*yetzer hara*). The righteous person, therefore, is one who has nurtured the former and restrained the latter by the power that comes from studying and obeying the Torah. Thus, at the Last Judgment, such people's good deeds will outweigh their bad deeds, and they will enter into the bliss of the age to come. Paul, however, modifies that understanding of righteousness at two critical points. First, God justifies the *ungodly* on the basis of Christ's death (vv. 25–26). Second, God declares the sinner righteous *now*, projecting, in effect, the divine verdict of the Last Judgment into the present moment. In other words, the righteousness of the age to come has broken into this age.[27]

Therefore, although we have not yet stood before God at the end-time judgment, we have already received our end-time verdict of "not guilty." And, having been justified, we are now charged with living a lifestyle that reflects justice and righteousness.

Kingdom Characteristics:
Death Destroyed ❖ *Newness*

One of the most dramatic blessings of the kingdom is the *destruction of death*,[28] prefigured by people like Lazarus whom Jesus raised from the dead,[29] and ultimately heralded by Jesus' own resurrection to a new dimension of life. Using already/not-yet terminology, Paul refers to Christ as the firstfruits of the resurrection. The firstfruits are the first ripened crops of a harvest. They are a real part of the harvest itself, but they are also tangible evidence that the rest of the harvest will follow. Jesus' resurrection, then, is not just an amazing historical event. It is proof that those who put their trust in him will also rise from the dead, experiencing the newness of life that is part of the *newness* of the kingdom.[30]

> Although we have not yet stood before God at the end-time judgment, we have already received our end-time verdict of "not guilty."

Although the new heavens and new earth predicted by Isaiah have not yet arrived, and although the end-time resurrection remains in the future, we can already experience much of the kingdom's newness. Author and scholar Stephen Travis reveals:

> We live in *a new era*. The letters of Paul, for example, exude this sense of newness. Because Jesus has come, has died and has risen, he has brought the life of God's longed-for kingdom into present experience. Through union with Christ we already, in a real sense, experience the blessings of the heavenly world (Ephesians 1:3). We are part of a 'new creation' (2 Corinthians 5:17). We have put on the 'new self,' 'the new being which God, its Creator, is constantly renewing in his own image' (Colossians 3:10). We are the people of a 'new covenant' (1 Corinthians 11:25). This sense of decisive fulfillment, the sense that God's purposes have entered a new stage and he is closer to men and women than ever before, is a powerful incentive to hope.[31]

Kingdom Characteristics:
Spirit Poured Out ❖ *God's Presence* ❖ *All Nations Included*

A major reason for this newness is the *outpouring of the Holy Spirit* at Pentecost, resulting in his indwelling and empowering of all God's people, just as Joel had predicted.[32] Paul uses another already/not-yet analogy when—in language so jarring we might think it irreverent if it didn't originate in Scripture—he calls the Holy Spirit a "deposit."[33]

If you buy a house, for example, you'd generally put down a deposit. The deposit is a real and present part of the purchase price. And, it's also a guarantee that the rest of the payment will follow in the future. The gift of the Holy Spirit functions in the same way. That which Moses desired has come to pass; God's Spirit has been poured out abundantly upon people from every station in life. This event is a guarantee that the rest of the kingdom's blessings will follow.

But, as O. Palmer Robertson points out, it is a tremendous present blessing as well:

> Often believers in Christ do not fully appreciate the significance of their possession of the Spirit. Because his work is generally done in quiet, unobtrusive ways, the fact that God's power is resident within them is not adequately appreciated. But divine power has been unleashed in the world by the outpouring of the Holy Spirit on the church. This power is nothing less than the realization of God's kingdom in the world, and its manifestation will continue until the end of the age.[34]

The indwelling of the Spirit turns us—both as individuals and corporately as the body of Christ—into a temple where *God's presence dwells*.[35] And one of the most shocking discoveries of the early church was that repentant Gentiles could experience this blessing as well, on an equal footing with repentant Jews, signifying that *all nations are included* in the inaugurated kingdom.[36] Together we await the consummation when, in John's vision, the New Jerusalem descends from heaven and God dwells forever with his people.

Kingdom Characteristic:
Peace (Shalom)

The work of Christ has resulted in reconciliation and *peace* that includes, but is not limited to, the relationship between Jews and Gentiles—a peace that is both already and not yet.[37] As New Testament scholar Andrew T. Lincoln says in his commentary on Ephesians,

> The gospel of peace is embodied in Christ who "is our peace," and this is a peace with both vertical and horizontal axes: peace with God the Father and peace between human beings, Jews and Gentiles, who were formerly at enmity. Since such peace is the pledge of future cosmic harmony (cf. 1:10; 3:10), its realization in the Church not only sounds the death knell for opposing cosmic powers but also, in the meantime, leads to the intensification of their opposition. A continuing preservation and appropriation of the gospel of peace is, therefore, necessary if the powers are to be resisted and if believers are to be ready to make their stand in the world, the stand that is in line with their calling.[38]

Kingdom Characteristic:
Messiah Will Rule

The Prince of Peace, the *Messiah* (or "Christ," which is the Greek translation of that Hebrew title), has now ascended to reign at God's right hand.[39] In the words of the writer of Hebrews, God "crowned him with glory and honor and put everything under his feet. In putting everything under him, God left nothing that is not subject to him. Yet at present we do not see everything subject to him" (Hebrews 2:7b–8).

Theology professor George H. Guthrie explains:

> This tension between the "now" and the "not yet," between what is present reality but not yet seen, expresses what may be referred to as "the inaugurated rule of Christ." That is, the reign of Christ and the reality of Christian experience have

begun, but will not be fully actualized until a final consummation at the end of the age. The Son's rule is already a reality; that reality, however, must be confessed by faith until we see its full impact at the end of the age.[40]

Kingdom Characteristic: Intimacy with God

This inaugurated rule has resulted in an *intimacy with God* that most who lived during Old Testament times could only dream of.[41] The New Testament writers taught that those individuals who trust in Christ become children of God, adopted into a deep and loving relationship with their father. No longer do God's people have to rely on human intermediaries who stand between them and the Lord. In fact, in language that would shock our Old Testament counterparts, the writer of Hebrews reveals that we are not only permitted, but we are actually exhorted, to enter God's intimate presence in the Holy of Holies to obtain his help in time of need.[42] All this is a prelude to the consummation of our relationship with God, which is depicted as a marriage between Christ and his bride, the church.

> In language that would shock our Old Testament counterparts, the writer of Hebrews reveals that we are not only permitted, but we are actually exhorted, to enter God's intimate presence in the Holy of Holies to obtain his help in time of need.

Kingdom Characteristics: Love ❖ Joy ❖ God's Glory Revealed

As his children and his bride, we are to be motivated by the *love* that God has shown us, the love that characterizes his kingdom.[43] Although we have not yet experienced the consummation of the kingdom, we who live in the inaugurated kingdom are already called to conduct ourselves according to its culture. As author and scholar Tom Wright says, "Love is the way of life in the new world to which, by grace, we are bound. We need to learn it here and now. It is the grammar of the language we shall speak there. The more progress we make in it here, the better we shall be equipped."[44]

And *joy* is a hallmark of the kingdom that is both already and not yet.[45] For the joy set before him, Jesus endured the cross. The early Christians rejoiced in the midst of suffering, knowing their trials were a prelude to eternal joy when the kingdom arrives in all its fullness. As biblical scholar S. S. Smalley says,

> Christian joy also anticipated the end of the age. The church already experiences, through the Spirit, the joy of the messianic kingdom heralded by the prophets of Judaism. But that joy is still to be consummated. In the future there will be rejoicing because evil, and opposition to God, will have been finally overcome (Revelation 12:7–12); God's salvific purposes will have been accomplished through judgment (Revelation 19:1–8); and the church will be presented blameless in the presence of God's glory, with rejoicing (Jude 24–25).[46]

Finally, with Jesus' first coming *God's glory was revealed* in surprising ways.[47] First, it was revealed through Jesus' own body, which is a new tabernacle or temple. As theologian P. E. Enns says,

> The glory that resided above the ark in the Most Holy Place, to which the high priest alone had access once a year, is now walking the streets of Jerusalem for all to see, a truly "portable" tabernacle. . . . Further, Christ is himself holy and sacred ground in whom the glory of God resides. With the spread of the gospel, God's glory can now be seen in new temples everywhere, wherever men and women repent, come to know him, and gather to worship. God's sacred space is no longer restricted to a building in one part of the world. Nor is it embodied only in his Son, as it was for a brief time two thousand years ago.[48]

Furthermore, not only is the body of each individual believer a temple where God's glory resides, but as Paul reveals, believers collectively comprise a vast temple complex where we reflect the Lord's glory and are transformed into his likeness with ever increasing glory.

All this is a precursor to the ultimate fulfillment of the Old Testament prophecies concerning God's glory. John tells us that the New Jerusalem will descend from heaven to earth with no need for the sun or moon because God's glory will be the source of illumination. All nations will walk by its light.

Unpredictable Fulfillments

The prophecies and fulfillments concerning God's glory illustrate a trait that runs throughout the predictions about the kingdom. Their already/not-yet fulfillments surpassed what everyone had anticipated, provoking confusion, amazement, and jubilation among Jesus' contemporaries.

These multifaceted fulfillments remind me of something that happened one day in my fifth grade science class. The teacher gave each of us a glass prism and a small flashlight. As we aimed the light through the prisms, small rainbows were projected on the white makeshift paper screens we had placed on the other side of the prisms.

Though they couldn't be seen, the white light from the flashlight actually contained all the colors of the spectrum, the teacher explained. But when the light passed through the prism, it was refracted (bent) and dispersed (broken by wavelengths into all the colors of the spectrum), making the colors visible to us.

When I read the New Testament with its Old Testament background in mind, I perceive something similar happening. As the white light of Old Testament prophecy shone through the prism of the resurrected Jesus it split into a million colors, startling and dazzling the earliest believers. In twenty-seven amazing documents (which we call the New Testament) some of these early believers chronicled the shock, celebration, and transformed lifestyles resulting from the discovery of this newly visible kaleidoscope.

The prophets had prepared them to expect that in the coming kingdom, Gentiles would one day worship the God of Israel. But nothing had prepared them for the fact that—though invisibly and inherently in the prophets' oracles—repentant Gentiles would be accepted as

---

Again and again, in reading the New Testament documents, we sense the astonishment of a generation discovering that the ancient predictions were exploding into fulfillment all around them in utterly unpredictable ways.

God's children on an equal footing with his people the Jews.

The prophets had awakened hopes of some sort of a blissful afterlife. But nothing had prepared them for a crucified Messiah whose resurrection would be the prototype for the resurrection that awaits all his people.

The prophets had predicted that one day when the kingdom arrived, God's glory would cover the earth. But nothing had prepared them for the fact that not only would God's people witness that glory; they themselves would share in it and be transformed by it.

Again and again, in reading the New Testament documents, we sense the astonishment of a generation discovering that the ancient predictions were exploding into fulfillment all around them in utterly unpredictable ways.

It is hard to imagine the amalgamation of joy, shock, and excitement that overtook the early Christians when they discovered that the kingdom had dawned and that they could already begin experiencing its blessings even as they awaited its fullness. We, like they, have to adjust to the paradoxes resulting from living in a kingdom that is both here and not here. As New Testament professor Richard N. Longenecker observes,

> The old age has been judged and is passing away, but the new age has not yet been fully brought about; the condemnation of sin has been dealt with and the compulsion of sin broken, but sin still is present to tempt and to frustrate; the tyranny of death has been crushed, but mortality and depravity still remain; the domination of the law is ended, but forms of legalism and our perverted desire to gain in divine favor by our own endeavors still exist; the supernatural antagonistic

powers have been disarmed and defeated, but they are not yet destroyed. Indeed, those who have become righteous still await righteousness, those who have been received as sons still await sonship, those who have been raised to newness of life still await resurrection, and those who have known Christ's coming still await His return. It is this temporal tension between the "no longer" and the "not yet" that lies at the very heart of the gospel and that contains the key to the understanding of the entire New Testament.[49]

Entering the Kingdom

So how do we enter this kingdom? Jesus and the New Testament writers taught that it's both the easiest and the hardest thing we could ever do.

It's easy because it's uncomplicated. A child can do it. We must recognize that we have sinned, that our sin separates us from God, but that Christ's sacrifice paid the price of our forgiveness, and that in order for our relationship with God to be restored we must receive his forgiveness as a gift that cannot be earned.

It's hard because entering the kingdom demands a breakneck about-face in the way we live, turning from our sin and self-centeredness and turning to God, committing ourselves to following his ways. The technical term for this hairpin U-turn is "repentance," though it's easy to forget that this pious-sounding word ever meant anything so radical.

> We are Jed Clampetts, tasting the splendors of Beverly Hills without having lost our Ozark accents or our fondness for fried possum and crow gizzards. Like Jed, we should not expect a seamless transition.

Jesus said that living out this commitment is like hauling a heavy cross around every day.[50] He warned us that before we make this decision we should count the cost (like a king calculating how much his coffers will be depleted if he goes to war).[51] But he also taught that it's worth the cost (like a man who sells all he has so he can buy a field with a treasure chest buried on it).[52] Paradoxically then (and the kingdom involves a lifestyle and lifetime of paradoxes), entering the kingdom means receiving an absolutely free gift that costs you absolutely everything you have.

Once we make that commitment, we become citizens of the coming age and, still living in the present age, we find ourselves squarely in the overlap. We who live in the overlap are amphibious creatures, navigating two worlds simultaneously as we begin our transition from one to the other.

We are Jed Clampetts, tasting the splendors of Beverly Hills without having lost our Ozark accents or our fondness for fried possum and crow gizzards. Like Jed, we should not expect a seamless transition.[53]

As pastoral counselor James Robert Ross says:

> But the blessings of the age to come, which the Christian experiences now, do not solve the problems of living in this age. In a very real sense the problems become more acute, or at least more acutely perceived. . . . In every relationship the demands of the kingdom of heaven are in constant tension with the way this world operates. The Christian, as it were, has already been fitted with wings for the life of the age to come, but he has to learn how to use those wings within an alien, earthbound environment.[54]

Having sprouted our wings, then, we may find ourselves desiring flight training. For we now face the awesome privilege—and bracing challenge—of living in the overlap.

PART TWO:
LIVING IN THE OVERLAP

Living in the overlap reminds me of the time I first went scuba diving in Australia's Great Barrier Reef. I knew nothing about diving until I got a brief lesson during the boat ride out to the reef. Then the instructor helped me "suit up." I had to wear an air tank on my back, fins on my feet, a weight belt around my waist, and a mask on my face. Walking around on the boat in this getup was awkward. I also had to learn to breathe slow, deep breaths through a regulator in my mouth.

Once we got into the ocean I had to practice expelling water from the mask by tilting my head back, putting a finger on the mask just above my nose, and exhaling sharply. The instructor also told me I had to refrain from taking any plane rides for twenty-four hours after the dive. (I've since been told that the change in atmospheric pressure can give you a potentially fatal case of the bends.)

Then we plunged below the water's surface. No underwater photos or videos, not even the semi-submersible craft ride I'd recently taken, prepared me for what I saw on the dive. Yellow-tailed damselfish swarmed all around me. I put my hand inside a giant clam (contrary to what we see in cartoons, they don't snap shut). I picked up a deep indigo sea star. I glided over rainbows of soft and hard corals. The soft corals swayed like wildflowers in a breeze. It looked like the landscape of a foreign planet. It was another world down there, a world I wanted to explore again and again.

Yet, if a landlubber who had never heard of scuba diving had watched me suiting up, he might have had a different opinion: "Poor guy. Those fins make it hard to walk. That tank makes it hard to balance. The mask makes it hard to see. The regulator makes it hard to breathe. And he's not allowed to go on airplanes—this guy's leading a clumsy, cramped existence." He would need to realize that all those "confining" things turned me into a creature that could explore the wonders of the ocean floor.

We who live in the overlap are like scuba divers. To outsiders we may appear to be confined by odd rules and rituals, by disciplines that seem awkward by this world's standards. But it's those unusual practices that turn us into creatures who can explore the wonders of a whole new world.

Living in the overlap involves a lifelong process of lifestyle adjustments, adjustments that equip us to function as creatures of the age to come, while temporarily remaining creatures of this present age. Part Two, then, examines some of the practical implications of living within the already/not-yet realities of these overlapping ages.

CHAPTER THREE

LIVING IN THE LIGHT

OF THE KINGDOM

What did Jesus mean by the kingdom of God? It's another name for heaven.
The kingdom of God means God's reign in our hearts.
The kingdom of God is a metaphor for Christianity and the Christian
life. We're supposed to bring people into the kingdom and build the
kingdom for God's glory.

I've frequently heard and read comments like these. You probably have, too. They're all well intentioned. But, ultimately, they miss the mark.

Scripture certainly teaches us about God's abode, heaven. But, it never equates the kingdom of God with heaven. And of course, the kingdom of God includes God's reign in our hearts. But his reign doesn't end there (even in this present age). The coming of the kingdom meant blind eyes seeing, deaf ears hearing, demons being expelled from human bodies, and corpses springing back to life. These and other kingdom events go far beyond a change in the human heart.

And although Scripture says that people can enter the kingdom, and inherit it, and pray for it to come (among other actions), the Bible never depicts the kingdom as something that people can build. (One look at The Kingdom Dartboard should affirm this. Who among us can, by our efforts, "build" any of the items listed there, let alone build all of them?)[1] Furthermore, Jesus never used "the kingdom of God" as a generic metaphor for Christianity or the Christian life. Instead, it had a precise technical meaning.

The kingdom of God, as proclaimed by Jesus, is God's end-time reign, predicted by the prophets, inaugurated by Christ at his first coming, and to be consummated at his second coming. We cannot divorce the kingdom from its Old Testament prophetic background or from the New Testament emphasis on its already/not-yet nature.

> The coming of the kingdom meant blind eyes seeing, deaf ears hearing, demons being expelled from human bodies, and corpses springing back to life. These and other kingdom events go far beyond a change in the human heart.

In seminary classes and Bible commentaries this is recognized as obvious. But is it obvious to the average churchgoer? Some prominent Christian leaders argue that, regrettably, the answer is *no*.

For instance, Peter Kusmic, founding president of one of Eastern Europe's largest evangelical schools, laments,

> The Kingdom has been *already inaugurated* with the arrival of the King, although it still *awaits its consummation* and fulness at the time of his second coming. . . . If this is the focus of the practice and teaching of Jesus, it should also be central to the teaching of evangelicals with their high regard for Scripture and the person of Jesus. . . . It is only more recently that, due to the importance of this concept in modern theological debates, some evangelicals are looking at the Kingdom with greater seriousness. That has hardly, however, filtered down from the biblical theological investigations to the pulpits and has yet to produce a desired change in evangelical behavior.[2]

Missiology professor Mortimer Arias echoes this concern: "The kingdom-of-God theme has practically disappeared from evangelistic preaching and has been ignored by traditional 'evangelism.' The evangelistic message has been centered in personal salvation, individual conversion, and incorporation into the church. The kingdom of God as a parameter or perspective or as content of the proclamation has been virtually absent."[3]

Author and church-renewal professor Howard A. Snyder offers a pithier analysis: "The Bible is full of teaching on the kingdom of God, and the church has largely missed it."[4]

In contrast, the already/not-yet kingdom was foundational for the early Christians, as New Testament scholar Gordon D. Fee explains:

> The early believers, therefore, learned to be a truly eschatological people. They lived between the times—that is, between the *beginning* of the end and the *consummation* of the end. At the Lord's table they celebrated their eschatological existence, by proclaiming "the Lord's death until he comes" (1 Corinthians 11:26). *Already* they knew God's free and full forgiveness, but they had *not yet* been perfected (Philippians 3:7–14). *Already* victory over death was theirs (1 Corinthians 3:22), *yet* they would still die (Philippians 3:20–21). *Already* they lived in the Spirit, *yet* they still lived in the world where Satan could attack (e.g., Ephesians 6:10–17). *Already* they had been justified and faced no condemnation (Romans 8:1), *yet* there was still to be a future judgment (2 Corinthians 5:10). They were God's future people; they had been conditioned by the future. They knew its benefits, lived in light of its values, but they, as we, still had to live out these benefits and values in the present world.[5]

How can we follow their example and live out the benefits and values of the age to come while living in this present age? As I've wrestled with what it means to live in the overlap of the ages, I've identified three areas in which I've needed to make some adjustments in order to become a more kingdom-oriented believer.

Kingdom Orientation: Studying and Applying Scripture

First, I've needed to let the kingdom impact my study and application of Scripture. This has involved a process of refocusing my attention on the kingdom while reading the Bible. The kingdom is in fact not only the central theme of Jesus' ministry, it is a theme that permeates the entire Bible as well. Each part of the Bible reflects the kingdom in its own way. The Bible tells the story of God establishing his kingdom on earth.

> The kingdom is not only the central theme of Jesus' ministry, it is a theme that permeates the entire Bible as well.

The Old Testament reveals the need, and the preparation, for the kingdom. In the early chapters of Genesis, God creates the heaven and the earth, and places Adam and Eve in Eden. They enjoy an intimate relationship with God. But sin and death enter the world because of the Evil One. He usurps and corrupts God's creation. Mankind's fellowship with God is broken. God then initiates a plan to destroy the Evil One, to create a new heaven and a new earth, and to restore his intimacy with mankind.

He chooses a people, Abraham's descendants, and through a long, arduous process teaches them what sort of God he is and what sort of people he expects them to be. Through them he will realize his plan to inaugurate his eternal kingdom. The story unfolds through books of history, poetry, and prophecy.

The Gospels reveal the inauguration of the kingdom. The Gospels, the first four books of the New Testament, tell the story of how God becomes a man in the person of Jesus. He proclaims the kingdom through his teachings, parables, healings, exorcisms, and forgiveness of sins. Through his sacrificial death on the cross, he defeats the Evil One, then rises from the dead.

The book of Acts reveals the advance of the kingdom. For forty days the risen Jesus appears to his followers and teaches them about the kingdom. Then he ascends to heaven. As his people proclaim the gospel, God reveals to them the astonishing truth that the gospel is for the Gentiles as well as for the Jews. The early Christians risk—and in some cases lose—their lives announcing the kingdom. They spread the gospel from Palestine throughout southern Asia and southern Europe, and finally to the capital of the Roman empire.

The epistles reveal the life of the kingdom. Early Christian leaders write letters instructing their fellow believers in how to live within the already/not-yet tension of the kingdom. These letters teach us to grow in kingdom character traits (such as love, joy, peace, righteousness) while we enjoy kingdom blessings (such as forgiveness, intimacy with God, abundance, newness). As citizens of the kingdom of light, we are to embody the life of the age to come while we shine in this present age of darkness.

The letters teem with reminders of the counterpoint between the present and future ages: we are to live godly lives in this present age while we wait for the appearing of Christ; God, who began a good work in us, will carry it on to completion until the day Christ returns; Christ gave himself for our sins to rescue us from this present evil age; our present sufferings are not worthy to be compared to the glory that will be revealed in us; through our generous deeds we are to lay up treasure as a firm foundation for the coming age.[6]

Although the kingdom theme pervades the letters, the actual term "kingdom" becomes less prominent than it is in the Gospels. There are apparently two reasons for this. In the first place, the kingdom of God is a Jewish concept that would not have been easily understood by Gentiles. In fact, it might have been misinterpreted by Rome as having political overtones. In the second place, now that the king has arrived, it is more natural to speak of him instead of the kingdom.[7] As theologian Lesslie Newbigin explains:

> What is new is that in Jesus the kingdom is present. That is why the first generation of Christian preachers used a different language from the language of Jesus: he spoke about the kingdom, they spoke about Jesus. . . . The kingdom, or kingship, of God was no longer a distant hope or a faceless concept. It now had a name and a face—the name and the face of the man from Nazareth.[8]

Thus, instead of talking about being "in the kingdom," Paul talks about being "in Christ." "The kingdom of God has come to you" becomes "Jesus Christ is Lord." The messenger has become the message. Moreover, the letters proclaim Jesus' kingship by constantly assigning to him the title "Christ," the Greek rendering of the Hebrew "Messiah." By proclaiming the king, therefore, the letters implicitly proclaim the kingdom.

But the kingdom theme is always below the surface even in passages that do not specifically mention the king, the kingdom, or the age to come. Every time the Holy Spirit is depicted as active among believers, every time the new covenant is referenced, every time resurrection or righteousness or God's glory or the inclusion of the Gentiles among God's people is discussed, every time the dualism of this age vs. the age to come is expressed (such as darkness/light, flesh/Spirit, old man/new man, death/life), something is tacitly being said about the arrival of the eschatological kingdom.

As New Testament scholar Greg K. Beale points out,

> The apostles understood that they were already living in the end-times and that they were to understand their present salvation in Christ to be already an end-time reality. *Every aspect of their salvation was to be conceived of as eschatological in nature.* To put this another way, every major doctrine of the Christian faith has an end-time tint.[9]

I have had to readjust my thinking in order to see the eschatological nature of the letters. For example, Paul writes to the Corinthian church, "Therefore, if anyone is in Christ, he is a new creation; the old has gone, the new has come!" (2 Corinthians 5:17). I had long interpreted this individualistically. I thought it meant that when I became a Christian, my life as an individual would be different because of my personal relationship with Christ. But while this is certainly true, it is not Paul's major thrust. As New Testament scholar George Eldon Ladd points out, he is actually saying something more cosmic:

> The Pauline statement that in Christ the old has passed away and the new has come is an eschatological statement. "The

> new aeon, which has dawned with Christ, brings a new creation, the creation of a new man.". . . . In Christ there is deliverance from the present evil age (Galatians 1:4). In Christ men no longer need be conformed to the old age (Romans 12:2). . . . Therefore to be "in Christ" means to be in the new sphere of salvation. To be in Christ means to experience the newness of the new aeon.[10]

Thus, this passage, like many passages throughout the letters, actually deals with a believer experiencing the blessings of the age to come. When we recognize the eschatological nature of the letters, we can see how—both explicitly and implicitly—they reveal the life of the kingdom.

The Book of Revelation reveals the consummation of the kingdom. In this final book of the Bible, the events in the early chapters of Genesis are reversed. The Evil One and death are cast into the lake of fire, this present sinful age ends, and the new heaven and new earth appear. God regains intimacy with his people, he wipes every tear from their eyes, and he reigns in glory.

You and I are not just readers of this story. We are characters *in* the story. We are part of the *whoever* in "whoever believes in him shall not perish but have eternal life" (John 3:16). We are part of the *anyone* in "if anyone is in Christ, he is a new creation; the old has gone, the new has come!" (2 Corinthians 5:17).[11] Living in the overlap we have the privilege and responsibility of allowing this story to shape our daily lives in the most trivial and most trying situations.

> You and I are not just readers of this story. We are characters *in* the story.

I recall a heartbreaking situation I witnessed many years ago. I attended the funeral of a friend who died instantly in an auto accident. She and her family were Christians who attended a solid evangelical church. Her grief-stricken brother stood to deliver the eulogy. Haltingly, he told stories of her kindness to family and friends.

Then in tears he said, "God needed an angel, so he called her home." I ached for him, not only because of his tragic loss, but also because of the way he was grasping at straws to summon some kind of comfort.

Years later I found myself dealing with grief. I had flown to Pittsburgh on Easter weekend to visit my terminally ill grandmother in the hospital. Both her body and her mind had become feeble. We knew that barring a miracle, she would not survive much longer. Sunday morning in her hospital room I kept looking at the clock on the front wall near the television set. I had to leave at two o'clock to catch my plane home. When one o'clock rolled around, I realized I only had one more hour to see her alive. I held her hand and smiled at her, occasionally turning to see the clock. Forty-five minutes, then thirty, then fifteen. I kept holding her hand. I didn't want two o'clock to arrive. I didn't want to let go of her.

When it was time to leave, we told each other that we loved each other, and I left the room to head for the parking lot with my mother. Nana died twelve days later of congestive heart failure.

As Mom and I drove away from the hospital, I realized that this was the first Easter I had ever missed church. Easter services at my church are always celebrations. In addition to a rousing sermon, I can count on joyful music from the choir and orchestra, and sometimes a parade of colorful banners depicting Scriptural names for Jesus, or even a special performance by a drama team. But I did not feel like celebrating anything this Sunday, not even Jesus' resurrection.

Two dissonant concepts—Nana's impending death and Jesus' triumph over the grave—clashed inside my head. Any celebratory notions seemed to mock the heartache of losing my grandmother. *This is a heck of a way to spend Easter*, I thought.

However, as Mom and I rode along in silence, the dissonance resolved itself. My mind drifted to the Scriptures I always hear during Easter sermons. And I saw that there was no more appropriate day to say goodbye to Nana before she died; her death had *everything* to do with Easter. I was reminded that Easter is not just the celebration of Jesus' resurrection. Rather, Easter is also the celebration of our own resurrection, and that of our loved ones who know him, because it's all part of the same harvest. The firstfruits have ripened; the rest of the harvest will follow. Christ has risen; we shall rise. The power of the kingdom of God has broken into this present age, and even death could not prevail against it. We know this is true, not just because the Bible tells us, but because an empty tomb in Jerusalem bears witness to the fact that the resurrection process has already begun.

Like Lincoln's assassination or Henry VIII's reign, Jesus' resurrection is a fact of history. And this sets Christianity apart from any other belief system. Other religions may speak about some sort of existence beyond the grave. But only Christianity offers a God who became a man, who lived and died and rose from the dead at a particular time and place in history, who then appeared to more than five hundred eyewitnesses,[12] and who promised that all who trust in him will follow him in resurrection from death.

Thus, our Savior is also our trailblazer. He has cleared our pathway from this world to the next. No other religion offers such emphatic assurance of eternal life. We must either commit ourselves to Jesus or forfeit this assurance.

Two deaths: my friend's and my grandmother's. Two ways of finding comfort: "God needed an angel" and "Christ is the firstfruits of the resurrection." One based on a sentimental fantasy, the other based on the fact of an inaugurated kingdom.

As I look at what life was like on this planet before Jesus inaugurated the kingdom, I am struck by the chasm between our situation and that of those who lived before him.

Living on this side of Calvary, we don't have to worry about what kind of verdict we'll receive when we stand before God's judgment seat. Living on this side of Easter, we don't have to worry about whether or not there's some sort of existence for us after death. Living on this side of Pentecost, we don't have to worry about how we'll find the strength and guidance to navigate through the hardships we experience in this present age.

> Living in the overlap means appropriating and enjoying the "already" blessings, while being motivated and encouraged by those that belong to the "not yet."

We do not have all the blessings that the kingdom will eventually bring. But what we already have is astonishing. Living in the overlap means appropriating and enjoying the "already" blessings, while being motivated and encouraged by those that belong to the "not yet." This will happen more and more as we immerse ourselves in the Scriptural story of the kingdom, and as we work to live out that story in our everyday lives.

Kingdom Orientation: Proclaiming the Good News

There's a second way in which I'm working to live out the benefits and values of the kingdom. In addition to letting the kingdom theme impact my study and application of Scripture, I am also working to let it impact my gospel proclamation.

For a long time I would have described the gospel as something like this: If I repent and accept Christ as my Savior, my sins will be forgiven, and I'll live with God eternally in heaven.

But Russell D. Moore, dean of the School of Theology at The Southern Baptist Theological Seminary suggests something far different: "Evangelical theology will remind Christians that the call to Christ is not a call to 'go to heaven when you die,' but instead a call to be 'joint-heirs' (KJV) with the Messiah who will inherit an all-encompassing Kingdom."[13]

The only gospel Jesus ever proclaimed was the gospel *of the kingdom.* And this all-encompassing kingdom includes each of the characteristics listed on The Kingdom Dartboard. Forgiveness of sins is one major kingdom blessing. But without de-emphasizing this cardinal facet of the kingdom, we must give appropriate emphasis to the other facets. Otherwise we'll fall into the trap of mistaking a part for the whole.

> The only gospel Jesus ever proclaimed was the gospel *of the kingdom.*

Gospel literally means "good news." When a triumphant army headed home from battle, it would send a herald to run ahead and announce the good news (or gospel) of victory. The gospel is the victorious proclamation that Jesus has defeated the Evil One; that the kingdom of God has arrived in Jesus' ministry, his sacrificial death, his resurrection, and his ascension to God's right hand; and that we can begin to experience the kingdom's blessings now even though we still await its fullness.

Of particular relevance here is the fact that the kingdom is characterized by peace, or in the Hebrew of the prophets, *shalom*. As biblical scholar G. R. Beasley-Murray says, "*Shalom* is the most comprehensive term for the salvation of the kingdom of God in the Old Testament; it includes not only the thought of the end of war, but that of the total well-being of man as he lives under the gracious rule of God, in harmony with heaven and earth, and so in joy and happiness."[14]

Thus, *shalom* refers to well-being in every area of life. The Old Testament used it to describe blessings such as physical health, prosperity, contentedness, good relationships between nations and between men, and salvation.[15]

We see the emphasis on *shalom* in Jesus' ministry, not only in his words that proclaimed the gospel of the kingdom, but in his actions. His table fellowship with outcasts, his patient conversations with honest inquirers, the healings, the exorcisms, the teachings on how to pray and how to live, the welcoming of children—these all demonstrate his concern for the whole person. As I've analyzed Jesus' holistic approach, I've had to rethink my concept of what it means to proclaim the gospel.

> We see the emphasis on *shalom* in Jesus' ministry, not only in his words that proclaimed the gospel of the kingdom, but in his actions.

I had long recognized that Christians should engage in activities such as feeding the hungry, caring for the sick, visiting those in prison, and working for racial harmony. But even so, I still tended to see such actions as ancillary charitable activities. I sometimes tended to think of them as bait on the hook of evangelism, as though one of their real purposes was to gain an audience for our "real business" of winning souls. I've heard other people express similar sentiments (such as workers in a soup kitchen telling how they give people a meal and then "give them the gospel").

However, I now see that such activities, in and of themselves, are part of our real business of proclaiming the gospel of the kingdom—an integral part. They proclaim what kind of kingdom we belong to. They proclaim what kind of king we serve. Proclaiming the gospel means that we will strive to help people experience the *shalom* that characterizes the kingdom, *shalom* that extends to every area of life.

Lausanne II, the Second International Congress on World Evangelization (held in the Philippines), affirmed the necessity for such ministry when it published the *Manila Manifesto*. The *Manifesto* says:

> Evangelism is primary because our chief concern is with the gospel, that all people may have the opportunity to accept Jesus Christ as Lord and Savior. Yet Jesus not only proclaimed the kingdom of God, he also demonstrated its arrival by works of mercy and power. We are called today to a similar integration of words and deeds. In a spirit of humility we are to preach and teach, minister to the sick, feed the hungry, care for prisoners, help the disadvantaged and handicapped, and deliver the oppressed. . . . Our continuing commitment to social action is not a confusion of the kingdom of God with a Christianized society. It is, rather, a recognition that the biblical gospel has inescapable social implications.[16]

For my own part, realizing this has given me a new appreciation for what I used to see as auxiliary activities. I now see that when I participate in the Red Cross blood drive sponsored by my church, or when I volunteer at an inner-city soup kitchen, I am engaging in gospel proclamation because I am helping to proclaim the character of the kingdom I belong to, and I am striving to help people experience *shalom*. Such projects are not optional undertakings that merely supplement more "spiritual" types of ministry.

But, conversely, they are not a substitute for more overt ways of communicating the gospel message of repentance and forgiveness. We live in a world where people need to hear clearly and loudly that Jesus died for their sins and that they can be forgiven and have eternal life. Living in the overlap, we are called to let our words and our actions merge to create a unified proclamation of the kingdom of wholeness we are privileged to inhabit.

Kingdom Orientation: Waging Spiritual Warfare

In trying to live out the benefits and values of the kingdom, there's one more thing I'm trying to do: I'm trying to let the kingdom impact my understanding of spiritual warfare. I admit that this is not one of my favorite topics, but I'm coming to see that it's critical to realize that when we enter the kingdom we become a special target of the Evil One.

As psychiatrist M. Scott Peck says, "In common with 99 percent of psychiatrists and the majority of clergy, I did not think the devil existed. Still, priding myself on being an open-minded scientist, I felt I had to examine the evidence that might challenge my inclination in the matter. . . . I now know Satan is real."[17]

Unlike Peck, I've never doubted Satan's existence. But I have often acted as though Satan's existence is irrelevant. My natural tendency is to treat Satan as a theoretical, rather than an actual, threat.

I think there are two reasons for this. First, I've been unconsciously influenced by a naturalistic world view that leaves no room for belief in a dark supernatural power. Second, I have a skeptical streak that causes me to question allegations that Satan is at work in any given situation.

I've heard people blame every kind of misfortune—from the tragic to the trivial—on the devil ("Satan's attacking me at work; my boss has been so hostile lately" or "The devil's causing my financial problems"). My natural inclination is to find a less sinister explanation ("Maybe she's just a lousy employee" or "He's probably just a bad money manager"). It often seems to me that naiveté causes people to blame Satan for events that have another explanation.

Yet, when we turn to Scripture, we see prominent warning signs reminding us that we can expect the Evil One to attack us: he is like a roaring lion looking for victims to devour; he is the "god of this age" who blinds the minds of unbelievers; he is a murderer and the father of lies; he masquerades as an angel of light.[18]

Scripture provides a balance to my natural skepticism. It helps me see that naiveté cuts both ways. It may be naive to assume that every misfortune is directly caused by an enemy attack, but it is equally naive to assume that we can breeze through life without experiencing such attacks.

When we look at Jesus' example, one thing becomes clear: kingdom ministry does not simply consist of doing good to other people; it also consists of overcoming the Evil One. John tells us, "The reason the Son of God appeared was to destroy the devil's work" (1 John 3:8). When Jesus inaugurated the kingdom of God, he assaulted Satan's kingdom.

Scripture reveals that the Evil One is crafty. It also reveals that he is destructive. But it also reveals—and this is paramount—that he is defeated. And it is only a matter of time until he will be destroyed. Author and pastor Calvin Miller describes the already/not-yet situation:

> The link in the chain of victory over Satan involves accepting the rumor of Satan's defeat. Why would I use the word *rumor*? Why would I not simply say the *fact* of Satan's defeat. Because we are still dealing in the area of faith. I trust a Christ whom I have never seen with my physical eyes. I believe that this yet-to-be seen Christ has defeated the devil. Yet I live in the confidence of something I cannot prove to unbelievers: this rumor, I do indeed trust as a fact. It is the trusting that gives Christ's victory real force in my life. Satan's threat to all of us was over the moment that our wounded Savior looked into the heavens and cried *"It is finished!"* (John 19:30). This was the final turn of the screw by which the enemy was forever barred from heaven. But more than

this, in that cry from the cross, evil was prohibited from ever being eternally effective in the lives of God's children. There exists all about us the rumor of Satan's defeat. He has been judged and banished from heaven. He can never enter that wonderful finality which will be our home forever.[19]

But right now, we live simultaneously in two clashing ages. Satan is still the god of this age. He is no match for the true God, but he can and will still strike at God's people. So, we have to battle this powerful, but already defeated, enemy. Just as Jesus defeated Satan on the cross, we have to defeat him on a daily basis in our own lives.

The works of New Testament professor Clinton E. Arnold are a great help in understanding the nature of the spiritual battle we all face. In particular, his book *3 Crucial Questions about Spiritual Warfare* provides a balanced and biblical overview. He affirms that spiritual warfare must be grounded in the fact that we live in the overlap of the ages, which inevitably results in conflict. He also affirms that in the overlap we face three forms of evil influence:

- The world (our ungodly social environment)
- The flesh (our inner inclination to do and think evil)
- The devil (an intelligent, powerful, and evil spirit)

These three work together like three strands of a single malignant rope, often making it difficult to distinguish between them.[20]

Paul describes how we in the overlap (not simply as individual soldiers but corporately as an army) should arm ourselves for the inevitable battle:

Put on the full armor of God so that you can take your stand against the devil's schemes. For our struggle is not against flesh and blood, but against the rulers, against the authorities, against the powers of this dark world and against the spiritual forces of evil in the heavenly realms. Therefore put on the full armor of God, so that when the day of evil comes, you may be able to stand your ground, and after you have everything, to stand. Stand firm then, with the belt of truth buckled around your waist, with the breastplate of righteousness in place, and with your feet fitted with the readiness that comes from the gospel of peace. In addition to all this, take up the shield of faith, with which you can extinguish all the flaming arrows of the evil one. Take the helmet of salvation and the sword of the Spirit, which is the word of God. And pray in the Spirit on all occasions with all kinds of prayers and requests. With this in mind, be alert and always keep on praying for all the saints.

—Ephesians 6:11–18

Clinton E. Arnold's interpretive summary of the armor of God is most helpful:

RESPONDING TO THE POWERS OF DARKNESS

You cannot succeed on your own. Draw on the strength that Christ promises to supply. Realize that you cannot count on life to be a smooth, easy path. There are evil supernatural forces out to destroy you.

1. Put On Your Trousers—Wear Truth: Know the truth of who you are in Christ (for the powers of darkness will try to deceive you). Practice honesty and live with moral integrity.
2. Put On the Breastplate of Righteousness: Realize your status before God as one who has been acquitted of all guilt. Acquire personal holiness and develop good character.
3. Put On Your Boots: Prepare to Share the Gospel of Peace. Prepare yourself for sharing the gospel wherever God calls you.
4. Take the Shield of Faith: Do not doubt! Believe that God will help you overcome.
5. Put On the Helmet of Salvation: Be secure in your identity in Christ—as one who has been saved, united with Christ, made alive, co-resurrected, and co-exalted.
6. Take the Sword of the Spirit, the Word of God: Devote your life to aggressively spreading the gospel. Know Scripture and apply it to every difficult situation.
7. The Bottom Line: Pray! Ask God to strengthen you and other believers to resist temptation and share the gospel effectively.[21]

Paul's admonition "put on the full armor of God" is deadly serious. But recently while meditating on it, I saw a grain of humor in it. After all, I thought, what dunderheaded soldier in the thick of battle would have to be reminded to use his armor and weapons? What excuses could he have for not using them? "I can sleep in an extra ten minutes if I don't bother to dress before combat"? "War is much more exciting when you're unarmed"? "It seems impolite to make things difficult for the enemy"?

Yet, I look back sheepishly on times when I've yielded to temptation. And I realize that often those periods were preceded by periods when my times of prayer and Bible study were on the superficial side. I realize that all too often I have been a dunderheaded soldier. I must remember that God has graciously provided his armor to me; I must take the time and effort to put it on.

I've made another mistake when it comes to spiritual warfare. I've often tended to see it as something special you do when confronted with extreme difficulty or oppression. If a missionary is suffering formidable persecution or if a friend is struggling with overwhelming emotional problems, I'd be inclined to think, "These situations call for spiritual warfare." And so they do. But *every* situation calls for spiritual warfare. No aspect of our life in the overlap is exempt from the enemy's influence. We are to adopt a lifestyle of warfare.

And herein lies a paradox. On the one hand we are called to a lifestyle of peace, wholeness, *shalom*. In order to experience this we are to practice spiritual disciplines like Bible reading, prayer, and exercising faith.

Yet, when we look at the armor of God we find the same things listed as instruments of battle. Thus, what from one standpoint look like

> The sweet-faced granny kneeling to pray is assuming a combat position, and the third grader memorizing Psalm 23 and John 3:16 is stockpiling an arsenal that makes a cache of nuclear weapons look like a bathtub full of rubber duckies.

placid spiritual exercises are, from another standpoint, downright devastating.

If you hammer a dent into one side of a piece of sheet metal, a corresponding bump automatically appears on the other side. In the same way, any advance for the kingdom of light is automatically an assault on the kingdom of darkness. Therefore, our most innocuous-looking spiritual disciplines are also acts of warfare. The sweet-faced granny kneeling to pray is assuming a combat position, and the third grader memorizing Psalm 23 and John 3:16 is stockpiling an arsenal that makes a cache of nuclear weapons look like a bathtub full of rubber duckies.

Herein lies our calling in the overlap. We are called to be healers, and we are called to be warriors, and we cannot be one without the other. A lifestyle of *shalom* is inevitably a lifestyle of warfare.

Living in the Light of the Kingdom

When I think about living in the light of the kingdom through a kingdom-oriented study and application of Scripture, through a holistic gospel proclamation, and through a lifestyle of spiritual warfare, I'm reminded of a paper inspired by the International Congress on World Evangelization in Lausanne, Switzerland. It reads in part:

> The *evangel* is God's Good News in Jesus Christ; it is Good News of the reign he proclaimed and embodies; of God's mission of love to restore the world to wholeness through the Cross of Christ and him alone; of his victory over the demonic powers of destruction and death . . . of the charismatic community empowered to embody his reign of shalom here and now before the whole creation and make his Good News seen and known. It is Good News of liberation, of restoration, of wholeness, and of salvation that is personal, social, global and cosmic. . . .
>
> There is no biblical dichotomy between the Word spoken and the Word made visible in the lives of God's people. Men will look as they listen and what they see must be at one with what they hear. The Christian community must chatter, discuss, and proclaim the Gospel; it must express the Gospel in its life as the new society, in its sacrificial

service of others as a genuine expression of God's love, in its prophetic exposing and opposing of all demonic forces that deny the Lordship of Christ and keep men less than fully human. . . .

The response demanded by the evangel is that men and women repent of their sin and every other lordship than that of Jesus Christ, and commit themselves to him to serve him in the world. . . . Salvation is by God's grace on the sole ground of Christ's death and resurrection and is received by obedient faith. Repentance is demanded; men must experience a change of understanding, attitude and orientation. But the new birth is not merely a subjective experience of forgiveness. It is a placement within the messianic community, God's new order which exists as a sign of God's reign to be consummated at the end of the age. . . .

We must allow God to make visible in the new humanity the quality of life that reflects Christ and demonstrates his reign.[22]

Wearers of armor and bearers of *shalom*. That's our calling. Every time we share Christ with an unbelieving friend, every time the Spirit empowers us to resist a temptation that has previously tripped us up, every time we pray for a missionary, or give a cup of water in Jesus' name, or apply God's Word to a difficult challenge in our personal lives, we are living out the benefits and values of the kingdom.

Our identity and our mission flow out of our citizenship in this age-straddling kingdom of God. For we are not merely nice people doing good deeds for others. We are not merely individuals struggling to make some small difference in our little corner of the world. We are not merely forgiven sinners telling other sinners how to find forgiveness.

Rather, we who live in the overlap are part of a worldwide army fighting an enemy who has already lost the decisive battle, and we are part of a worldwide family of healers helping people find wholeness in every area of life.[23] And as we strive to flesh out Scripture's kingdom theme, every day provides new opportunities for us to proclaim—through our words and through our actions—the present reality and the future victorious consummation of our king's reign.

CHAPTER FOUR

PRAYING FOR HEALING

The doctor told Linda and J (his name is John but he goes by his initial) that the ultrasound taken during the seventeenth week of pregnancy revealed a problem. She immediately sent them to a perinatal specialist. After taking a second ultrasound, the specialist told them that in addition to a live fetus—a boy—there was an abnormal mass of tissue in the womb, which he called a mole. It was impossible to tell if the mole, caused by an irregularity in an egg or sperm (or both), was attached to the baby. The five obstetrician/gynecologists monitoring Linda's pregnancy agreed with the diagnosis.

The specialist warned Linda and J of the ramifications of this molar pregnancy, each one more dire than the one before. The baby's genetic condition was unknown and the specialist feared that the child might be triploid, having an extra set of chromosomes. This meant that he could not survive outside the womb. Other defects, such as Down syndrome or spina bifida, would be more likely if the child were connected in any way with the mole.

The strongest probability, however, was that the baby would not live long enough to be born. Ordinarily, a woman's body will spontaneously abort a mole, eighty percent of the time by about the twentieth week. In this case, the baby would be aborted along with the mole. The spontaneous abortion protects the mother. If there were no such abortion, molar cells could enter Linda's blood stream and lodge in her heart, brain, or liver and become malignant.

Linda and J asked their friends to pray. Friends from their church and other churches responded. People from all over the country, people they had never met, prayed for them. Linda and J invited a deacon from our church (also named John) and me to their house to pray with them. We anointed Linda with oil, laid hands on her, and asked God to grant her a healthy pregnancy and delivery.

At the specialist's request, they had amniocentesis done, so they and the doctors could be prepared for an early delivery in case such a procedure was necessary to try saving the baby. If the baby survived in the womb until the twenty-sixth week of pregnancy, the doctors could take him by caesarean section, if necessary. Linda and J had already decided to do all they could to save the baby, even if his chances for survival outside the womb were almost nonexistent. J wept as he told me, "Linda said if they took him by C-section, she wanted me to hold him until he died."

Then came the first good news. Contrary to the doctors' expectations, the amniocentesis demonstrated that the baby was perfectly healthy. He had no genetic abnormalities. In addition—and again, contrary to the doctors' expectations—Linda's body was showing no signs, of trying to abort the baby. He was developing normally. Weeks passed with Linda getting routine ultrasounds and blood tests. The ultrasounds continued to show the grapelike sacs the doctors identified as the mole. But for some reason it was not affecting the health of either the mother or the baby.

Three weeks after the final ultrasound, having been carried full term, healthy little Zachary was born. And there was no sign of the molar tissue the doctor expected to find in the afterbirth. The pathology report stated no molar tissue was present, though there were some abnormalities on the placenta. Could it have been a misdiagnosis? It seemed unlikely. Nine health care professionals—the perinatal specialist, five obstetrician/gynecologists, and three ultrasound technicians—had concurred that the ultrasounds indicated the presence of molar tissue.

Referring to the mole, the senior obstetrician/ gynecologist assured them after the delivery, "There was something there." But something had rendered the mole harmless and eventually caused it to vanish. Something the doctor could not explain. . . .

What Does Scripture Really Teach about Healing?

Healing—there's no shortage of conflicting opinions about the Bible's teaching on the subject. I once saw a healing evangelist gently chide a woman he had just prayed for.

"Are you healed?" he asked after the prayer.

"I hope so," she replied.

"You *hope* so?" he asked with a frown. "Sister, the Bible says you are healed. Just confess that." He implied that if she didn't confess it, the healing might not "take."

On the other hand, I recall a Sunday school teacher explaining why Jesus left certain sick people unhealed.

"Jesus didn't come to heal people, but to save their souls." She implied that healing was a sideline in Jesus' ministry, not a major part of what he came to accomplish. And not something people could expect either in Jesus' day or our own.

How should we handle the issue of divine healing? Is it something we can claim? If people are not healed, is it because they've done something wrong? Or is it misguided to emphasize prayer for healing? Is it presumptuous to pray for it at all? Was it or was it not a major focus of Jesus' ministry? Should it or should it not be a major focus of ours?

My experience with praying for healing began when I was in high school. My Campus Life club (part of Youth for Christ's ministry to high school students) had a singing group that sang in various churches on

> How should we handle the issue of divine healing? Was it or was it not a major focus of Jesus' ministry? Should it or should it not be a major focus of ours?

Sunday nights. One Sunday we were rehearsing in an Assemblies of God church. I struck up a conversation with a church member I had just met.

"This is a great church," he said. "We had several healings here last month." At the conclusion of a service, people would pray for healings in the front of the sanctuary.

Healings? At my church, people would come forward after the service to become Christians or rededicate their lives. But we didn't do healings. That is not to say we never prayed for sick people. We did, though not in front of the whole congregation. But our prayers seemed more like verbalized wishes than confident requests. Sort of like telling somebody, "Have a nice day," without thinking about what that really means. I got the impression that it was okay to pray for healing as long as you didn't expect much to happen. This church obviously took a different view. I wasn't sure what to make of it.

Then one Saturday my father rushed my mother to the hospital emergency room. She was having extreme abdominal pains. The doctor diagnosed it as a problem with her gall bladder. It was probably gall stones, he said, though she would have to come back Monday for more extensive tests. He prescribed a painkiller, Darvon, in the meantime.

The Darvon did its job, and Mom just rested that evening and the next day. Sunday evening I was getting a snack in the kitchen when she walked in. I asked her how she was feeling.

"The painkiller's wearing off," she said. "It's really starting to hurt."

I assumed she would just pop another pill. I was not prepared for what she said next.

"Marilyn says you and Teri should lay hands on me and pray for healing." I didn't know if she was saying this because she thought it was funny or because she wanted us to do it.

"Oh?"

"Would you do it?"

Marilyn was a family friend. About a week earlier when my sister Teri and I were talking with her, the subject of divine healing came up. I had listened politely to what she had to say, though the subject did not interest me. I had seen evangelists on television promising healing to people, and I was not impressed. I thought they were weird. The people who were allegedly healed must be stooges who fake illnesses and healings, I figured. Or they were very suggestible people who allowed a manipulative evangelist to convince them they'd been healed. Besides, the entire emphasis seemed wrong. *The gospel is about getting people saved, not healed,* I thought.

But Marilyn said that praying for the sick was a legitimate ministry, and she shared some Scripture verses about it. I trusted Marilyn. She was a solid Christian with a good grasp of the Bible and was one of the most levelheaded people I knew. Maybe there was something to this after all. I recalled that some people seemed to have been healed at the Assemblies of God church. After our conversation I was willing to admit that maybe praying for healing was a valid ministry (though I still had my doubts about the "healers" I'd seen on television). But although I thought it might be okay for some people to get into, it was not something that appealed to me. I never expected to go to a healing service or see a healing.

And I certainly never expected my mother to ask me to pray for one. It was the kind of request my charismatic friends might make, not my fundamentalist mother. *She must really be in pain,* I thought.

Before I could answer Mom, Teri walked into the kitchen. Mom asked Teri if she'd join us in praying for healing. Teri was no more eager than I.

"Let me go upstairs and brush my teeth and think about it," she said. She headed upstairs. I hoped she would take a long time and maybe Mom would change her mind. In my own mind I was wishing Marilyn had kept her mouth shut. *If Marilyn's so into this healing thing, why doesn't she come over here and lay hands on Mom?* I thought.

I considered offering just to go into my room and pray alone for Mom. I could handle that. But laying hands on her and praying with her was something else. For some reason it felt threatening, it raised the stakes to a higher level. Yet I knew I'd feel guilty if I refused. So I told Mom I'd pray with her. Teri came back downstairs. She agreed to do it, too. The three of us went into the living room. My ever practical father stayed in the family room and read the newspaper. This was too strange for him.

We sat on the couch, Teri on Mom's right and I on the left. I asked Mom where it hurt. She patted her abdomen, and I placed my right hand there. Teri put her hand on Mom's shoulder. During our talk, Marilyn had briefly mentioned some of the things that should be said during a prayer for healing. Now I wished I had paid better attention. We bowed our heads, and I started to pray. It may have been the most unemotional prayer I've ever prayed. I wasn't thinking about Mom's pain or the fact that we were asking for some kind of miracle. I was just trying to remember all the points Marilyn had made, and to recite them in the right order. It was like praying the grocery list.

When the prayer was over, I took my hand off Mom. I was sure nothing had happened.

"How's it feel?" I asked, assuming she'd say there was no change. Marilyn had said that even if it seems like nothing has happened, sometimes healings take place gradually. You just have to keep praying for them. I was going to tell Mom this after she confirmed that the pain was still there. Then the unexpected happened. She patted her stomach and stared straight ahead.

"The pain's gone," she said.

"What?"

"It's a little stiff where the pain used to be but it doesn't hurt anymore."

The pain never returned. She slept through the night without taking any more Darvon. The next day Dad took her to the hospital for the test. She told the doctor that the pain had gone away.

"Even if it doesn't hurt, you can still have problems with the gall bladder," he said. He told them the test would reveal those problems; then he ran the test and gave them the results.

"You have a perfectly working gall bladder," he said. "I can't find anything wrong." Never again did Mom experience the abdominal pains. Was she healed through prayer? Initially my parents disagreed.

"It must not have been your gall bladder if the pain went away all by itself like that," Dad said.

"It didn't go away all by itself," Mom responded. "God healed me." (Subsequent experiences with other healings have since caused Dad to reverse his skepticism.)

This experience changed my antipathy toward the subject of healing. It became something of great interest to me. I read everything I could about it. Most of the books I read quoted the following passage from Isaiah as the foundation for belief in divine healing:

> Surely he took up our infirmities and carried our sorrows, yet we considered him stricken by God, smitten by him, and afflicted. But he was pierced for our transgressions, he was crushed for our iniquities; the punishment that brought us peace was upon him, and by his wounds we are healed.
> —Isaiah 53:4–5

According to these sources, this passage teaches that Christ died for our sicknesses as well as for our sins. As proof of this, they cited two New Testament passages that refer to the quotation in Isaiah. The first came from Matthew's Gospel:

> When evening came, many who were demon possessed were brought to him [Jesus], and he drove out the spirits with a word and healed all the sick. This was to fulfill what was spoken through the prophet Isaiah: "He took up our infirmities, and carried our diseases."
> —Matthew 8:16–17

The second came from Peter's first epistle:

> He [Jesus] himself bore our sins in his body on the tree, so that we might die to sins and live for righteousness; by his wounds you have been healed.
> —1 Peter 2:24

Therefore, according to the books I was reading, just as we prayed to receive forgiveness of sins we can also pray to receive healing of sickness. The authors argued that we can claim that we are healed even if our symptoms of sickness continue. When we ask God to forgive our sins, we may not feel any different. But instead of trusting our feelings, we must trust God's Word that tells us we are forgiven. Similarly, when we pray for healing we may not "feel healed." But, they said, we must trust God's Word that tells us we have been healed. If we stand firm in believing we've been healed, the books said, then the symptoms will eventually disappear, though it may take some time.

With this theology in mind, I would sometimes pray for healings as a need arose. The results seemed mixed. Usually people would recover from an illness or an operation at about the same rate you'd expect them to recover naturally. Some people with serious illnesses did not recover. But there were a couple of instances where recovery seemed to have more than a purely natural explanation.

My brother Dave had a chronic pain in his right elbow. The doctor said it developed because of his playing Little League baseball, and the doctor could do nothing for it except advise him to stop playing Little League. Yet when we prayed for healing with the laying on of hands, the pain left during the prayer and never returned.

Years later my friend Greg asked me to pray for him right before a doctor's appointment. A few days earlier the ophthalmologist had examined his right eye, which had been hit by a racquetball. He had told Greg that the eye had suffered serious trauma and that he expected Greg to have permanent vision impairment. Greg and I prayed for healing with the laying on of hands, right before the second appointment.

The doctor was amazed at the improvement. "He said it didn't look like the same eye," Greg said. "He called it a miracle." The eye eventually healed completely and has never given Greg any problems since.

I choose to believe that I have occasionally seen people healed through prayer. Others may disagree. A skeptic can insist that there are natural explanations for any alleged accounts of divine healing. To some people the words "psychosomatic" and "misdiagnosis" can explain anything. I have no desire to argue with such people. In fact, sometimes I almost envy them. If I could believe that nobody was ever healed through prayer then I would not have to grapple with the question of why some people seem to be healed and some don't.

Yet, the more I prayed for the sick, the more I concluded that there often seemed to be a discrepancy between my theology—which said that we can claim healing—and the medical facts of a particular situation. Many people were not healed through prayer. Why? Did they lack sufficient faith? Had they committed some sin that inhibited the healing process?

That's what my theology tended to say. My understanding of Scripture was that our healing had already taken place. We just had to accept it. And if we were still sick, we hadn't fully accepted our healing. The implication was that if we were not healed, we were doing something wrong; we needed to change something in our lives. Maybe we needed to increase our faith. Maybe there was some hidden sin we needed to confess. Maybe we needed to take some action that illustrated faith, like throwing away our medicine. Maybe we just needed to keep confessing that we were healed in spite of our symptoms.

> Many people were not healed through prayer. Why? Did they lack sufficient faith? Had they committed some sin that inhibited the healing process?

I acknowledged that there may be instances when lack of faith or unconfessed sin may block a healing. However, I began questioning the idea that when we are not healed, it is generally because we are doing something wrong. It seemed to put us in the same category as Job's friends—automatically blaming an innocent man for his afflictions. It seemed to have unhealthy consequences both physically and spiritually. People blamed a quadriplegic for lacking the faith to get healed, and "negatively confessing" that his neck was broken. People died from easily treatable diseases, "confessing their healing" and refusing medical treatment. People who couldn't muster enough faith to get healed wondered if they ever really had enough faith to receive forgiveness of sins.

The issue became more complex as I searched the Bible for a balanced view on healing. Scripture reveals a paradox concerning the apostle Paul. The book of Acts depicts Paul with almost magical healing powers. People received healings simply by touching handkerchiefs and aprons he had touched.[1] But, though Paul's own letters make passing reference to miracles, they depict numerous failures to obtain healings. He tells the Philippians that Epaphroditus became ill and almost died.[2] He tells Timothy that he left Trophimus sick in Miletus.[3] Surely Paul must have prayed for these men. He also tells Timothy, "Stop drinking only water, and use a little wine because of your stomach and your frequent illnesses" (1 Timothy 5:23). He did not tell Timothy to claim his healing, but rather to take his medicine. Paul himself was not exempt from physical affliction. He reminds the Galatians that it was because of his illness that he first preached the gospel to them.[4] Clearly Paul did not believe that all our sicknesses would go away—even over a period of time—in response to a prayer of faith.

How do we explain the paradox between Paul's healings in Acts and his failure to obtain healings in the epistles? Moreover how do we explain the apparent mixture of success and failure we experience in praying for healings today?

Healing and the Overlap

I never wavered in my conviction that the Bible teaches us to pray for healings, and that we may experience healings today. But I wondered if Scripture might not provide a more sufficient foundation for divine healing than I was aware of. And as I surveyed Scripture, I came to see that the key lies in understanding the "already" and "not yet" reality of living in the overlap.

We know that when the kingdom of God arrives in all its fullness, disease and death will be eradicated. But we live in this present evil age where they can still strike. However, since the kingdom of God has been inaugurated, we can begin to experience some of its blessings. And at times those blessings may take the form of healings, foretastes of the physical wholeness that the consummated kingdom will bring. We are God's army, fighting to win back territory that the Evil One has usurped. And praying for healings is one of the weapons in our arsenal.

> We are God's army, fighting to win back territory that the Evil One has usurped. And praying for healings is one of the weapons in our arsenal.

Twice, using almost identical language, Matthew describes Jesus' threefold strategy to advance the kingdom: teaching, preaching the kingdom, and healing.[5] Healing the sick was an integral part of Jesus' proclamation of the kingdom. Therefore, shouldn't it be an integral part of our ministry as well? Missiology professor Mortimer Arias says:

> The good news of the kingdom is for the whole person—physically (healing), intellectually (teaching), and spiritually (preaching). . . . The healing ministry, then—whether healing through prayer, medicine, pastoral counseling, group therapy, nutrition and mental health services, rehabilitation from drug addiction, or social reconciliation and the defense of human rights, in whatever form—is not merely a secondary social service of the church but also an inseparable part of the announcement of the good news of the kingdom of life revealed in Jesus Christ.[6]

Theologian Michael Green concurs:

> Kingdom ministry embraces preaching, teaching and healing. When the church exercises this ministry, she will often lack the power, immediacy, and effectiveness of Jesus; he shared God's nature in a way the church does not. But wherever the church is truly carrying out the work of the kingdom, those three stands—challenging preaching, clear teaching and healing (of physical disease, inner hurts and grip by dark forces)—will be seen.[7]

Thus, understanding the kingdom of God helps us understand the incomplete nature of divine healing. Why are some people healed? At least a partial answer is that the age to come has arrived, and sometimes its power reveals itself through healings. Why are some people not healed? At least a partial answer is that we are still living in the present evil age where we are subject to disease and death. Perfect health will not be ours until the kingdom of God arrives in its fullness.

Then what about Isaiah's statement that by his wounds we are healed? Did Christ die for our sicknesses as well as our sins? Or to put it more theologically, is physical healing in the atonement?[8] Respected scholars disagree. Some contend that healing is in the atonement. However, they hasten to add that not all the benefits of the atonement are ours yet, whether it comes to being saved from sin or from sickness.

For example, there is a sense in which we *were* saved from sin when we were first converted. Our sins were forgiven and we were declared "not guilty" before God. There is another sense in which we *are still being* saved from sin, as we resist temptation and grow in holiness. There's a third sense in which we *will be* saved from sin, when we are resurrected with new bodies that will never get sick or die. When it comes to sin, we have not yet received all the benefits of the atonement.

Similarly, some scholars believe healing from sickness is in the atonement, but stress that we have not yet received its full benefits. Biblical scholar Charles Farah, Jr., affirms that healing is in the atonement but adds:

> We may liken the benefits of the Atonement to one of the new, super cold pills that boasts it releases its medication at properly spaced intervals. In our dispensation, salvation is universal for all who sincerely repent and receive Christ as Lord and Savior. I have yet to meet a man or woman who sincerely called upon the Name of the Lord who was not saved. But I have met many godly saints who have called upon the Lord but have not been healed. The time release for that particular medication from the Atonement has evidently not yet been universally released.[9]

But Gordon D. Fee questions whether physical healing is in the atonement at all. He says,

> While there are scores of texts that explicitly tell us that our sin has been overcome through Christ's death and resurrection, there is *no* text that explicitly says the same about healing, not even Isaiah 53 and its New Testament citations.
>
> Matthew's use of Isaiah 53:4 does not even refer to the cross; rather he clearly sees the text as being fulfilled in Jesus' earthly *ministry*. . . . Matthew clearly saw Isaiah 53:4 as referring to *physical healing*, but as part of the Messiah's

ministry, not as a part of the atonement. Peter, conversely, saw the "healing" of Isaiah 53 as being metaphorical and thus referring to the healing of our *sin* sickness. Thus *neither* New Testament reference sees the "healing" of Isaiah 53 as referring to *physical healing in the atonement*. But what did Isaiah himself intend? Almost certainly his first reference is metaphorical, as the Septuagint[10], the Targums[11], and Peter all recognize. Israel was diseased; she was grievously wounded for sins (Isaiah 1:6–7). Yet God would restore His people. There would come one who himself would suffer so as to deliver. In grand cadences of Hebrew poetry (note the synonymous parallelism), Isaiah says of him: "The *punishment* that brought us peace was upon him, and by his *wounds* we are *healed*." In the context of Isaiah, that refers first of all to the healing of the wounds and disease of sin. Yet, since physical disease was clearly recognized to be a consequence of the Fall, such a metaphor could also carry with it the *literal* sense, and this is what Matthew picked up.

The Bible, therefore, does not explicitly teach that healing is provided for in the atonement. However, the New Testament does see the cross as the focus of God's redemptive activity. In this sense (and in the sense that sickness is ultimately a result of the Fall), one may perhaps argue that healing also finds its focal point in the atonement. [12]

Thus, whether we share Farah's convictions or Fee's reservations about healing being in the atonement, we arrive at the same practical conclusion—the atonement does not *guarantee* physical healing at this moment in time. But this does not mean that we should refrain from earnestly *praying* for healings. Indeed, such prayer is one of our primary tools for helping people experience the wholeness, the *shalom*, that characterizes the kingdom. The

> The atonement does not *guarantee* physical healing at this moment in time. But this does not mean that we should refrain from earnestly *praying* for healings.

kingdom of God has arrived, and we can expect at times to witness its healing power. Referring to the healing of Peter's mother-in-law[13], Michael Green says:

> In recent years I have repented of my earlier skepticism in the matter, and have often followed the example set out here. And I have often seen healings result. But many people are not healed. It is a mystery which we shall never plumb. We can never be dogmatic about when God will heal and when he will not. But what happened regularly and without a failure rate in the life of Jesus does happen occasionally and with many failures when his disciples pray in faith and call on God to heal. It is a sign of the kingdom. We should be surprised if we never see it. The powers of the age to come have broken into our world; but the powers of this age are there too. We have to live with that ambivalence. We are in a "betwixt and between" state in this mortal life: we shall see the pain and the failure, but we shall also see the power and the glory, at least sometimes, if we maintain that attitude of simple trust in the heavenly Father which Jesus so movingly displayed.[14]

There's another way the kingdom of God impacts our understanding of divine healing. Because the kingdom has arrived, we can all experience the supernatural empowering of God's Spirit.

In a naturalistic generation like ours, it is easy to overlook the supernatural. But as author and apologist Francis Schaeffer says:

> The supernatural does not touch the Christian only at the new birth and then at his death, or at the second coming of Christ, leaving the believer on his own in a naturalistic world during all of the time in between. Nothing could be further from the biblical view. Being a biblical Christian means living in the supernatural now, not only theoretically but in practice.[15]

The supernatural power of the Holy Spirit is ours today. Some may experience this power through physical healing of their bodies. Some may experience it through an inner strengthening that occurs in spite of the fact that they are not physically healed. We cannot predict what God's plan for any individual is.

The twelfth chapter of Acts tells of the divergent paths taken by two men of God. Both James and Peter were arrested for their faith. James was martyred and Peter was miraculously freed from prison. Their task was to glorify God and minister in the power of the Spirit, no matter what their situation.[16] Living in the overlap, our task is the same.

The issue of divine healing reminds me of an old story about a drunken man riding a horse. First, he falls off the right side. Then, determined not to make the same mistake again, he climbs back onto the horse and promptly falls off the left side. Like the drunken man, we may find ourselves leaning too far in one direction or the other. Some of us may approach the subject of divine healing by expecting almost nothing. Some of us may approach it by demanding just about everything.

As one who has repeatedly fallen off both sides of the horse, I acknowledge how slippery the saddle can be. Yet, somewhere between the two extremes is a biblical middle ground that recognizes the power, wisdom, and sovereignty of a loving God. And that middle ground rests squarely on our already/not-yet status of living in the overlap. We who have the privilege of living in the overlap also have the privilege of asking our all-powerful, all-wise, and all-sovereign God for healing, and then leaving the results in his loving hands. As Fee says:

> The first sentence of a sound biblical theology may well be, God *must* do *nothing*. God is free to be God. He is sovereign in all things and is simply not under our control. The second sentence of a sound biblical theology will be: Although God *must* do *nothing*, in grace he does *all things*. No healing has ever been deserved; it is always an expression of God's grace. Some have asked, If God must do nothing, then why pray at all? Why not simply wait for Him to act sovereignly? The answer is simple: because God answers prayer. The mystery of faith is that there is a wonderful correlation between our asking and trusting, and what goes on about us. God doesn't

have to answer prayer, but He does. God doesn't have to heal, but He graciously does. Healing, therefore is not a divine obligation; it is a divine gift. And precisely because it is a gift, we can make no demands. But we can *trust* Him to do all things well![17]

CHAPTER FIVE

BEING USED BY GOD

When I was four years old my parents bought me a new raincoat. Thrilled with the purchase, I couldn't wait for a rainy day. Finally nature smiled on me. I begged my mother to let me play outside in the rain, and she agreed. After bundling me in the yellow coat and tying the matching hood around my head, she let me out the front door with a strict, "Stay in the driveway." Periodically she'd glance out the living room window to make sure I was okay.

After a while she looked out the window and couldn't see me in the driveway. But up the street in a neighbor's yard stood a little figure that seemed to be dressed in the same yellow coat and hood I was wearing. She assumed it was me.

With all the frustration of a mother disobeyed, she threw on her coat and grabbed an umbrella. Marching outside into the rain, which had become torrential, she yelled, "Stevie! Stevie!" at the object of her ire. There was no response. Then she heard a little voice behind her say, "What, Mommy?"

Turning around, she saw me standing against the garage door, taking refuge under the overhang. Then she turned back toward the neighbor's yard and realized her mistake. She had been screaming at a yellow fire hydrant.

I think this may be symbolic of what happens to a lot of us. Probably more often than we realize, we go through life seeing things that aren't really there, and assuming things that aren't really true. This may be especially true when it comes to living in the overlap; we are citizens of an unseen kingdom that deals with invisible realities. The tension between the "already" and "not yet" is something we deal with on a daily basis; while dwelling in this present age, we must already live as citizens of a kingdom that is not yet seen. We know that an invisible God is at work in the world around us using certain people to accomplish his purposes. But how can we know that we will be numbered among those people? How can we know that God will use us?

> An invisible God is at work in the world around us using certain people to accomplish his purposes. But how can we know that we will be numbered among those people?

One Pattern

Maybe the most obvious way to answer this is to look at people God used during Bible times, determine what they have in common, and then try to follow their example. For a long time I saw only one pattern for this. When we look at a Moses or a Joshua or a Paul, we see such a pattern.

First, God calls them to do something. From a burning bush, God tells Moses to venture into Egypt and tell Pharaoh to let his people go.[1] God tells Joshua to parade around Jericho seven days in a row, blowing trumpets and shouting on the last day.[2] Through a vision of a Macedonian man, God directs Paul to travel to Macedonia and preach the gospel there.[3]

Second, they obey God. Moses (after unsuccessfully trying to get out of this assignment) gives the message to Pharaoh. Joshua and his men employ the unconventional military strategy. Paul sails to Macedonia and proclaims the gospel.

And finally, they see the results of their obedience. Moses leads the Jews out of Egypt and to the brink of the Promised Land. Joshua sees Jericho's walls come tumbling down. People throughout Macedonia respond to Paul's message. Many of us may have experienced this pattern in our own lives—God calls us to do something, we obey, and we see results.

This is certainly one way God works. For a long time I wasn't aware of any other way. This frustrated me because often I did not feel any particular leading from God to perform certain deeds. If only God would speak to me like he did to Moses or Paul, I'd obey, I thought. But I didn't experience the guidance from God that those men experienced.

Not that I expected to hear his voice booming out of a blazing shrub; I recognized that God reveals his will to us through such avenues as Scripture, the advice of godly friends, circumstances, and inner impressions by the Holy Spirit. But what if specific instructions didn't seem to come? The very invisibility (or inaudibility) of the kingdom became a source of frustration. Was I to remain stuck in a holding pattern, unable to be used by God until I deciphered some clue that would reveal what precise act God wanted me to perform next? Or was there another pattern for being used by God—one that didn't depend on perceiving detailed directions from him?

A Less Obvious Pattern

As I examined the Scriptures I saw that there's another less obvious, but equally valid, way God can use us.

For example, a young woman goes to a well and grants a thirsty stranger's request for water, giving water to his camels as well. No voice from heaven tells her to do this, but because of this gesture Rebekah becomes a matriarch of God's people, the Jews.[4]

Then there's a man sitting at the city gate, who just happens to overhear an assassination plot. When he reports it he knows he's saving the king's life, but Mordecai has no idea his deed will also start a chain reaction that will save all the Jews in Persia from slaughter.[5]

And it isn't a divine dream or vision that starts a young shepherd boy on his trip. He's just obeying his father's order to take grain and bread to his older brothers in the military. But when he arrives at the camp, David encounters a certain giant who needs to be disposed of.[6]

Scripture is full of instances where God uses his people without their even realizing it; they just do what comes naturally and somehow wind up in the right place at the right time to be used by God.[7]

We see examples of this today. Evangelist Leighton Ford tells of a Christian who had no idea of the impact his life was having on another:

> Jim Petersen, who worked with The Navigators in Brazil, tried for a long time to reach a Communist student for Christ. This student was a tough case. Jim taught him, befriended him, and debated spiritual issues with him for months. Finally, this student gave his life to the Lord. Jim later asked him, "What did I say that reached you?"
>
> "Nothing," the student replied.
>
> "Nothing!" Jim was dumbfounded.
>
> "Oh, I listened," the student went on. "I was searching and questioning, and you answered a lot of my intellectual questions. But it wasn't what you *said* that changed my heart. It was what you *did*."
>
> Now Jim was *really* baffled. "What did I do?" he asked.
>
> "Nothing spectacular," the student replied. "It's just that you were a friend to me. You invited me into your home. And that's how I got to find out what kind of guy you really are. Jim, I watched the way you disciplined your children—with grace and toughness, and above all with love. *And I saw God in the way you lived with your children.*"[8]

Probably most of us can relate similar occurrences we've witnessed. Many years ago my father worked with a woman named Lois. At first she was his secretary, and then, she became secretary to his supervisor, the president of the corporation. She knew Dad as someone who was honest, who kept calm under pressure, and who treated people the way they would like to be treated. She knew my mother as a warm, outgoing person who took a genuine interest in the people Dad worked with. Although Mom and Dad don't broadcast the fact that they're Christians, most people who have known them for any length of time realize their faith is important to them.

One day Lois attended a special service at her church, led by an evangelist. He said that Jesus offered forgiveness and eternal life to those who committed themselves to him. And Lois thought, *That must be what happened to the Schaefers.* She wanted in her life what she had seen in theirs. So when the evangelist invited people to make a commitment to Christ, she responded to the invitation.

The next day at work she told Dad about the decision she had made and the influence he had on it. As the weeks passed it was our privilege as a family to see Lois grow rapidly in her Christian walk. However, it wasn't long after this that Lois discovered she had cancer. In spite of the prayers of God's people and the best medical care, she died. But she died knowing that she would spend eternity with God because of her relationship with Jesus Christ.

As I look back on that episode with Lois, I wonder what might have happened if Dad had been the kind of Christian who sometimes set aside his principles at work—who wasn't always honest, who lost his temper easily, and who didn't treat people right. What if Mom had been the kind of woman who made life miserable for her husband's secretary? And I visualize Lois sitting in church listening to the evangelist, thinking, *This must be what the Schaefers are into. And if it is, I don't want any part of it because I don't want to be like them.*

I can't help but wonder what a difference there may have been in Lois' life and eternal destiny. And through it all my folks would never have known the consequences of their lack of Christian commitment in this area.

> Every day we have encounters with people that can lead them one step closer to God or one step farther away. And in many, maybe most, cases we may not have a clue about the impact we're having.

This incident reminds me that, living in the overlap, every day we have encounters with people that can lead them one step closer to God or one step farther away. And in many, maybe most, cases we may not have a clue about the impact we're having.

Perhaps one reason I feel so strongly about this is that my own Christian walk is partially the result of this kind of encounter. When I was a sophomore in high school I got involved with Campus Life. And although I had been brought up in the church I realized I didn't have the relationship with God that a lot of the other Campus Life kids had. I remember a particular turning point. When we were sharing prayer requests a girl stood up, choking back tears, and said, "Please pray for me. I've been treating my mother so badly, and I feel terrible about it—I need your prayers."

I thought, "How can she admit that in front of all these people?" I wouldn't have admitted my faults before a roomful of people. I could barely admit them to myself. But I realized that she and the other kids were free to be real with each other because they knew God loved them exactly the way they were and he was helping them become the people he wanted them to be. They were not Super-Christians. They were just real people struggling to follow a real God. I realized I wanted what they' had. And it wasn't much later that I made my commitment to become a Christian.

I don't remember that girl's name. I don't even remember what she looked like. But there are two things about her I do know. First, I know that God used her to give me a glimpse of what it meant to be a Christian and to help turn my life around. Second, I know that during the exact moment God was using her in a mighty way to help draw me into the kingdom, she felt like a total failure as a Christian.

And this is why I think it may be a mistake to be preoccupied with our own usefulness. When we strive to be useful, there's a tendency to look around us to see what kind of impact we're having on people. And chances are we'll either overestimate or underestimate what God is really doing with us.

Jesus' parable of the talents can help us here.[9] Jesus compared the kingdom to the situation of a man going on a long journey. Before leaving, the man gives five talents to one servant, two talents to another one, and one talent to a third. (A talent is a weight of money, like a gold brick.) When he returns, the man finds that the first two servants had put their wealth to work, doubling its value.

"Well done, good and faithful servant! You have been faithful with a few things; I will put you in charge of many things. Come and share your master's happiness," he tells each of them.

But when he discovers that the third servant had merely buried his talent, the master reprimands him for being wicked and lazy. He tells the servant that he could have at least earned some interest on the money by putting it into a bank. Then he decrees that the talent be taken away from that servant and given to the first servant.

It's significant that the master does not tell the profitable servants, "Well done, good and *useful* servant." He praises them instead for their faithfulness. And he condemns the unprofitable servant, not for lack of results but for lack of effort. Faithfulness, not usefulness, is what's emphasized in the kingdom; the implication is that if we focus on faithfulness, usefulness will follow. When we adopt a lifestyle of faithfulness we become more like Jesus. And the more we become like Jesus, the better equipped we are to be used by God.

> Faithfulness, not usefulness, is what's emphasized in the kingdom; the implication is that if we focus on faithfulness, usefulness will follow.

God's All-Stars

Some of us may feel we don't have what it takes to be somebody God uses. We may need to take a second look. When I think of the heroes of the faith, I think of the people listed in Hebrews 11 as "God's All-Stars." They're held up to us as models we should follow. And I tend to put people like David and Abraham and Moses on pedestals, as if they were made of different stuff from you and me—as if they were born to be religious because they had holy chromosomes in their genes. But recently, in rereading the chapter, I took a look at what kind of a past some of these people had.

On two occasions a fearful Abraham palmed off his wife to a foreign king, pretending she was just his sister.[10] His son Isaac pulled the same stunt with his wife.[11] Rahab was a prostitute.[12] Moses murdered a man in anger.[13] Noah disgraced himself in a drunken stupor.[14] Jacob was a cheat.[15] Samson was a playboy.[16] David committed adultery with Bathsheba, then had her husband killed.[17] In fact, of the fifteen heroes of the faith mentioned by name in this chapter, over half of them had some major sin or weakness in their past that we might think would disqualify them from being a role model for godliness. And I mean no irreverence here, but I concluded that from a certain standpoint this looks like a pretty sorry group of people.

True, nobody's perfect. But when God was choosing role models, couldn't he have picked people whose worst sin was overeating, or fudging on their taxes, or maybe just having a really cranky temper? Do we really have to go this route of adultery and prostitution and murder? Then I realized that if Hebrews 11 means anything, it means there's hope for those of us who feel deep down inside that we don't have what it takes to be a man or woman of God.

> If Hebrews 11 means anything, it means there's hope for those of us who feel deep down inside that we don't have what it takes to be a man or woman of God.

Those of us who struggle with a poor self image can look at Moses, who resisted God's call by insisting he was a talentless nobody. Those of us who struggle with anxiety can look at Abraham, whose fear caused him to abandon Sarah. Those of us who feel that the world has chewed us up and spit us out so badly we'll never be of use to anybody can look at Rahab, who was used and abused by so many until she found God's direction for her life. And those of us who feel we've sinned too badly to ever be one of God's special people can look at David, who sinned deeply, but also repented deeply and remained a man after God's own heart.

In fact if Hebrews 11 tells us anything, it tells us that none of us has an excuse *not* to become the kind of person God uses. And what kind of person is that? When we look at Scripture, we see he uses people who fail and struggle, people who feel like nobodies, who fight against him and who sin tragically—but who eventually raise their hands in surrender, saying, "Not my will but yours be done," and who endeavor to live out that commitment moment by moment, one day at a time.

Living in the Overlap

This has a couple of ramifications for us. First, it means we may be in for some surprises when we arrive at the pearly gates. We may have assumed that our most effective works for the kingdom were the highly visible or "spiritual" deeds—the solos we sang in church, the Sunday school classes we taught, the testimonies we gave before the congregation. However, we may discover that we did our most valuable work through our seemingly inconsequential acts—the phone calls made to a friend, the kindnesses shown to that co-worker who grates on our nerves, the hugs we gave our children. As soldiers in the invisible kingdom we will be sent on secret missions, sometimes so secret that we ourselves are not aware of them. In his devotional classic *My Utmost for His Highest*, Oswald Chambers reminds us, "If you want to be of use to God, get rightly related to Jesus Christ, and He will make you of use unconsciously every moment you live."[18]

> As soldiers in the invisible kingdom we will be sent on secret missions, sometimes so secret that we ourselves are not aware of them.

Second, we may need to encourage ourselves not to give up. There are days when our five senses will tell us that we're not accomplishing anything and the Christian life doesn't seem worth living; when God seems deaf, blind, and mute, if he seems to exist at all. But when we feel like shucking the whole thing and railing against heaven, I suspect we're really just screaming at fire hydrants—perceiving something that's just not true, and reacting to it. The apostle Paul reminds us, "Let us not

> We do not yet know what our faithfulness will accomplish, but already we can be confident that it will reap a harvest.

become weary in doing good, for at the proper time we will reap a harvest if we do not give up" (Galatians 6:9). Again we see the tension between the "already" and the "not yet" of living in the overlap. We do not yet know what our faithfulness will accomplish, but already we can be confident that it will reap a harvest.

It's easy to get discouraged if we constantly look around us to see if we're making an impact on people. I have found a role model in the villager that pastor Ron Lee Davis describes in *Gold in the Making*. Davis tells of a friend who visited a leprosarium in a Third World country:

> As he was talking with some of the people there who were afflicted with this terrible disease, he met one particular man who had a vital, glowing love for Jesus Christ. The two of them began to visit together.
>
> The leper said to my friend, "You know, I didn't always have this joy, this love of God in my heart. When I first came to this leprosarium, I was the most angry and bitter man here.
>
> "But there was one man from the village nearby who came out every day to visit me. Every single day he came out and brought me food, and at first I threw it back in his face. He'd come out and offer to play cards with me, but I shouted at him to leave me alone. He wanted to talk with me, but I would have nothing to say to him. Still, he kept coming to visit me, day after day after day after day.
>
> "Finally I could do nothing else but ask him, 'Why? *Why* do you keep coming to see me, to love me, when all I ever show you is bitterness and hatred?'
>
> "And he told me, 'It's because of the love of Jesus Christ Himself.'"

Then my friend asked the leper, "How long did your friend from the village come out to see you before you gave your heart to Christ?"

The leper's answer: "He came every day for thirteen years."[19]

If this villager had focused on his own usefulness he almost certainly would have given up after a year or five or ten. But he was content to be a faithful servant, obeying his master without looking for results or recognition.

As we seek to serve God we may sometimes relate to a Moses or a Paul, who got direct guidance through a burning bush or a vision; but at other times we may feel relatively "bushless" or "visionless." Yet though we may not hear that voice from heaven telling us specific actions to perform, we already have definite guidance in Scripture concerning what kind of people we should be—people who love God and each other, people who cast their burdens on the Lord and who bear each others' burdens, people who walk as Jesus did, people who seek the kingdom above all else. And God has a habit of using people like that every day of their lives without their even realizing it.

Living in the overlap, we are like actors in a stage play that is still being performed. The house lights are dimmed and we're not in a good position to gauge the impact we're having on our audience. After the play is over we'll discover how effective our performance has been from their standpoint. But our task for the present is to portray our roles in a way that will please our director. And he has already revealed to us, by his example and by his Word, what sort of performance he expects.

CHAPTER SIX

LOVING OTHERS

God's love brings us into the kingdom in the first place; that same love must have a practical outworking in our lives," says theologian Michael Green.[1] But for a long time it seemed to me that this kind of love was anything but practical. In inaugurating the kingdom, Jesus went beyond conventional religious teachings about love, and demanded something radical. As George Eldon Ladd says:

> In inaugurating the kingdom, Jesus went beyond conventional religious teachings about love, and demanded something radical.

Jesus redefines the meaning of love for neighbor: it means love for any person in need (Luke 10:29ff.), and particularly one's enemies (Matthew 5:44). This is a new demand of the new age Jesus has inaugurated. Jesus himself said that the law of love subsumes all the ethical teaching of the Old Testament (Matthew 22:40). This law of love is original with Jesus, and is the summation of all his ethical teaching.[2]

I used to consider the kingdom's "law of love" to be an admirable but impossible ideal. I struggled with Jesus' frequent exhortations to love others, such as this discourse from the Gospel of Luke:

> But I tell you who hear me: Love your enemies, do good to those who hate you, bless those who curse you, pray for those who mistreat you. If someone strikes you on one cheek, turn to him the other also. If someone takes your cloak, do not stop him from taking your tunic. Give to everyone who asks you, and if anyone takes what belongs to you, do not demand it back. Do to others as you would have them do to you.
>
> If you love those who love you, what credit is that to you? Even "sinners" love those who love them. And if you do good to those who are good to you, what credit is that to you? Even the "sinners" do that. And if you lend to those from whom you expect repayment, what credit is that to you? Even "sinners" lend to "sinners," expecting to be repaid in full. But love your enemies, do good to them, and lend to them without expecting to get anything back. Then your reward will be great, and you will be sons of the Most High, because he is kind to the ungrateful and wicked. Be merciful, just as your Father is merciful.[3]

Not only did Jesus command us to love our enemies; he also commanded us to love our neighbors as ourselves, and to love each other as he loves us. Living in the overlap means that we are obligated to love *everybody*, an obligation that, for a long time, I considered unrealistic.

In the first place, if love means having affectionate feelings toward somebody, I didn't see how you could command somebody to love. You can command people to do things but you can't command people to feel things. When I was a child my mother could command me to clean up my room, but she couldn't command me to *enjoy* cleaning up my room. How could we be expected to whip up loving feelings for anybody, let alone people Jesus himself actually identified as "enemies"?

But I tried. Some people said if you pray for God to give you love for people, he will. I tried this but my prayers seemed to go unanswered. No amount of praying changed my feelings toward people.

84

Some people said you have to ask God to love other people through you. The idea was that you are like a pipeline between God and another person, and God's love will flow through you to that person. But I evidently needed the spiritual equivalent of Roto-Rooter to unclog me because, aside from the fact that I felt silly doing my pipe imitation, none of my feelings changed.

Some people argued that when you have trouble loving certain people, you have to emphasize their good points and try to ignore the bad. So I tried to pretend that some cruel or malicious people weren't so bad after all. I tried to manufacture positive feelings toward people I thought were obnoxious. But this was not only unsuccessful, it was dishonest. Jesus never asked us to pretend that some people aren't so bad. In fact he emphasized just how bad some people can be (as in the above quotation from Luke's Gospel). As a realist he told us that people will be hateful. Then like an idealist (to my way of thinking) he told us to love them anyway. And this command seemed like the impossible dream.

Compounding the problem was the fact that, even if by some weird miracle it were possible to love everybody like Jesus said, it didn't seem right. At least not to the degree that we are commanded to do it. We who live in the overlap are not merely told to "put a little love in your heart," as the old song says; we're told to love our neighbor as ourselves. This seemed to be his way of saying there should be no limit to the amount of love we have for anyone, even relative strangers. It sounded like he was commanding us to have the same overwhelming feeling of affection for everybody. Not only did this seem impossible, it seemed wrong. Shouldn't a man feel more love for his daughter than for the little girl down the street? Shouldn't you feel more love for your best friend than you do for some stranger standing next to you

> Compounding the problem was the fact that, even if by some weird miracle it were possible to love everybody like Jesus said, it didn't seem right.

in an elevator? Shouldn't a woman feel more love for her husband than she does for the mailman?

What Is Christian Love?

I realized I needed to take a deeper look at exactly what kind of behavior Jesus expected from citizens of the kingdom. As I investigated, I discovered I was mistaken in assuming that Christian love is a feeling. Jesus was not commanding us to *feel* a certain way toward people; he was commanding us to *act* a certain way toward them.

Some Christians tried to clarify this issue by pointing out that there are various categories of love. Many argued that Greek—the original language of the New Testament—was more nuanced than English when it came to the language of love, and that we can understand this issue better if we understand the ancient Greek words for love.

Their argument went like this: "There were four major words for 'love' in Greek. The first was *erōs*. It tended to refer to the passion between a man and woman. It could refer to crude lust or to a more exalted romantic passion. The second was *storgē*. It tended to refer to family affection, especially the love between a parent and a child. The third was *philia*. It tended to refer to friendship between people who cherish each other and have some shared bond. The fourth was *agapē*. Until it appeared in the New Testament, it was a relatively obscure word. Christianity infused it with new meaning. It tended to refer to Christian love, which is not something you feel, but something you do."

But while agreeing that Christian love is not a feeling, some Christian scholars discouraged using these four terms to discuss love. They considered such an approach to be oversimplified. They argued that this approach overlooks the fact that the connotations of the Greek words changed over time, that each word had a range of meaning that sometimes overlapped with others, and that the New Testament does not use these words to refer to four different kinds of love.[4]

I acknowledge the validity of these scholars' arguments. But I still believe it is important to recognize distinctions between various categories of love. And for discussion purposes I believe it can be valid and helpful to use the four Greek words as a "shorthand" for what otherwise might be called romantic love or passion, affection, friendship, and Christian love. In contemporary popular usage it seems that the Greek words have come to stand for such concepts, regardless of how they were used in antiquity. Therefore, it is in this sense, as contemporary operational definitions, that I choose to use the terms here.

Thus, although the words *erōs*[5] and *storgē*[6] are not used in the New Testament, and *philia* (almost always appearing in its cognate verb form *phileō*) appears relatively infrequently, the concepts they represent can be seen in the Bible as images of God's love for us. We see the passion of *erōs* in the picture of an ardent God loving Israel as a husband loves his wife, and Christ loving the church as a bridegroom loves his bride. We see *storgē* in the picture of God loving us as a father loves his children. We see *philia* in the picture of friendship Jesus and his disciples enjoy. In these pictures we see the passion and deep affection God has for us.

But these three kinds of love, which we may call natural affections, contrast with Christian love. *Agapē*, the love Jesus commanded from citizens of the kingdom, focuses on recognizing a person's value, being concerned for that person's welfare, and committing yourself to bring about the best for that person. It differs from our natural affections in two important ways. First, it is an action, not a feeling. Although it may be accompanied by a feeling of affection, it doesn't have to be. You can have *agapē* for a person without feeling any attraction to him at all. Second, it's voluntary. You choose to do it. It has to do with your will and your actions, not your emotions. As New Testament scholar William Barclay says:

> Let a man be a saint or let a man be a sinner, God's only desire is for that man's highest good. Now, that is what *agapē* is. *Agapē* is the spirit which says: "No matter what any man does to me, I will never seek to do harm to him; I will never set out for revenge; I will always seek nothing but his highest good." That is to say, Christian love, *agapē*, is *unconquerable benevolence, invincible good will.* It is not simply a wave of emotion; it is a deliberate conviction of the mind issuing in a deliberate policy of the life; it is a deliberate achievement

and conquest and victory of the will. It takes all of a man to achieve Christian love; it takes not only his heart; it takes his mind and his will as well.[7]

Author Keith Miller, in his book *A Second Touch*, gives a picture that helps clarify the nature of *agapē*. He was struggling with the fact that he did not often feel loving toward others. He says that as he was thinking about the question of Christian love, a scene flashed onto the screen of his imagination. In this scene, his daughter was riding her tricycle onto the street into the path of a moving van with failed brakes. He ran and pushed her out of the way but was run over by the moving van in the process, feeling and hearing a horrible crunch as the wheel ran over his back. Then another scene replayed itself in his mind. This time a nasty little kid from down the street, one that he didn't even like, was riding into the path of the moving van. Miller hesitated at first but then dove to push the tricycle out of the path of the van and, again, was run over in the process. He continues:

> In thinking about these two experiences, the haunting question came to my mind: *Which of these two was the greater act of Christian love? To save your own daughter or the kid from down the street?* And the answer I could not shake was *to die for the child down the street.* Any pagan would try to save his own daughter. And yet there was *no warm feeling of love at all* in the second loving act. I had not even *wanted* to help him.[8]

If we take a second look at the above quotation from the Gospel of Luke, we see the same thing. Jesus tells us to love our enemies. Then he lists several examples of what this means. Bless those who curse you, pray for those who mistreat you, turn the other cheek, and so forth. All of these examples deal with our actions, not our feelings. We are told to *do* to others as we would have them do to us, not *feel* for others what we'd like them to feel for us. Our actions, not our feelings, are what are commanded by the kingdom's law of love.

We see here a contrast between *agapē* and natural affections. Our natural affections make us look inward and ask, "How do I feel about this person?" *Agapē* has us look outward and ask, "How am I acting toward this person?" Natural affections are involuntary. We naturally feel an attachment to certain people. *Agapē* is voluntary. We choose to extend *agapē* to people.

When we realize what *agapē* is, a couple of things happen. First, we are freed from experiencing false guilt over the fact that we don't feel affection toward somebody. I may naturally like pizza and not sauerkraut. There's nothing wrong with that. I may naturally like jogging and not playing tiddlywinks. There's nothing wrong with that. And I may naturally like Joe and not John. There's nothing wrong with that. But, in spite of my feelings, I do have to extend *agapē* to John.

> Our natural affections make us look inward and ask, "How do I feel about this person?" *Agapē* has us look outward and ask, "How am I acting toward this person?"

The command to love our neighbors as ourselves gives us an insight here. As Princeton University professor Paul Ramsey observes:

> You naturally love yourself for your own sake. You wish your own good and you do so even when you may have a certain distaste for the kind of person you are. Liking yourself or thinking yourself very nice, or not, has fundamentally nothing to do with the matter. . . . Regardless of fluctuations in feeling, you love yourself on one day about as much as on any other. And regardless of differences in temperament or capacity for deep emotion, one person probably wishes for his own good about as much as another person wishes for his.
>
> Christian love means such love for self *inverted*. Therefore, it has nothing to do with feelings, emotions, taste, preferences, temperament, or any of the qualities in other people which arouse feelings of revulsion or attraction, negative or positive preferences, in us. Christian love depends on the direction of the will, the orientation of intention in an act, not on stirring emotion. The commandment requires the

Christian to aim at his neighbor's good just as unswervingly as man by nature wishes his own. [9]

My ability to love myself doesn't depend on feeling an overwhelming affection for myself. I'm aware of at least some of my faults and weakness but that doesn't stop me from having *agapē* for myself. I take care of myself. I make sure I get three meals a day, a roof over my head, and clothing on my back. When I'm depressed, I do something to cheer myself up. When something good happens to me, I'm happy for myself. If I am to show *agapē* to John, I will need to show similar concern for his welfare, even though I don't feel an emotional attachment to him, or even though he may have many faults.

Something else happens when we make a distinction between our natural affections and *agapē*. We realize that sometimes the presence of natural affections can make it easier to show *agapē* to someone, but sometimes it can make it more difficult. We must avoid mistaking our natural affections for *agapē*. Suppose that after a while I actually start to like John. This may make it more pleasant or natural to show *agapē* to him. But my newfound affection is not the same thing as having *agapē* for him.

> We must avoid mistaking our natural affections for *agapē*.

Actually, the natural affections can often get in the way of our showing *agapē* to people. Sometimes our emotional attachment to people can prevent us from looking out for their best interests. When we're attracted to people we want them to be happy. But we might also want them to make us a principal source of their happiness. We want our loved ones to need us, and may feel threatened if they find happiness outside of a relationship with us.

Andy Gibb sang a song, *I Just Want to Be Your Everything*. It was catchy but unrealistic. I can't be another person's "everything," and I can't expect another person to be mine. My friends Bonnie and Gene have a great marriage, but Bonnie freely admits, "Gene's athletic and has a need to go skiing with somebody from time to time. However,

I can't meet that need. I ski on my rear end. So I'm glad he has other people who can ski with him."

We can fool ourselves into thinking that because we have an emotional attachment to somebody, we are obeying the command to love that person. But the opposite is often true. Look at the mother who won't untie the apron strings and whose children are growing up overly dependent on her. If you suggest she's not really loving her children, she'll deny it. She'll protest that she has great affection for her children. And she does. She has *storgē* for them, but not *agapē*. If she had *agapē* for them, she'd strive to raise them to become independent adults.

Or look at the unmarried teen couple who is getting sexually intimate. If we suggest that they don't really love each other, they'll object, "What do you mean? Of course we love each other—we can't keep our hands off each other." They may have *erōs* but not *agapē*. If we have *agapē* for a loved one, we won't coax that person into sin and force that person to deal with its emotional and spiritual consequences. Our tendency to confuse sex with love, and our ability to dismiss casual sex with a "nudge-nudge, wink-wink" mentality, reveal how tragically our society has fallen into the trap of using people instead of loving them.

As C. S. Lewis points out, we choose an unfortunate phrase when we say that a man looking for easy sex *wants a woman*: "Strictly speaking, a woman is just what he does not want. He wants a pleasure for which a woman happens to be the necessary piece of apparatus."[10]

Paradoxically, the people we feel the most attracted to (and therefore "love" most, as far as our natural affections go) may be the people for whom we have the least *agapē* (and therefore love least, as far as Christian love goes). Living in the overlap, part of our job description is to bring our natural affections under the discipline of *agapē*.

Watching *Agapē* in Action

When I first became aware that Christian love is an act of the will instead of a feeling, I felt disenchanted. It seemed that Christian love was being reduced to having a general concern for someone or just performing cold charitable deeds. But in watching *agapē* in action, I've come to see how demanding it can be.

One year a Sunday school class in my church solicited names of families who needed financial help during the Christmas season. Class leaders were given the name of a seventeen-year-old unwed girl with an infant daughter. The girl's alcoholic mother had kicked them out of her house. The girl's father, also an alcoholic, was unable to support them in any way. She worked at a Burger King, feeding the baby with restaurant food. She paid one hundred dollars a month to live in a filthy cockroach-infested apartment with a family. Both she and the baby slept on the floor. It quickly became apparent that this was going to be more than a simple holiday project.

Two women spearheaded an effort to make a permanent difference in the young mother's situation. They contacted the state department of health and enrolled her in a program that provided milk and cereal for the baby. They found out that the girl could not get full benefits unless she was legally emancipated. After her parents agreed to it, the two women helped her through the legal process of becoming emancipated. One of the women wanted to have the girl move in with her. But the girl, who had no car and could not drive, could not get to her job from there. Plus, in order to become emancipated, she had to show that she was supporting herself and the baby.

A Sunday school class member contacted a friend who managed apartments. The friend agreed to lower the rent on a small apartment near a bus stop where the girl could catch a bus to work. Class members donated furniture, kitchen supplies, food, and clothing, and moved the mother and baby into the apartment. They collected money to help with the initial rent payment. They helped find affordable child care. The two women handled the paperwork for getting the utilities connected. They took the girl shopping for clothes before her court appearance for the emancipation, and accompanied her to the hospital when the baby needed tests to determine how severe a congenital medical problem was. They continue to support her as she learns how to live on her own.

This ongoing relationship has meant a substantial investment of time, money, and energy for these women. But it has grown into a relationship of deep affection. "At first I was just trying to help somebody in need," one of them says. "But now I feel like I have a new daughter and granddaughter." Because of their continuing *agapē*, a young girl and her baby now face a future with hope.

But things don't always work out happily. Several people in my church befriended a Sunday school class member who was struggling with drug and alcohol abuse. It too meant a huge investment of time and energy. It meant long hours of encouraging him on the phone. It meant insisting he stick with his weekly counseling sessions. It meant bailing him out of jail at two o'clock A.M. when he was arrested for attempting to purchase drugs from an undercover police officer. It meant praying and studying the Bible with him. It meant taking out-of-town trips together to go skiing or to the beach. It meant spending countless evenings together having dinner or going to the movies or just talking. And ultimately it meant gut-wrenching grief and anguished questioning ("What more could we have done?") after a dealer shot him dead as he reportedly tried to buy cocaine. Sometimes *agapē* can be almost unbearable.

How Can We Cultivate *Agapē*?

God does not guarantee that *agapē* will always yield positive results, but he does command citizens of his kingdom to always cultivate this kind of love. How do we develop it? Author Tom Sine tells of an unexpected answer a respected Christian leader once gave to this question:

> During one of his many speaking tours, the late E. Stanley Jones, missionary and author, was asked by a listener, "How can I love others more?" As I heard the question, my mind immediately filled with possible responses, but I failed to anticipate Jones' reply to this earnest question. He simply instructed the listener to allow God to love him more. He explained, "If you allow God to share the profound unconditional love he has for you, then it is much easier for you to discover he has the same love for others . . . and we can participate with him in his agape love."[11]

"We love because he first loved us," says John in his first epistle (1 John 4:19). God's love for us is the key that unlocks our love for others. How does this happen? I think several factors are involved.

First, it provides the *motivation* for us to love. God's love brought us into the kingdom. It nurtures us as we grow in the kingdom. Thus, out of gratitude to God and a desire to express the *shalom* of his kingdom, we are motivated to love.

Second, it provides an *example* for us. Jesus modeled for us what it means to love. Through his servanthood on behalf of others, culminating in his sacrifice on the cross, he showed us what love truly is.

Third, it provides the *power* for us to love. God in his love has welcomed us into his kingdom. As citizens of his kingdom we receive the Holy Spirit, who empowers us to love. As religion professor Roger Mohrlang says:

> As the guarantee of the life to come (2 Corinthians 5:5; cf. 1:22), the Spirit effects the power of the new age in the believer's life here and now, making a form of eschatological existence actually possible in the present. Thus, freed from the enslaving powers of sin and the Law, the believer is empowered to produce real "fruit" for God (Romans 7:4), the "fruit of righteousness" (Philippians 1:11)—which for Paul is always the "fruit of the Spirit"; and the most important "fruit" is love.[12]

The ability to love is part of the overall transformation that results from a close walk with God; it is part of the eschatological "newness" of the kingdom.

I am coming to see that my ability to bear this fruit depends on my overall spiritual health. In contrast to a weight trainer who might focus on developing his biceps while ignoring his quadriceps, we cannot develop the ability to love while ignoring the other aspects of our Christian walk. The ability to love is part of the overall transformation that results from a close walk with

94

God; it is part of the eschatological "newness" of the kingdom. As theologian Leon Morris says:

> The cross shows us the self-sacrificing love that has made us Christians, the kind of love that is looked for from us. This kind of love is not the achievement of the natural man. True, the natural man feels certain kinds of love, but *agapē*, love as the New Testament writers understand it, is not among them. It is brought about in man by God himself, a most important part of the transformation that turns a worldly man into a Christian.[13]

Agapē and the Overlap

My understanding of the overlap has changed my perspective on *agapē*. I used to see *agapē* as the great Christian "obligation." But I am now coming to see it as the privilege that it is. Here again, the "already" and "not yet" of the kingdom come into play. Though the kingdom of God has not yet arrived in all its fullness, God is already bringing the *shalom* of his kingdom to people through his redemptive love. He allows us to participate in the process by acting as his ambassadors.

Catherine Marshall gave an example of this in her book, *Something More*. She told of meeting a former Nazi storm trooper, trained in hatred and destruction, who had become a Christian. In fact, he became a Lutheran pastor. He told her the story of how an elderly woman's *agapē* led him into the kingdom.

In December 1941 he had invaded Russia with the German armies. As his regiment was pushed back, he became separated from the others

Though the kingdom of God has not yet arrived in all its fullness, God is already bringing the shalom of his kingdom to people through his redemptive love. He allows us to participate in the process by acting as his ambassadors.

and found himself behind Russian lines. He crept up to a small hut in the forest where he found a tiny old Russian woman living alone. She offered him food and drink. Neither spoke the other's language but she risked her life to hide him for three days and nights, feeding him and caring for him. The woods around her hut swarmed with Russian soldiers. She could have easily turned in the Nazi. In fact, her refusal to do so meant that she could have been shot if she were found harboring him. He could not fathom why she would care for him like this.

Finally, he communicated his question to her through gestures and facial expressions: "Why have you risked your life to hide and befriend me?" She looked at him in silence and then pointed to something on the wall above her bed. It was a crucifix.

"After I escaped from enemy lines," he said, "try as I would I couldn't forget what had happened. I hadn't known love like that was possible. In the end, I was drawn irresistibly to the One who enabled the little Russian lady to prefer another to herself—even when that other was a cruel and deadly enemy. I wanted to know the power of the Cross in my life too. That's why I'm a Christian today."[14]

For most of us, *agapē* will never require literally risking our lives. But the consequences of our loving acts may have as much impact as the old woman's. Pastor D. L. Dykes, Jr., tells the story of Dr. Nat Long, pastor of Glenn Memorial Church in Atlanta. One Sunday morning Dr. Long stepped into the pulpit and was shocked to see one of the city's most powerful businessmen, an outspoken atheist, in the congregation. The man began attending regularly. Dr. Long started preparing his sermons with this man in mind, feeling that if he could convert him it would have a powerful impact on the community. Finally, one morning at the conclusion of the service the avowed atheist walked down the aisle, with tears streaming down his face, to profess faith in Christ.

Later, when they were alone, Dr. Long said to him, "I want to ask you a question. If you can answer it, it might help me to help a lot of other people. Which one of my sermons was it? What idea was the turning point for you, and what started you in the other direction?"

The man said, "Dr. Long, I've enjoyed and appreciated your sermons, and I wouldn't hurt your feelings for anything, but it was none of your sermons. It was the fact that for forty-one years I've lived with two of the kindest, most loving people that God ever made. I want to be able to love like my wife and daughter love. I want a God in my life like my wife worships."[15]

I am sometimes amazed at the tiny acts of love that become turning points in people's lives. A deacon pays a hospital visit to the mother of a friend who has drifted away from the church; as a result, the friend resumes his church attendance and becomes a joyful servant of God. A woman leaves an encouraging message on the telephone answering machine of a Sunday school classmate who—unbeknownst to her—is considering suicide; as a result, the classmate realizes that life is worth living after all. A mother impulsively hugs her rebellious teenage son who is overwhelmed by a messy breakup with his girlfriend; as a result the son weeps in his mother's embrace and begins a journey of reconciliation with his parents and with the God they serve. Somehow, little acts of *agapē* can become pivots that help turn their recipients toward a God of hope and *shalom*.

To use a jarring analogy, we find ourselves in a similar position to a woman who lived in New York a century ago. Mary Mallon came down with a bacterial disease that causes weakness, fever, and sometimes death. She recovered, but her body still harbored the *salmonella typhi* bacterium. She became a carrier, someone who could spread the disease to others. This disease is caught through contact with contaminated food or water. The simple act of peeling a potato or washing an apple could have fatal consequences. Unfortunately, Mary Mallon was employed as a cook.

The health department discovered she was the source of major typhoid outbreaks and made her agree to abandon her profession. But she secretly continued working as a cook, including laboring in a sanitarium and a maternity hospital. Authorities eventually found her, and "Typhoid Mary," as she came to be known, spent the rest of her life forcibly quarantined in a hospital. She was directly responsible for infecting over fifty people (three fatally), and causing at least six major outbreaks in New York. As the disease spread exponentially, the full extent of the damage she caused in incalculable.

We who live in the overlap are also carriers of something powerful that once laid hold of us, something called the love of God. We can spread it to others, deliberately or unknowingly, through our smallest acts. We may never know in this life what chain reactions we may set into motion. But as *"Agapē Johns"* and *"Agapē Janes"* we have the privilege of occupying strategic posts in the divine epidemic.

CHAPTER SEVEN

KEEPING OUR FOCUS

N o one who puts his hand to the plow and looks back is fit for service in the kingdom of God" (Luke 9:62). Jesus' maxim applies both to farming and to living. How can you plow a straight furrow in front of you when you're looking behind you? How can you serve effectively in the kingdom when rival priorities keep stealing your focus?

Alan's Story

This maxim comes to mind when I think of my friend Alan.[1] Most people would say he's got the world on a string, yet I don't think I've ever seen him happy. I've known him since my senior year of college. He's intelligent with an easygoing sense of humor, has the good looks of a tanned blond surfer, and has a well-paying job as a sales representative with a major corporation. On a recent trip to the Midwest I looked him up, and we grabbed lunch at a Mexican restaurant.

To hear him talk, nothing was going right with his life. His job was becoming routine, and he didn't get along with some of his co-workers. He's been on a constant, and unsuccessful, search for "Miss Right" since college. However, the women he was attracted to weren't interested in him, and the women who were interested in him weren't attractive to him.

Alan is a Christian, though his involvement with church has generally been sporadic. He says he's been unable to find a church where he feels at home. He will go through periods of time where he "tries to do right" by attending church, reading the Bible, and "being a good Christian." But at other times he puts Christianity on the shelf. Instead of attending church on Sunday morning, he will visit bars on Saturday evening, primarily in hopes of finding female companionship.

"Funny thing," he said, sitting across the table from me. "Even when I do everything right and try to put God first, it doesn't make any difference in my job or my dating situation."

I wished I had some profound answer for him. But I just mumbled something about keeping him in my prayers, and reminded him that a bar was not a place where he'd be likely to find prospects for a Christian wife. Part of me felt helpless because I just didn't know what to say. Part of me recalled that in college people perceived him as having made up his mind to be unhappy no matter what. That didn't seem to have changed. I decided, rightly or wrongly, that the best thing I could do was listen to him and pray for him without trying to give advice.

For weeks afterward I found myself thinking about Alan's situation. It's not that he was rejecting Christianity. He just moved it several notches down his priority list while he focused on other things. He had a certain idea of what Christianity was supposed to do for him—improve his work situation and his love life—and when that didn't happen he felt justified in relegating the kingdom to the back burner. In his mind, Christianity was not living up to its claims, so why not look for fulfillment elsewhere?

An Occupational Hazard

I admit I think sometimes certain Christians may unintentionally make inflated claims for Christianity (or at least claims that can be interpreted as inflated). I've heard some evangelistic sermons and Christian songs implying that God will grant us a problem-free existence or make us feel happy all the time. Yet, Jesus plainly warned us, "In this world you will have trouble," (John 16:33) and the most cursory look at his life or those of his early followers bears that out. The overlap is a war zone. Battles are to be expected.

But setting aside some of the more exaggerated claims, Christianity does make some claims to meet our needs. Jesus tells us that God will feed us as he feeds the birds of the air and clothe us as he clothes the lilies of the field.[2] And when I look at these claims in light of Alan's feeling that Christianity is just not working for him, I can identify three responses I've traditionally heard in situations like his.

> The overlap is a war zone. Battles are to be expected.

First, "God promises to provide our needs, not our wants." But Alan would probably say that his career and romantic situations involve genuine needs.

Second, "God's promises are conditional. You have to meet certain conditions in order for God to provide your needs." But Alan would say that he has met the conditions, at least at certain times in his life.

Third, "God's timetable is different from ours. You have to keep waiting and trusting." Alan would probably admit that he had fallen down here. His spiritual attention span seems to have been pretty short.

Yet, though these responses may be valid, after reflecting on Alan's situation, I don't think we can just leave it there. I think there are some other issues that run deeper. As I pondered Alan's plight, I came to an uncomfortable realization—I'm just as guilty as he is. I saw that taking my focus off the kingdom is a trap I've often fallen into without even being aware of it. It's an occupational hazard of living in the overlap. My ways of doing it may be less visible than abandoning church in favor of bars. But when a difficult situation arises at work, I can fret about it without even recognizing that I should be trusting God with it. I have gone for weeks without a meaningful quiet time. I can live on my own steam instead of seeking

> Though I believe in God, I function as an atheist much of the time.

God's direction and empowering. Though I believe in God, I function as an atheist much of the time. My hand may be on the plow but instead of focusing on the kingdom, I am looking elsewhere.

As I pondered why people like Alan and I find it easy to take our focus off the kingdom, I concluded it's often because we're forgetting three truths. I find that I must periodically remind myself of them as a precaution against future slip-ups.

Christianity is True

First, we may find it easy to take our focus off the kingdom when we forget that Christianity is true. When I became a Christian, it was primarily because I had a need that I thought Christianity could meet. My Christian friends had demonstrated an ability to cope with problems ranging from poor self-images to the death of a father. I wanted that ability to cope, so I became a Christian. And as I learned, little by little, to trust God in my everyday life I found that I was beginning to experience that same ability.

My friend Don became a Christian about the same time as I did, at a Campus Life meeting. He and I would sometimes get together to pray. But as the weeks went by I found him to be a somewhat frustrating prayer partner, for one simple reason. He didn't have any problems.

Don was one of those enviable people who seemed to have absolutely everything going for him. Good grades came easily to him; he was great looking; the girls were all crazy about him; he lettered in football, gymnastics, and track; he came from a happy, affluent family; he had a winning personality. When we'd get together I'd share my anxieties and struggles and he'd say, "I really don't have much to pray about. I don't have any problems." Finally the week came when I'd heard "I don't have any problems" one time too many.

"If you don't have any problems," I asked him, "then how come you became a Christian?" He paused a second as though he were thinking about this for the first time.

"Well, when I first heard about asking Christ into my life, I just realized it was the right thing to do," he said. I don't remember what I said in response, but I do remember what I thought. I thought, *That's the dumbest reason I've ever heard for somebody to become a Christian. I* have since come to appreciate the integrity of a teenager who came to Christ without primarily being motivated by self-interest. But at the time my brain could not compute that.

I was raised in the church and was used to hearing people "give their testimony" about how they became Christians. And without fail they would talk about how there was some need in their life, ranging from a vague feeling of discontent to drug addiction, before they met Christ. Then they would explain how Christ met that need when they accepted him into their life. My own experience fell into this pattern. But here was Don saying everything was great in his life before he became a Christian. It was not a sense of need that brought him to Christ, but a sense of responsibility. It was the right thing to do. And his example has reminded me that there are two approaches to the issue of why we become and remain Christians. One is subjective, and the other is objective.

The subjective approach tells us, "Christianity will do something for you." There is nothing wrong with this approach. Jesus used it. We see him, for example, telling the woman at the well that he would give her living water.[3] Probably most people become Christians because (at least in part) they want God to do something for them.

The objective approach tells us, "Christianity is true." We see this approach used several times in the book of Acts,[4] in such contexts as Peter's sermon on the day of Pentecost. It goes something like this: "It is true that the long-awaited Messiah has come in the person of Jesus of Nazareth. It is true that he was crucified for our sins, buried, then raised on the third day. We know this is true for two reasons. First, it is the fulfillment of Scripture. Second, we ourselves are eyewitnesses. Because this is true, it is appropriate to respond by repenting and being baptized. Those who do will receive the forgiveness of sins and the empowering of the Holy Spirit."

It seems to me that in order to live successfully in the overlap, we need to balance these two approaches. They are like the two wings of an airplane, or the two wheels on a bicycle, both equally important. If I think of Christianity merely as a set of doctrinal truths that I must acknowledge, I miss out on experiencing God's blessings in my daily life.

But if I think of Christianity solely in terms of "what's in it for me," it's easy to neglect the Christian life when things don't go my way. Christianity is not just something that's supposed to do us some good. It claims to give us the facts about the world we live in, about God, about ourselves, about how we can know him and live our lives the way he intends. Either it's telling us the truth or it isn't.

If Christianity is true, we should embrace it even if it doesn't seem to do us any good at all. If Christianity is false, we should reject it even though a belief in it may be helpful in some way. The only reason to commit ourselves to any religion—indeed to any belief at all about anything—is that it's true.[5]

> The only reason to commit ourselves to any religion—indeed to any belief at all about anything—is that it's true.

I have a friend who says that when the Jehovah's Witnesses or Mormons knock on her door she simply responds, "I'm not interested in your religion, thank you, because I'm happy with mine." This may be an excellent way to rid your doorstep of unwelcome visitors, but as justification for practicing a religion it leaves much to be desired. Being happy with a belief is not enough. Believing I am Superman may make me feel happy. But the first time I leap off a skyscraper or tear off my clothes in a public phone booth I may be in for a rude awakening. Any number of religions, cults, and philosophies are competing for our attention. Many of them may make us happy, or give us peace or strength or whatever we're looking for—at least for a while. But since at some point they begin to contradict each other, they can't all be true. And ultimately the ones that aren't true will leave us splattered on the sidewalk or shivering in our skivvies.

I have another friend who, until relatively recently, didn't know what he believed about God. He decided to investigate the world's major religions to see which one had the most evidence behind it. He did a preliminary survey of the various religions and realized something.

"Out of all the world's major religions, only one had a founder who claimed to be God," Bill said. "Buddha never claimed to be God, Mohammed never claimed to be God, only Jesus claimed to be God. So I decided to start with Christianity and see what evidence there was to support Jesus' claim. And I realized the evidence was there, and I became a Christian."[6]

I admire people like Bill who were driven to Christ by a search for truth. I think they may have an advantage, at least initially, over those of us who became Christians out of a sense of need. Their Christian walk is not as dependent upon subjective factors such as their perceptions of what God is doing in their lives. Perceptions can be misleading. My perception tells me that every day the sun moves westward across the sky above a stationary earth. My knowledge of the truth tells me that, in fact, the earth moves around the sun. If my Christian walk depends on my perception of how well God is meeting my needs at any given time, I'm in trouble.

> If my Christian walk depends on my perception of how well God is meeting my needs at any given time, I'm in trouble.

However, if I've taken the time to examine the evidence for the truth of the Christian faith, and if I'm convinced that the evidence is solid, I'll be much less likely to bail out of the boat during those times when life seems hard and God seems a million miles away.[7] Those of us who became Christians because we wanted God to do something for us would do well to examine the evidence for our faith. Living in the overlap, we may need to periodically remind ourselves that we are Christians not just because God meets our needs, but because Christianity is true.

Christianity Costs

Second, we may find it easy to take our focus off the kingdom when we forget that Christianity costs. Pastor Wilbur E. Rees sums up an attitude I find myself relating to all too often:

I would like to buy $3 worth of God, please, not enough
to explode my soul or disturb my sleep, but just enough to
equal a cup of warm milk or a snooze in the sunshine. I don't
want enough of him to make me love a black man or pick
beets with a migrant. I want ecstasy, not transformation; I
want the warmth of the womb, not a new birth. I want a
pound of the Eternal in a paper sack. I would like to buy $3
worth of God, please.[8]

Periodically I find myself trying to get by on three dollars worth of
God, wanting enough of him to make my life pleasant but not so much
as to make it costly. There's a temptation to assume that Christianity
should make life easier. Adrian Plass and Paul McCusker's adaptation
of a well known Scripture verse sums it up:

For God so loved the world that he gave his only Son, that
whoever believes in him, keeps his nose clean and makes a
significant but sensibly balanced contribution to church life
in terms of time and cash, shall have a reasonable expectation of material comfort, physical good health, and ongoing
prosperity in the fields of business and emotional relationships, with guidance provided as and when necessary so that
opportunities in all these areas shall not be missed or wasted.
Oh, yes, I nearly forgot—he won't perish, and eternal life
gets thrown in as well.[9]

I wouldn't mind having that verse in my Bible. But the fact is, Jesus
did not make such guarantees. In fact, Jesus plainly warned potential
followers that there is a cost to entering the kingdom—a cost that must
be counted ahead of time like the cost of building a tower or the cost
of waging a war on a foreign king.[10] In a world that prizes instant
gratification this is easy to overlook.

"Our visitation teams have led forty people to Christ, but not one
of those forty has become involved in church," a pastor once lamented
to my mother. I can't help but wonder what sort of invitation these
people thought they were responding to. Jesus' invitation to enter the
kingdom was unambiguous.

When a rich young ruler asked Jesus what he had to do to inherit eternal life, Jesus first reminded him of the commandments of the Torah. After the ruler said he'd kept all those since he was a boy, Jesus did something surprising. Mark tells us, "Jesus looked at him and loved him. 'One thing you lack,' he said. 'Go, sell everything you have and give to the poor, and you will have treasure in heaven. Then come, follow me'" (Mark 10:21). Jesus loved the man, and because of his love he made the man realize the cost of becoming a disciple. I don't believe Jesus' directive here was a universal command for all Christians, but was something this man had to do because of his attachment to his possessions. But the man would not pay the price. Instead, he sadly walked away from Jesus, who observed, "'How hard it is for the rich to enter the kingdom of God'" (Mark 10:23).

I wonder what would happen if the rich young ruler visited the average evangelical church today and asked what he had to do to inherit eternal life. Would he be met by someone who would love him enough to insist that he count the cost of entering the kingdom? Or would he be met by someone who would say in effect, "Great, all you have to do is accept these four principles, pray this simple prayer, and you're in"?

Jesus did not simply call people to accept a free gift called salvation; he also called them to embrace a costly lifestyle called discipleship. Repentance is the entrance to this lifestyle. The Holy Spirit—God's own Spirit indwelling us—provides the power to live it. How well are we getting this message across to potential Christians?

Yesterday I bought fifteen different gospel tracts at a Christian bookstore. When I first became a Christian I

> Would he be met by someone who would love him enough to insist that he count the cost of entering the kingdom? Or would he be met by someone who would say in effect, "Great, all you have to do is accept these four principles, pray this simple prayer, and you're in"?

learned how to share my faith through courses that used these kinds of tracts. I have relied on them when I've counseled at evangelistic rallies. As a youth worker, I used similar leaflets to train teenagers to share their faith. I'm convinced of their value, and I'm grateful for the considerable good that has been done through such literature. But today I did something different with them. I pretended I was a non-Christian who was encountering the gospel for the first time. I wanted to see what I could understand about Christianity simply by reading the tracts.

Six of them used a four-step approach that contained variations on the following:

1. God wants us to have abundant life in a relationship with him.
2. We have all sinned, and our sin separates us from God.
3. Jesus died for our sins, so that we could be forgiven.
4. We must receive God's forgiveness by faith as a free gift; we cannot earn it.

Each point was illustrated with appropriate Scripture verses. Nine of the tracts contained a sample prayer (sometimes called "the sinner's prayer") that incorporated the above points. I believe those four points with all my heart. If I were a non-Christian I believe these tracts would have done an excellent job of communicating them to me. Yet, I felt disturbed when I read the literature—not at what was said but at what was not said.

In the first place, only seven of the tracts specifically mentioned repentance. Three of those did not define it. The others defined it as turning away from sin (or self) and turning to God. One tract that didn't specifically mention repentance did say we have to turn from our sin. Another said we have to turn away from whatever we were trusting to get us to heaven and turn to Jesus instead. Yet my Bible dictionary describes repentance like this: "not just as a feeling sorry, or changing one's mind, but as a turning round, a complete alteration of the basic motivation and direction of one's life."[11] If I were not a Christian I don't think I would understand from reading these tracts how demanding repentance is. I might view it as turning away from past sins, but I would not know that it's something that should transform my life's whole direction. I would not understand that the decision to receive Christ is no less life-changing or irrevocable than the decision to get married.

Also, none of the tracts specifically mentioned discipleship. Five of them did give some guidance on living the Christian life (such as reading the Bible, praying, and having fellowship with other Christians). Seven others invited people to write for follow-up literature if they responded to the message.

My Bible dictionary gives this description of discipleship: "It involved personal allegiance to him [Jesus], expressed in following him and giving him an exclusive loyalty (Mark 8:34–38; Luke 14:26–33). In at least some cases it meant literal abandonment of home, business ties and possessions (Mark 10:21, 28), but in every case readiness to put the claims of Jesus first, whatever the cost, was demanded."[12]

If I were not a Christian, I believe some of these tracts may have informed me that I would need to perform certain spiritual disciplines as a Christian. But I would never have understood the depth of commitment Jesus calls us to. Perhaps some of the follow-up literature would have explained it. But shouldn't we make people aware of the cost of discipleship *before* we ask them to become Christians, not *after*?

Furthermore, only three tracts mentioned the Holy Spirit. One of them had only a one-sentence mention of the Spirit's role in the new birth, but said nothing of his role in our daily lives. If I were not a Christian, I would understand nothing about the Holy Spirit from most of these tracts.

This exercise spawned some questions. In our admirable desire to make the gospel of the kingdom understandable in a post-Christian world, have we accidentally watered down the message? Is evangelism about getting people into heaven, or turning people into disciples? What would Peter and Paul think of

> What would Peter and Paul think of evangelism that mentions repentance, discipleship, and the Holy Spirit only parenthetically if at all?

evangelism that mentions repentance, discipleship, and the Holy Spirit only parenthetically if at all? Might a primary cause of lukewarmness in today's church be that people are "praying the sinner's prayer" without understanding the depth of the commitment they're supposed to be making? By neglecting to put discipleship in the proper perspective, might we be influencing people to pay the cost of nondiscipleship instead? As philosopher and theologian Dallas Willard says:

> In 1937 Dietrich Bonhoeffer gave the world his book *The Cost of Discipleship*. It was a masterful attack on "easy Christianity" or "cheap grace," but it did not set aside— perhaps it even enforced—the view of discipleship as a costly spiritual excess, and only for those especially driven or called to it. It was right to point out that one cannot be a disciple of Christ without forfeiting things normally sought in human life, and that one who pays little in the world's coinage to bear his name has reason to wonder where he or she stands with God. But the cost of nondiscipleship is far greater—even when this life alone is considered—than the price paid to walk with Jesus.
>
> Nondiscipleship costs abiding peace, a life penetrated throughout by love, faith that sees everything in the light of God's overriding governance for good, hopefulness that stands firm in the most discouraging of circumstances, power to do what is right and withstand the forces of evil. In short, it costs exactly that abundance of life Jesus said he came to bring (John 10:10). The cross-shaped yoke of Christ is after all an instrument of liberation and power to those who live in it with him and learn the meekness and lowliness of heart that brings rest to the soul. . . . The correct perspective is to see following Christ not only as the necessity it is, but as the fulfillment of the highest human possibilities and as life on the highest plane. [13]

We will either pay the cost of discipleship or the greater cost of nondiscipleship. But it is foolish to think that we can avoid payment altogether. In New Testament times few potential converts would have been ignorant of the cost of following Jesus. He himself proclaimed, "If anyone would come after me, he must deny himself and take up his cross daily and follow me" (Luke 9:23). Moreover, the unspoken footnote to any evangelistic invitation in the early church was "and, of course, if you do respond you may lose your life." And many did.

> We will either pay the cost of discipleship or the greater cost of nondiscipleship. But it is foolish to think that we can avoid payment altogether.

Jesus used a couple of analogies that illuminate this issue. He compared the kingdom to treasure buried in a field. A man uncovered it and reburied it. Then he joyfully sold all he had, and used the proceeds to buy the field so he could legally own the treasure. Jesus also compared the kingdom to a precious pearl found by a merchant. He sold all he had and used the money to buy the pearl.[14]

A paradox emerges here about the cost of entering the kingdom. Compared to what we have, the cost is everything. But, compared to what we gain, the cost is nothing. Sacrifice, in the alchemy of the kingdom, becomes abundance. And slavery becomes emancipation. This brings us to a third point.

Christianity Offers Ultimate Freedom

Finally, we may find it easy to take our focus off the kingdom when we forget that Christianity offers ultimate freedom. My friend Alan seems to think Christianity is too restrictive. He has the idea that his evenings of drinking and meeting women in bars conflicts with his commitment to Christ, and he's vaguely uneasy about it. But he continues to do it. He wants his freedom.

When I think about this issue of freedom, I think about the time I tried tandem skydiving. When I arrived at the skydiving company office, the manager gave me all sorts of options. The basic jump was from eight thousand feet, but for fifty dollars more I could get a ten-thousand-foot jump, and for fifty dollars more than that I could get a twelve-thousand-foot jump. I decided, "Let's go for it. I'll probably only do this once in my life," so I went for the twelve-thousand-footer. Then he told me that for additional money they'd send a photographer up with both a still camera and a video camera mounted on his helmet. He'd parachute out of the plane and document my jump. I decided to go for that, too.

After signing forms absolving the company from all blame in case anything went wrong, I put on the suit they gave me—a neon blue one with pink and yellow sleeves—along with a gray harness that would hook me to the dive master who was jumping with me. The dive master, Chris, gave me basic instructions. During the free fall I was to extend my arms and bend my legs back. When he tapped me on the shoulder to signal that he was going to activate the parachute, I was to fold my arms in front of me.

The photographer, Hank, sat in the back of the small plane with me while Chris sat in the front next to the pilot. I was especially glad for the seat belt strapping me in when I discovered there was no door on the plane—just a yawning hole where the door would have been. I wasn't too nervous at first. But as the trees and cars and people on the ground looked smaller and smaller, I felt a little apprehension. After a while they looked so tiny that I thought we had to be close to twelve thousand feet. I checked the altitude gauge on my suit. It read four thousand feet. I felt a lot more apprehension.

"Twelve thousand feet is a good jump," Hank said about that time. "That's over two miles." I wished he hadn't said that. Feet are such small units that even a lot of them didn't seem that high. But, two miles seemed very high indeed. I got more apprehensive.

It got even worse when we flew through a layer of clouds and continued climbing. The dense clouds blocked my view of the ground. We could be a million miles in the air for all I knew. Ideally, once we reached twelve thousand feet, we could have jumped immediately. But because of the cloud layer we could not jump. We had to find a hole in the clouds so we could see what was underneath us—otherwise we could have hit a flock of birds or a plane or something. So we kept circling and circling, looking for a clear spot to jump through. And as we circled I had more time to think about what I was doing. Thoughts popped into my head like unwelcome surprise house guests. Thoughts such as, *What kind of idiot would fork over a lot of hard-earned cash for the privilege of jumping out of a perfectly good airplane more than two miles in the air?* Now I was really apprehensive. I tried to make my mind go blank, and just act like an unthinking robot.

Finally, we found a clear spot. Chris had me crouch in front of him while he hooked our harnesses together, his front against my back. Then, like a pair of conjoined twins, we inched to the doorway and stretched out our left feet out so we could step on the plane's wheel. Then the right feet came out to rest on a bar. Chris counted me down, and we somersaulted forward into the air. I stretched out my arms and bent my legs back as I had been told, and we free fell in this birdlike position for about forty-five seconds. The brisk air rushing at me and the spectacular view of the ocean, mountains, and trees made me feel exhilarated. Excitement had replaced the fear.

Once, when I accidentally unbent my legs, my lower body dropped and I started thrashing around. Chris immediately tapped me on the shoulder and told me to get back in position. I did, and I stabilized. Then he tapped me again and told me to fold my arms in front of me. When I did, he opened the chute and we immediately shot straight up into the air. Then we hung in the sky, upright this time as though we were standing on air. We floated gently to earth like a dandelion seed wafting in the breeze. Our goal—which we reached—was to land inside a circle that was marked on the ground.

After the dive was over, I realized something. When I was safe in the circling airplane, securely strapped in, I was nervous. But after I had leapt from the plane and was plummeting toward the ground at 120 miles an hour with nothing but a piece of fabric to keep my body from smashing into the earth, the nervousness had gone. Why was this?

Part of it may be that I often find the anticipation of an uncomfortable experience—such as a visit to a dentist or having to speak in public—to be worse than the experience itself. But I think the major reason is that while I was in the plane I had a couple of options available to me, and being torn between them was stressful. When I got on the plane I fully intended to make the jump, but there was also the realization that at any time I could tell the pilot, "I've changed my mind. Let's land this thing." The more the plane kept circling and circling, the more I felt like not making the jump. But once we had somersaulted out of the plane, I was committed to a single course of action. In fact, I remember a specific point during the free fall when I told myself, "It's too late to change your mind now. You might as well focus on enjoying the jump." And I did.

This experience taught me something about freedom. I tend to equate freedom with having many options. My fifth grade teacher told our class that a free country is a country in which you can do whatever you want, provided you don't hurt someone else. The abortion debate has made "freedom of choice" a catchphrase in our society. But that is only one side of the coin. Being torn among competing options can be stressful, sometimes brutal. There is also a freedom that comes from eliminating all but one option and being single-mindedly committed to it. While I was freefalling I had the freedom to focus on enjoying the skydiving, without being distracted by the option of staying on the plane. Such lack of choice can be liberating.

> Lack of choice can be liberating.

And so it is with Christian freedom. If we allow the old life to distract us after we've leapt into the new life, we rob ourselves of the freedom of single-mindedness. If after leaping into the new life we neglect to do whatever is necessary to make it successful, we will thrash around like I did when my legs got out of position. Paul's strategy for Christian living could have been lifted from a handbook on skydiving: "Forgetting what is behind and straining toward what is ahead, I press on toward the goal" (Philippians 3:13b–14a). He was free to pursue the new life without the distraction of the old.

Scripture presents us with a paradox when it comes to the issue of freedom. At first glance the Bible is filled with images of restricted freedom. We are to take up our cross daily and follow Jesus; when we're nailed to a cross we don't have options to do many other things. We are the bride and Christ is the bridegroom; the bride pledges to forsake all others. We are parts of the body of Christ; the hand is not free to become a foot or an ear. But amidst the flurry of such images—like the eye in the middle of the hurricane—stands our Lord's affirmation, "If the Son sets you free, you will be free indeed" (John 8:36).

And it happens. The bride who forsakes all but her groom is free to experience a deeper intimacy, a deeper expression of love, than she had known before. The hand that resigns itself to being a hand is free to play a piano concerto or pitch a baseball or dress a wound. Those who submit to a cross are free to be resurrected.

It may help if we think of ourselves as grains of sand in the top of an hourglass. As we move downward we begin to notice that our world is shrinking. The glass seems to be closing in around us. Our freedom is eroding with the sand underneath us. Finally, the glass seems to close in so tight we think we'll suffocate. It looks like we'll spend eternity in a cramped glass prison.

Then, after we feel that the life has been squeezed out of us, we notice something. There's a little more space around us than there was a minute ago. And the more we travel downward, the wider our world gets. After a while, it seems we're in a place that will never stop expanding, that offers more and more freedom the deeper we go.

I think it's that way with life in the kingdom. Initially, it may look like we're giving up our freedom. But after squeezing through the narrow place we realize we've exchanged a shallow freedom for a deeper one. At first the narrowness may look like it's going to be an eternal situation, but it's not. It's just what we have to pass through on our journey to an ever-widening destination. The proverbial camel was not expected to take up permanent residence inside that needle's eye.[15]

Living in the Overlap

The temptation to take our focus off the kingdom is one that many of us will struggle with as we navigate between two worlds. Remembering three truths may help us resist: *Christianity is true. Christianity costs. Christianity offers ultimate freedom.* By God's grace may we keep our hands on the plow and our eyes on the kingdom. That's the only way to live effectively in the overlap. And as my friend Don would say, it's the right thing to do.

CHAPTER EIGHT

BUILDING FENCES

Sometimes when I visualize the literal meaning of Jesus' words, I feel queasy: "If your hand causes you to sin, cut it off. It is better for you to enter life maimed than with two hands to go into hell, where the fire never goes out. And if your foot causes you to sin, cut it off. It is better for you to enter life crippled than to have two feet and be thrown into hell. And if your eye causes you to sin, pluck it out. It is better for you to enter the kingdom of God with one eye than to have two eyes and be thrown into hell" (Mark 9:43–47).

How would it feel to pry your own eyeball out of its socket with a knife? How would it feel to hack through your own wrist or ankle with a hatchet? If it weren't for the fact that Jesus himself used these images, I would probably think them too revolting to be mentioned from a pulpit or in a Sunday school class.

Yet, through this hyperbole, Jesus made his point. These images may be horrifying, but they are tame compared to the consequences of sin. When it comes to sin, we who live in the overlap must reckon with the tension between the "already" and the "not yet"; we are already free from the penalty of sin, but we are not yet free from the temptation to sin. Because the kingdom of God is a kingdom of righteousness, we

> Living in the kingdom may require spiritual amputation.

must deal ruthlessly with such temptation. Living in the kingdom may require spiritual amputation; we have to cut ourselves off from anything that might lead us into sin.

As I've pondered this command, I've come to a conclusion that surprised me: there is a correlation between this teaching of Jesus and a major teaching of the Pharisees. In fact, I've come to believe that the Pharisees—at least some of them—can be role models for us when it comes to avoiding temptation.[1]

The Truth about the Pharisees

I admit that for most of my life as I've read the Bible, I've regarded the Pharisees as "the enemy." I saw them as a monolithic group of self-righteous hypocrites who reduced religion to an intolerable system of ridiculous rules, while ignoring the need for true devotion to God. In my mind they all thought alike, acted alike, and dressed alike (pious expressions, flowing white garments, and sandals—looking like See No Evil, Hear No Evil, and Speak No Evil in bathrobes and shower thongs). If the Gospels were a cowboy movie, the Pharisees would be the guys with black hats and curly mustaches who tie sweet Nell to the railroad track in the path of a rapidly approaching locomotive because she cooked a pot of stew for some starving orphans on the Sabbath. At least that was my impression.

Certainly there was some justification for such a viewpoint. After all, the Pharisees were on the receiving end of blistering words from Jesus. "Whitewashed tombs," "blind guides," and "brood of vipers" are not considered compliments in any culture I'm aware of. According to Jesus, Pharisees "shut the kingdom of heaven in men's faces" and they themselves would not enter in. "How will you escape being condemned to hell?" he exclaimed.[2] The Pharisees are even pictured as plotting to kill Jesus.[3] On the surface, it might seem impossible to say anything in their defense.

Yet, when I took a closer look, I saw that the New Testament also paints sympathetic portraits of Pharisees, portraits I've usually overlooked.[4] Nicodemus, a prominent Pharisee, affirmed that Jesus had come from God. He sought Jesus out to learn more about his teachings. He also spoke in Jesus' defense when other Pharisees and chief priests sent the temple guard to arrest him. After Jesus' death, Nicodemus helped prepare his body for burial.[5]

> The New Testament also paints sympathetic portraits of Pharisees, portraits I've usually overlooked.

Furthermore, given the close association between scribes and Pharisees, the scribe who told Jesus, "Teacher, I will follow you wherever you go" (Matthew 8:19), was probably a member of the Pharisaic party. The same can be said of the scribe to whom Jesus said, "You are not far from the kingdom of God," when he agreed with Jesus' teaching about the greatest commandment (Mark 12:28–34).[6] Also, Joseph of Aramathea, a disciple who provided the tomb for Jesus' body, was probably a Pharisee.[7]

And when the members of the Sanhedrin wanted to put the apostles to death, Gamaliel the Pharisee was the voice of wisdom who persuaded them to let the apostles go. "If what they're doing is of human origin it will fail," he said, "But if it's from God you won't be able to stop them—you will only be fighting God."[8] A sizable number of Pharisees became Christians, as evidenced by the mention of the Pharisaic party representing the conservative viewpoint at the Jerusalem Council.[9] And when Paul was tried before the Sanhedrin, certain Pharisees argued vigorously in his defense.[10] An objective reading of the New Testament reveals that although many Pharisees may have been judgmental and hypocritical, others were tolerant and devout seekers of truth and justice. As New Testament professor James A. Brooks observes, "Not all scribes and Pharisees were bad. Indeed, at their best they represented the finest element in Judaism."[11]

Then what about Jesus' rhetoric against them? We must keep in mind the fact that like other teachers, Jesus sometimes used sweeping generalizations to make a point. Thus he could characterize Jerusalem as "you who kill the prophets and stone those sent to you"[12] though the city also had many holy men and women who sought to obey God, and he could denounce a "wicked and adulterous generation"[13] or an "unbelieving and perverse generation"[14] although there were many people in that generation who had become his followers. By the same token it would be inaccurate to insist that all Pharisees were guilty of the sins Jesus attacked in his broad denunciations.[15] As New Testament scholar R. V. G. Tasker said (referring to Jesus' castigation of the Pharisees in Matthew 23), "It is important to remember in reading this chapter that not *all* the Pharisees came under the condemnation of Jesus, and that there were good and bad Pharisees just as there have always been, and still are, good and bad Christians."[16]

I had always seen the Pharisees as shining examples of how *not* to live. However, I've come to appreciate a strategy they pioneered that—when rightly applied—can help keep us from temptation.

The Pharisees' Fences

The Pharisaic movement arose at a time when pagan Greek culture was luring God's people away from their holy lifestyles. The Pharisees, whose name probably means "Separated Ones," called people back to following Israel's God. They studied the Scriptures but they were not content with mere head knowledge. They strove to live out their beliefs in their everyday lives, even if it meant great difficulty. Obeying God was of utmost importance to them. In order to keep from transgressing God's commands, they developed the practice of "making a fence" around the law.[17] These "fences" consisted of rules that would keep them a safe distance from violating God's laws ignorantly or accidentally.

For example, the law of Moses prohibits working on the Sabbath. But it does not explicitly identify what is meant by "work." So the Pharisees devised a list of thirty-nine categories of work.[18] They believed that if you kept yourself from these activities on the Sabbath, you wouldn't accidentally transgress the command to avoid work.

The reasoning went like this. God prohibits work on the Sabbath. Kindling a fire is work, so we will "build a fence around" (or prohibit) the kindling of a fire on the Sabbath. However, if we are reading by lamplight, the light might flicker, and we might unthinkingly tilt the lamp so the oil in the lamp will flow more freely. Technically, that is kindling a fire. So we will build a fence around this situation and prohibit reading by lamplight on the Sabbath. This will keep us a safe distance from transgressing the prohibition against work.[19]

Or take the case of a tailor. Sewing more than one stitch on the Sabbath was one of the thirty-nine forbidden activities. But if a tailor carried a needle outside on the Sabbath people might think he's soliciting work, since carrying one's tool of trade was considered solicitation of business. So we will build a fence and prohibit the tailor from carrying a needle outside on the Sabbath, or even walking around with one stuck in his garment. But what if he is carrying a needle around before nightfall (when Sabbath officially starts) and forgets he has it? We will build another fence and prohibit him from carrying a needle during the daylight hours immediately before the Sabbath.[20]

A final example: cutting your hair was forbidden on the Sabbath. However, suppose you looked in the mirror and saw that some of your locks were uneven? You might unthinkingly trim them up. So we will build a fence and prohibit looking in the mirror on the Sabbath.[21]

We can see that not only did the Pharisees build fences around the original prohibition against work; they also built fences around their fences, just to be sure they wouldn't transgress the original commandment. Their rules may seem ridiculous to us. But, behind these rules was a serious determination to obey God even if it were inconvenient.

These fences of the Pharisees have often been compared to the rules some Christians make. For example, some Christians have followed the logic that since we are to keep ourselves from premarital sex, and dancing can stir up lustful feelings, we should build a fence and say that Christians shouldn't dance. Some have built a fence around this fence and said that since roller skating is nothing more than "dancing on wheels," Christians should not skate either.

Growing up in a conservative church I heard prohibitions against such things as dancing, card playing (the joker was said to represent Jesus), and movies (many of which were considered "sordid" and all of which were considered "worldly"). Innocuous family movies were still to be avoided because "even good food is thrown out with the garbage."

My family took a more liberal stance than others in our church. We were allowed to play cards and go to movies (though we were careful not to mention them in front of certain other church members). And after originally abiding by my church's prohibition against dancing, I capitulated and asked a girl to my senior prom. Mom tried valiantly (and not too successfully due to ineptness on my part) to teach me a few dance steps before the big day.

By the time I got to college I had pretty much rejected what I considered the "legalism" of both the Pharisees and my church background. After all, I reasoned, what matters is our internal attitude. There was no place for "fences" in the life of a truly liberated Christian whose attitude was right. In my mind, people who built them were missing the point. As a Baptist, I was amused at the comment of a friend who said, "Baptists are against premarital sex because it can lead to dancing." The quip highlighted what I saw as the problem with fences. They put the cart before the horse. Man's rule replaced God's rule.

Fences Can Be Our Friends

I've had to rethink my position about "fences." It started a few years ago in my doctor's office. He decided to put me on hypertension medication, since my blood pressure had been elevated. I had been trying to deal with the problem through lifestyle factors like exercising and cutting down on my sodium intake, but it had not been successful. He thought my problem may be hereditary since my mother also had high blood pressure. But there was one more factor that was a potential cause of the problem. Over the past few years I had allowed about twenty pounds to creep onto my frame. I had not been motivated to take it off, but now that it was a possible health hazard, I decided to get serious about losing the weight.

It proved to be more challenging than I had anticipated. I tried to diet and exercise conscientiously but I lacked the discipline to stick with it. Eventually I signed up for one of the nationally known weight loss programs. There I found two factors that helped turn the problem around—accountability and encouragement. Every Saturday morning I would go to the center and empty my pockets so a relative stranger could weigh me and hold me accountable for my commitment to lose the weight. Some weeks I did well. Other weeks were not so good. But even on the 'off' weeks, nobody scolded me for departing from the program. They would just ask me where I had gone wrong and how I would change things to do better in the future. Then they would encourage me to stick to the program and tell me they knew I'd be successful.

In addition to the accountability and encouragement offered by the weight loss center, there was one more crucial factor in my eventual success. The program allowed me to eat at restaurants, provided I would stick to prescribed portions of certain foods. But I frequently ate at my favorite Italian restaurant, which offered all the soup, salad, and breadsticks you could eat. And, inevitably, I would make a pig of myself. So I did something drastic. I built a fence around that restaurant. I decided not to eat there until after I had lost the twenty pounds.

It worked. Although I was unsuccessful in resisting temptation when I was eating in the restaurant, building that fence kept me away from the source of the temptation. There was no way I could be a glutton in a restaurant I never patronized. By avoiding it and other all-you-can-eat places, I eventually lost the twenty pounds and lowered my blood pressure to the point where the doctor decreased the dosage of my medication.

I wish I were the kind of disciplined person who could make all the right choices without having to resort to something like this. But, because I have a weakness in this area I found it necessary to build the fence. And for the rest of my life as I struggle to maintain my appropriate weight, there will probably be times when I will need to rebuild it.

I've noticed other people discovering the benefits of fence building. A man told me that when he got married twenty-five years ago, he and his wife decided not to have a television set. "I knew if we had one we'd spend a lot of time watching it, and I don't have that kind of time," he said. "We've never regretted that decision."

I know of a young couple who built an almost literal fence by putting a Bible between them on the front seat of the car when they went on dates. It was a reminder that there was a certain line they would not cross in their physical expression of affection. I know a man, struggling with temptation to overspend, who cut up all his credit cards.

Another friend, a relatively new Christian, built a fence that I had previously dismissed as a silly taboo. When the movie *Chariots of Fire* first came out I asked him if he was going with our church group to see it. "No, I don't go to movies," he said. "I'm weak and I don't want to expose myself to certain temptations." I almost told him I didn't think he'd find anything objectionable in this film. Then I realized such a response would be beside the point. His one-time decision to avoid movies freed him from having to decide on a case-by-case basis if any given movie might cause a problem. By avoiding all movies he guaranteed that no movie would ever tempt him to violate his standards.

Jesus did not condemn Pharisees for *using* fences, but for *abusing* them. In fact, it seems to me that his command about spiritual amputation is just a more graphic version of the Pharisees' command to build fences. Rightly applied, these commands can keep us from sin. Wrongly applied, they can lead us into sins like pride and hypocrisy. Several principles emerge here as we seek to live effectively in the overlap.

The first is that each of us may need to be a fence builder in some area of our lives. While rejecting the "one size fits all" approach of blanket taboos for Christians in general, we can analyze our own situation and respond appropriately. One of the most effective things we can do as individual Christians is to identify our weak areas and use our creativity to build fences that will keep us from temptation in those areas.

A second principle is that we mustn't expect other people to abide by the fences we've established for ourselves. I needed to build a fence around my favorite Italian eatery, but it would be arrogant for me to announce that, "Christians don't

> One of the most effective things we can do as individual Christians is to identify our weak areas and use our creativity to build fences that will keep us from temptation in those areas.

patronize all-you-can-eat restaurants." We may be tempted to judge people's spirituality by observing whether or not they share our fences, but we need to remind ourselves that this is an unfair and often highly inaccurate yardstick.

A third principle is that we should not make it difficult for other people to abide by the fences they've established. I would have been wrong to try talking my friend into going to the movie. I'm thankful that my friends did not try to coax me into relaxing my self-imposed restaurant ban. We may not always relate to the reasons why people build certain fences but we should always respect them.

This may sometimes require our submitting to other people's fences. Author Paul E. Little tells of an incident that took place at a conference in New Jersey. He suggested to a friend that after the conference they go to Connie Mack Stadium and see the Phillies play the Cards. An acquaintance who overheard the conversation exclaimed, "How can you as a Christian go to a baseball game?" Little was flabbergasted and didn't know what to say. He had heard a lot of taboos in Christian circles but baseball was a new one.

"How can you and Fred claim to be Christians and then go out to a ball game?" the man asked again. When Little and Fred talked to their acquaintance, they began to realize what the problem was. The man had worshiped baseball before he became a Christian. For something like twelve years he'd seen every game in Philadelphia. He knew every batting average since 1910. Baseball had been his idol. When he became a Christian, he abandoned his old idol. But now he assumed that anybody who saw a game was worshiping baseball like he used to.

Little and Fred canceled their plans to go to the game, since their going would have needlessly disturbed him at a sensitive time in his Christian life. But they also counseled with him. He knew that baseball would probably be a temptation to him for the rest of his life. But gradually he came to see that not all Christians have such a problem with baseball, and he couldn't expect others to abide by his convictions. Although Little and Fred did not have a problem with baseball, out of concern for him they were willing on this occasion to change their plans because of another person's fence.[22]

The apostle Paul dealt with a similar situation in his letter to the Christians at Rome. Some people there had chosen not to eat meat (possibly because it had been offered to idols, or because it had not been slaughtered according to Jewish dietary laws). Others felt it was perfectly permissible to eat it. Paul agreed with those who did not have a problem eating meat, but exhorted those who had a problem to continue abstaining. He warned each party not to judge the other.

He then continued, "For the kingdom of God is not a matter of eating and drinking, but of righteousness, peace and joy in the Holy Spirit. . . . Let us therefore make every effort to do what leads to peace and to mutual edification. Do not destroy the work of God for the sake of food. All food is clean, but it is wrong for a man to eat anything that causes someone else to stumble. It is better not to eat meat or drink wine or to do anything else that will cause your brother to fall" (Romans 14:17–21).

> Christian freedom includes the liberty to voluntarily restrict our freedom.

If our participation in an activity will tempt a brother to do something that violates his conscience, then out of love for our brother we should abstain. Christian freedom includes the liberty to voluntarily restrict our freedom. In the words of biblical scholar F. F. Bruce:

> Paul enjoyed his Christian liberty to the full. Never was there a Christian more thoroughly emancipated than he from un-Christian inhibitions and taboos. So completely was he emancipated from spiritual bondage that he was not even in bondage to his emancipation. He conformed to the Jewish way of life when he was in Jewish society as cheerfully as he went along with Gentile ways when he was living with Gentiles. The interests of the gospel and the highest well-being of men and women were paramount considerations with him; to these he subordinated everything else.[23]

This brings us back to the paradox of fences. For a long time the whole practice of building fences seemed restrictive to me. And certainly it can be. Jesus took to task those Pharisees who laid intolerable burdens on people by devising innumerable fences and demanding that they keep them all. But the other side of the coin is that fences, properly used, can be liberating. There were people for whom certain Sabbath fences were a source of joy. In fact, some of the Sabbath laws (such as Rabbi Shammai's prohibition against comforting mourners or visiting the sick on the Sabbath) were instituted to prevent people from spoiling the celebration with depressing activities. As Dr. J. H. Hertz, former chief rabbi of the United Hebrew Congregations of the British Commonwealth, says:

> Amid all the misery and slavery that for so many centuries were the lot of Israel, once a week the home of the humblest Jew was flooded with light. The Sabbath banished care and toil, grief and sorrow. . . . It was their love for the Sabbath which led them to exert all their ingenuity in discovering ways of differentiating it from other days and making it more thoroughly a day of rest, a day in which man enjoys some foretaste of the pure bliss and happiness which are stored up for the righteous in the world to come.[24]

The Old Testament scholar Rudolph Kittel agrees:

> Anyone who has had the opportunity of knowing in our own day the inner life of Jewish families that observe the Law of the fathers with sincere piety and in all strictness, will have been astonished at the wealth of joyfulness, gratitude and sunshine, undreamt of by the outsider, with which the Law animates the Jewish home. The whole household rejoices on the Sabbath, which they celebrate with rare satisfaction not only as the day of rest, but rather as the day of rejoicing. Jewish prayers term the Sabbath a "joy of the soul" to him who hallows it: *he* "enjoys the abundance of Thy goodness." Such expressions are not mere words; they are the outcome of pure and genuine happiness and enthusiasm.[25]

Fences and the Overlap

If a fence is something arbitrarily imposed upon us, it is a burden. But, if a fence is freely and thoughtfully chosen, it can be a source of joy. Living in the overlap, we can take comfort in the fact that our struggles with temptation will end when the kingdom is consummated. Until then, fences can be our secret weapon in keeping us from temptation and turning us into the kind of people God wants us to be.

Most of us have probably heard warnings about the dangers of becoming "Pharisaical." Perhaps it's time we also took a look at the *benefits* of becoming Pharisaical, in the good sense of the word. With their determination to obey God and their use of fences to keep them from sin, some of those wise old Pharisees may still be able to teach us a thing or two.

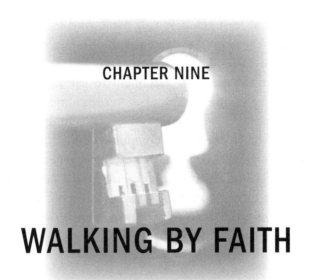

CHAPTER NINE

WALKING BY FAITH

"Is there a God?"

"Did Jesus really rise from the dead?"

"If I trust in God will he sustain me after my divorce?"

"Will he provide for me now that I've lost my job?"

Honest answers to these questions will reveal the presence of faith or doubts, or possibly a mixture of both. Whether we're dealing with intellectual questions or experiential ones, we who live in the overlap cannot avoid the need for faith. It is the optic nerve of the kingdom: we are to walk by faith, not by sight. But how do we do this? For a long time my concept of walking by faith was something like this: Faith is good. Doubts are bad. Faith is something I am supposed to conjure up. Doubts are something I am supposed to suppress.

Putting this into practice was no mean feat. On the surface, some of Jesus' pronouncements (telling his disciples their faith could cast a mountain into the sea, for example[1]) seem as idealistic as fairy tales. They appear to require a "believing makes it so" mentality like that of children at a Peter Pan performance affirming their belief in fairies by applauding to revive Tinkerbell. They seem to require closing our eyes to reality, or at least giving it a sly wink. And Jesus' anger seemed to burn against those doubters who wouldn't join in such a pious charade—those he labeled "you of little faith."[2]

Then, as I combed the New Testament to get a clearer picture of Jesus' perspective on faith and doubts, a more complex and decidedly un-fantasy-like point of view emerged. Jesus' central message of the kingdom helped me appreciate his emphasis on faith. I saw that—far from being a denial of reality—faith is the bridge between the visible realities of this age and the invisible realities of the next. We who live in the overlap of those two ages must deal with both realities. As the writer of Hebrews says, "Now faith is being sure of what we hope for and certain of what we do not see" (11:1). George Eldon Ladd explains further:

> The person of faith is the one who does not consider the visible world of human experience to be the world of ulti-mate values. He or she recognizes that above are the spiritual realities of God's Kingdom, which cannot be perceived with the physical senses but which are more real than the phe-nomenal world.[3]

As citizens of the kingdom we do not have to conjure up faith, nor do we have to feel guilty about having doubts.

In studying Jesus' teaching on the subject I was relieved to discover that as citizens of the kingdom we do not have to conjure up faith, nor do we have to feel guilty about having doubts. I saw that not all doubts earned a rebuke from Jesus; he seemed to divide doubts into three categories, two of which often sparked his wrath, but one of which sparked his sympathy.

Honest Doubts

This latter of the three categories (the one that evoked Jesus' sympathy) could be called "honest doubts." In fact when confronted with honest doubts, Jesus not only refrained from attacking the doubters, he some-times praised them and offered evidence to help them move beyond their doubts.

This happened with Nathaniel.[4] Nathaniel was not impressed when Philip first told him that Jesus of Nazareth was the one about whom Moses and the other prophets had written.

"Nazareth! Can anything good come from there?" he asked.

It was an understandable (if tactless) retort. Some expected the Messiah to come from Bethlehem. Others weren't sure where he'd come from. However, the unimpressive town of Nazareth wouldn't have made anybody's list.

We might have expected Jesus to rebuke Nathaniel for his skepticism. But as soon as they met, Jesus praised him for his honesty instead.

"Here is a true Israelite, in whom there is nothing false," Jesus said. Then he offered Nathaniel evidence that he was, in fact, the Messiah.

"How do you know me?" Nathaniel asked.

"I saw you while you were still under the fig tree before Philip called you."

How could he have known that? Nathaniel realized that this was no ordinary man.

"Rabbi, you are the Son of God; you are the king of Israel," Nathaniel said. Jesus had offered evidence and affirmation. And the honest doubter became an honest believer.

Jesus responded the same way to John the Baptist's doubts.[5] He was not embodying John's preconceived notion of how the Messiah would usher in the kingdom. John sent word to him from prison, asking, "Are you the one who was to come, or should we expect someone else?"

Jesus could have lambasted him for doubting. But, instead, he invited John to examine the evidence for his messiahship.

"Go back and report to John what you have seen and heard. The blind receive sight, the lame walk, those who have leprosy are cured, the deaf hear, the dead are raised, and the good news is preached to the poor." His miracles comprised twofold evidence. First, they revealed that in Jesus the power of the kingdom was at work. Second, they fulfilled Isaiah's prophecy that such healings would take place when the kingdom came.[6]

Then again Jesus praised a doubter. After John's disciples had left, Jesus said to his own disciples, "Among those born of women there is no one greater than John; yet the one who is least in the kingdom of God is greater than he."

Despite his doubts, John still represented the standard by which greatness in the kingdom would be measured. Once again Jesus responded to an honest doubter by providing evidence and affirmation.

He provided evidence again in his encounter with the Bible's most famous doubter, Thomas.[7]

After the other disciples had told Thomas that they had seen the risen Christ, Thomas had retorted, "Unless I see the nail marks in his hands and put my fingers where the nails were, and put my hand into his side, I will not believe it."

A week later Jesus entered the locked room where Thomas and the other disciples had gathered, and invited the skeptic to make good on his claim.

"Put your finger here, see my hands. Reach out your hand and put it into my side. Stop doubting and believe," Jesus said. We're not told if Thomas followed through with the examination. But he did cross the line from skepticism to belief.

"My Lord and my God!" he said.

"Because you have seen me, you have believed; blessed are those who have not seen and yet have believed," Jesus responded, evidently referring primarily to those who would become believers after his ascension.

Should Thomas be faulted for his doubts? Perhaps in light of Jesus' repeated assertions that he would rise from the dead (and his disparagement of "sign seekers"), Thomas was guilty of unjustified disbelief. Probably this is the most common view.

But might Thomas have been responding to something else Jesus had said?[8] Jesus had warned his disciples, "Watch out that no one deceives you. For many will come in my name, claiming, 'I am the Christ,' and will deceive many. . . . At that time if anyone says to you, 'Look, here is the Christ!' or, 'There he is!' do not believe it. For false Christs and false prophets will appear and perform great signs and miracles to deceive even the elect if that were possible" (Matthew 24:4–5, 23–24).

Thus, Jesus not only commanded his disciples to have a robust faith, but a robust skepticism as well. Whatever Jesus meant by having faith, he obviously did not mean that his disciples should unquestioningly accept every sanctimonious claim that came their way.

Might Thomas' skepticism about the risen Christ have been the result of trying to obey this command? He had previously shown himself to be a loyal, if pessimistic, disciple. ("Let us also go, that we may die with him," he had said when Jesus announced his intention to make a potentially dangerous trip to Bethany.[9])

If this is so, Jesus' command to stop doubting and start believing should not be considered a rebuke, but a command to move forward in his understanding. As seen in his dealings with Nathaniel and John the Baptist, Jesus viewed honest doubts as a prelude to belief. They were something to progress through, like a math student progresses through the multiplication tables before tackling the fundamentals of algebra. Perhaps Thomas' doubts fell into this category, too. In any case, Scripture makes it obvious that honest doubts are not something to suppress; indeed they can lead us to deeper faith.

> Jesus viewed honest doubts as a prelude to belief.

"Doubt must precede every deeper assurance; for uncertainties are what we first see when we look into a region hitherto unknown, unexplored, unannexed," says author George MacDonald.[10]

Author and pastor Frederick Buechner gives a more earthy description: "Doubts are the ants in the pants of faith. They keep it awake and moving. . . . Tillich said that doubt isn't the opposite of faith; it is an element of faith."[11]

Honest doubters had nothing to fear from Jesus. He accepted them as they were. But two kinds of doubts angered him. His enemies exemplified the first kind, and his own disciples exemplified the second.

Obstinate Disbelief

The first kind may be called "obstinate disbelief." It was the refusal to consider believing in Jesus despite the evidence. Some privileged people would have had much to lose if they had followed Jesus. To believe in him would have jerked the rug out from under everything upon which they'd built their lives. They didn't want his teachings to be true, so they shut their minds to his message.

"Give us a sign," they taunted, as if the sight of formerly lame (and formerly dead) people walking around did not constitute some sort of evidence.[12] Jesus refused to jump through their hoop. He opened the eyes of those who were blind through no fault of their own, who came to him for healing. But he would not pry open the eyes of those who chose blindness because "they loved darkness instead of light."[13]

They may have prided themselves on taking the intellectually "respectable" route, assuming their skepticism was more rational than the glad belief in Jesus that the common people—people they regarded as gullible—often displayed. But it's not just the gullible who are guilty of intellectual sloth; the skeptical can be equally guilty. Blind disbelief is as anti-intellectual as blind belief. And Jesus had no patience with those skeptics who reveled in their blindness.

Thus Nicodemus, a sincere Pharisee with honest questions, could have an earnest discussion with Jesus concerning spiritual matters. But those who had made up their minds to reject him, who would not be convinced "even if someone rises from the dead,"[14] were the targets of his reproof.

Unjustified Doubts

And surprisingly enough, his own disciples were a similar target. They embodied the second kind of doubt that angered him, what we might call "unjustified doubts." We may compare and contrast the disciples' situation with that of certain Gentiles who exemplified great faith: the Canaanite woman whose demonized daughter was delivered,[15] the Samaritan leper who was cleansed,[16] and the Roman centurion whose sick servant was healed.[17]

At times the disciples seemed to display similar faith. When Jesus sent them out to proclaim the kingdom of God, they too cast out demons and healed the sick.

"Lord, even the demons submit to us in your name," they exclaimed when they returned from one of their assignments. [18]

Yet, at times their faith was notable only for its Lilliputian dimensions.

On one occasion a squall threatened to sink the boat they were sailing in.[19] The frantic disciples woke Jesus and said, "Teacher, don't you care if we drown?"

Jesus rebuked the storm, then rebuked the disciples.

"Why are you so afraid? Do you still have no faith?"

The terrified men asked each other, "Who is this? Even the wind and the waves obey him!"

On a second occasion another storm buffeted the boat the disciples were in. Jesus walked toward them on the water.[20]

"It's a ghost!" the terrified disciples cried out.

"Take courage! It is I. Don't be afraid," Jesus answered.

"Lord, if it's you," Peter called out, "tell me to come to you on the water."

"Come."

Peter jumped out of the boat, walked toward Jesus, then started sinking. Jesus caught him.

"You of little faith," he said, "why did you doubt?" They climbed into the boat and the men worshiped Jesus.

"Truly you are the Son of God," they said.

On a third occasion the disciples were unable to drive the demon out of a boy whose father then went to Jesus.[21]

"Oh unbelieving generation," Jesus said, "how long shall I stay with you? How long will I put up with you? Bring the boy to me."

As the boy convulsed on the ground, foaming at the mouth, Jesus told the father, "Everything is possible for him who believes."

"I do believe; help my unbelief!" he exclaimed,[22] and Jesus drove out the demon.

Privately the disciples asked Jesus, "Why couldn't we drive it out?"

"Because you have so little faith," he answered.

When we read the Gospels we can't avoid the paradox. Jesus told people who had only one encounter with him, even despised Gentiles, that their faith had caused miracles. However, Jesus' closest disciples only demonstrated that kind of faith at certain times. Other times, according to Jesus, their faith was woefully inadequate. In fact, at times Jesus' favorite nickname for them seemed to be "you of little faith."

How do we explain this? Were the disciples exceptionally weak? Or is it harder to sustain faith for an extended duration than it is for a short burst of time? Or was Jesus calling his disciples to a higher standard, a deeper faith? Scripture doesn't spell out a definite answer, but a combination of the last two possibilities seems likely.

We may glean a clue from an exchange between Jesus and Philip.[23]

"Lord, show us the Father and that will be enough for us," Philip said.

> He didn't dispense the reasoned rebukes of a guru chiding his disciples for the inadequate execution of certain spiritual exercises. Instead he exploded with the passion of a wounded lover saying, "You should know me better than that!"

"Don't you know me, Philip, even though I have been among you such a long time? Anyone who has seen me has seen the Father," Jesus answered.

Don't you know me? This seemed to be the undercurrent in Jesus' continuous frustration with his disciples. He seemed to take their doubts personally, as though they were a breach of the relationship. He didn't dispense the reasoned rebukes of a guru chiding his disciples for the inadequate execution of certain spiritual exercises. Instead he exploded with the passion of a wounded lover saying, "You should know me better than that!"

It is harder for spouses to maintain a devoted marriage than it is for strangers on a blind date to maintain a cordial evening together. People expect more from their best friends than they do from casual acquaintances. Jesus' relationship with his disciples embodied similar challenges and demands. Jesus' anger over the disciples' weak faith seemed to reflect his basic concern about the inadequacies of their relationship.

He did not simply desire to perform a few miracles through these men; he planned to transform the world through them. Their doubts would have more disastrous consequences than other people's. These men had to develop a deeper faith in Jesus. They had to become intimate with him.

The two accounts of the storms on the sea may provide an insight. Each began with the disciples displaying a mistaken perception of Jesus ("He doesn't care if we drown."/ "That must be a ghost walking toward us"). Then Jesus issued a rebuke ("Do you still have no faith?"/ "Why did you doubt?"). Finally the disciples expressed a deeper perception of Jesus ("Who is this? Even the wind and the waves obey him!"/ "He is the Son of God").

There seemed to be a link between the disciples' inadequate perception of Jesus and their inadequate faith. And the only solution was for them to become better acquainted with him.

This is certainly true of other relationships. A happily married woman trusts her husband, not because she has sat around mastering some esoteric technique for having faith in spouses, but because she knows the man to whom she's married. Her faith in him is the by-product of a healthy relationship. And so it is with us. The kind of faith Jesus expects from disciples is the by-product of a thriving relationship with him. Such faith cannot be conjured up on demand.

It is probably no accident that the same seemingly extravagant promise that Jesus made about those who had faith ("If you believe, you will receive whatever you ask for in prayer"[24]) he also promised those who enjoyed an intimate relationship with him ("If you remain in me and my words remain in you, ask whatever you wish, and it will be given you"[25]). The faith is linked to the intimacy.

> A man who wants to experience mountain-moving faith without developing his relationship to Jesus is like a husband who wants to experience a glorious marriage without having to spend time with his wife.

There is no sense in trying to find a shortcut to acquiring this kind of faith. A man who wants to experience mountain-moving faith without developing his relationship to Jesus is like a husband who wants to experience a glorious marriage without having to spend time with his wife.

When we are in a relationship with someone who consistently shows himself to be faithful, our trust in that person should grow accordingly. The Old Testament periodically offers examples of this. Sometimes while reading the Old Testament I used to become annoyed at what I considered to be an irritating habit of the writers. In the middle of a perfectly good story the action would screech to a halt, and somebody like Joshua[26] or the Levites of Nehemiah's day[27] would launch into a lengthy speech reminding people of past events like the call of Abraham or the deliverance of the Israelites from Egypt. For a long time I saw this as a quaint redundancy—a misplaced history lesson.

However, I have since come to appreciate it. I've come to realize that at least part of the reason for it was to remind the readers of God's faithfulness in the past, so they'd have faith to keep trusting him in the future.

"Remember the days of old," Moses told Israel (Deuteronomy 32:7). God's enduring commitment to them was the basis for them to develop a trusting relationship with him.

Once when I was going though hard times I followed the lead of the Old Testament writers. I wrote my own chronicle of God's faithfulness to me. I jotted down a list of the trials he had seen me and my family through—illnesses, pressures at work, financial problems, joblessness, a dreaded IRS audit. My faith was reinforced by looking at this reminder of how God had provided for me in the past. I no longer remember what crisis prompted me to write the list, but I still have the yellow paper that gives chicken-scratched testimony to God's faithfulness in my life.

On at least one occasion Jesus issued this kind of memory jogger to his disciples. "You of little faith. . . . Don't you remember the five loaves for the five thousand, and how many basketfuls you gathered? Or the seven loaves for the four thousand, and how many basketfuls you gathered?" he demanded after they mistakenly concluded he was upset because they hadn't brought bread on a trip (Matthew 16:8–10). If their memories were so short, how could he ever inculcate the kind of faith he yearned for them to have?

But somehow it happened. In the end, their dogged doubts were no match for his dogged faithfulness. They became the people he needed them to be, and he changed the world through them.[28] Those of us who struggle with doubts can draw encouragement from their example. There is hope for us as well.

Yet, whether we come to Jesus as honest doubters who need evidence, or as disciples who need a closer relationship with him (or as a combination of both), there is one more factor to consider.

Taking a Leap

Examining the evidence may lead us to conclude that Jesus' teachings are probably true. Reminding ourselves of his past faithfulness may lead us to conclude that he will probably be faithful in the future. But faith goes one step beyond simply acknowledging the probable.

Actually, "one step" is an understatement. "A flying leap" is more like it. Author Sheldon Vanauken tells of a time he was confronted with such a situation:

> Christianity—in a word, the divinity of Jesus—seemed probable to me. But there is a gap between the probable and proved. How was I to cross it? If I were to stake my whole life on the Risen Christ, I wanted proof. I wanted certainty. I wanted to see Him eat a bit of fish. I wanted letters of fire across the sky. I got none of these. And I continued to hang about on the edge of the gap. . . .

The position was not, as I had been comfortably thinking all these months, merely a question of whether I was to accept the Messiah or not. It was a question of whether I was to accept him—or *reject*. My God! There was a gap *behind* me too. Perhaps the leap to acceptance was a horrifying gamble—but what of the leap to rejection? There might be no certainty that Christ was God—but, by God, there was no certainty that he was not. If I were to accept, I might and probably would face the thought through the years: "Perhaps, after all, it's a lie: I've been had!" But if I were to reject, I would certainly face the haunting, terrible thought: "Perhaps it's true—and I have *rejected my God!*"

This was not to be borne. I *could not* reject Jesus. There was only one thing to do, once I had seen the gap behind me. I turned away from it and flung myself over the gap *towards* Jesus.[29]

> The gap between the probable and the proved—it's understood by anyone who has ever weighed the pros and cons of buying a particular house or accepting a particular job. It may look like the right decision, but we won't know for sure unless we commit ourselves to it. We must fling ourselves over the gap.

The gap between the probable and the proved—it's understood by anyone who has ever weighed the pros and cons of buying a particular house or accepting a particular job. It may look like the right decision, but we won't know for sure unless we commit ourselves to it. We must fling ourselves over the gap.

When I think about making such a leap, I think of the time I tried bungee jumping. While visiting a resort city with a couple of bungee jumping sites, I investigated what it would be like. I talked with people who had done it. I checked into the safety record of the major bungee company. I even inspected a bungee cord—sort of a rope woven from hundreds of elastic strands no thicker than an ordinary rubber band.

I decided it looked safe enough. I would probably not die. But when the bungee crew started prepping me for the jump, I had some reservations. They wrapped a towel around my ankles, then tied a strap around the towel. They hooked the cord onto the strap. I had never specifically asked how the cord was attached to the jumper, but I had assumed it would be hooked to something that seemed more substantial, like a harness.

"What if the towel or strap comes loose?" I thought. I reminded myself that this company had a perfect safety record. But the nagging doubt persisted. As I stood at the top of a forty-meter platform (which is not particularly high as bungee jumps go, but was plenty high enough for me), one of the crew members gave me instructions.

"I'll give you the countdown. On the count of three, take a deep breath. On the count of one, dive off."

I felt like backing out. But another crew member, on the ground, was videotaping and I didn't want my cowardice preserved for posterity.

"Five . . . Four . . . three . . ."

I took a deep breath.

"Two . . . one!"

I jumped. I fell for several seconds until the cord stretched to its limit, then I ricocheted back into the air, and repeated the process a few times like a human yo-yo. The cord did not snap. The towel and strap did not slip. I did not die. The probable had become proven.

When I think of the ambivalent feelings I had with the bungee jump (as well as those I sometimes have when it comes to Christian faith), I think of the ambivalence certain Bible characters displayed. And I gain comfort from it. Faith unmixed with doubt may be preferable. But faith mixed with doubt can still get results.

"I do believe; help my unbelief," a father says. His son is delivered from the demon. But what if the father had refused to bring his son to Jesus until he had banished all unbelief from his mind?

Peter's friends pray for him after he's imprisoned. Yet, after his miraculous release they keep him waiting outside the house in which they've gathered, because they can't believe God has answered their prayers.[30] But what if they'd refused to pray until they had no doubts God would give them a miracle?

Probably most of us will struggle with some mixture of faith and doubt much (if not most) of the time. But the ultimate tragedy does not consist in having doubts; it consists in allowing our doubts to prevent us from doing what God wants us to do.

Faith and the Overlap

My understanding of the overlap is helping me come to terms with the fact that in this present age I will routinely have to make leaps of faith. After all, how could such leaps not be necessary for those who live between the "already" and the "not yet"?

> In this present age I will routinely have to make leaps of faith. After all, how could such leaps not be necessary for those who live between the "already" and the "not yet"?

Eugene H. Peterson's paraphrase of a passage in Corinthians 13 captures Paul's assessment of our challenge as we navigate between two ages: "We know only a portion of the truth, and what we say about God is always incomplete. But when the Complete arrives, our incompletes will be canceled. . . . We don't yet see things clearly. We're squinting in a fog, peering through a mist. But it won't be long before the weather clears and the sun shines bright! We'll see it all then, see it all as clearly as God sees us, knowing him directly just as he knows us! But for right now, until that completeness, we have three things to do to lead us toward that consummation: Trust steadily in God, hope unswervingly, love extravagantly."[31]

Thus Scripture plainly warns me that my sight and knowledge will be incomplete until the kingdom comes in all its fullness. I can strengthen my faith by becoming familiar with evidence that supports it, and by becoming more intimate with Jesus. But leaps of faith and battles with doubt will continue until we make that final leap from this age into the next.[32] Until then, whether I like it or not, I must get used to strapping the cord onto my ankle and jumping off the platform.

Examining the evidence. Deciding it looks valid. Affirming "I do believe; help my unbelief." Taking a flying leap. Then seeing what happens.

That's a pretty good picture of a bungee jump. It's not a bad picture of the faith God requires from us, either. And if we're willing to risk our necks, we'll find that God's grace, like the bungee cord, is worth trusting with the plunge.

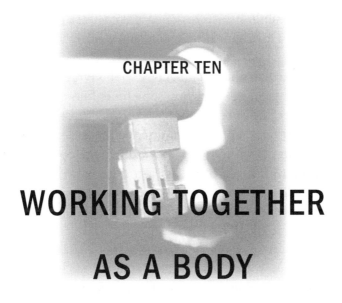

CHAPTER TEN

WORKING TOGETHER

AS A BODY

It was one of those times when I feel embarrassed to be a Christian. I was watching a television documentary about a battle raging at a certain seminary. The faculty was divided over the issue of women's roles in the church.[1] One group supported the practice of permitting women to serve in certain capacities. The other group opposed the practice. Passions ran deep on both sides.

I grieved as I watched. Not because of their lack of agreement, but because of the way their disagreement was expressed. Neither side seemed to base its arguments upon a careful study of Scripture. Each side seemed to assume that those on the other side were motivated exclusively by dishonorable motives. Therefore, instead of an honest discussion based on the Bible, the debate largely took the form of attacks on the motivations and character of those on the other side.

Proponents of one view accused their opponents of misogyny. Proponents of the other view accused their opponents of abandoning the Bible's authority and allowing their theology to be shaped by contemporary culture instead. Perhaps some of their more balanced and biblical comments wound up on the editing room floor. (Admittedly, this is a real possibility since reasoned theological arguments cannot easily be reduced to captivating sound bites, especially for a secular audience.)

But, as depicted in the documentary, nobody acknowledged that godly scholars of great integrity may sometimes find themselves in disagreement on certain issues. Nobody acknowledged that at times it is possible for Christians equally committed to the authority of Scripture to reach different conclusions because of different approaches to biblical interpretation. Instead, those on each side seemed to regard those on the other side as enemies. And so, viewers were treated to the sight of Christians taking potshots at each other in living color on coast-to-coast television. So much for Christian unity.

Living in the overlap, we are not Lone Ranger Christians who practice our faith in isolation from each other. Whether we like it or not, we collectively form the church, a body of believers that owes its existence and its mission to the kingdom Jesus inaugurated. As New Testament scholar Darrell L. Bock says:

> Thus the new community, the church, is the showcase of God's present reign through Messiah Jesus, who inaugurates the fulfillment of God's promises. . . . The current phase of the kingdom has continuity with the kingdom to come, because it shares the call to reflect the activity and presence of God's righteousness in the world. Such benefits come for the one who trusts Christ. If people are to see God at work and humankind living in righteousness and in love, they will see it in the church, where the Spirit is the active expression of Jesus' rule. The church's mission is the expression of love and righteousness not only to its own but to all those who are in need, the "tax collectors and sinners" of the world.[2]

Therefore, as the church or the body of Christ, we have a two-fold mission: to build up other members of the body, and to evangelize those who are not yet believers.[3] Both tasks require us to work together in harmony.

Body Building

When I think about Christians working together despite their differences, I think about a conversation I had with my friend Benjie. I met Benjie years ago when he joined our church as the new minister to singles. I came to appreciate him right away. He was one of the most dynamic Bible teachers I'd ever heard. Moreover, he had a servant's heart and a strong commitment to God. Shortly after his arrival, I became the vice president of our church singles group, which meant I planned and supervised the group's activities.

Benjie invited me to lunch one afternoon so we could discuss some matters pertaining to the singles group. During the conversation he asked me what I thought about speaking in tongues. The question made me uncomfortable, because I sensed that he and I probably did not agree on this issue. After a slight hesitation, I told him that I believed that speaking in tongues was a legitimate gift for Christians today. The look on his face told me that I was right to think that we did not see eye to eye on this issue.

There was an awkward pause. I had seen other friendships fall apart over this issue, and I wondered if this might strain our relationship. I even wondered if he might think there would be a problem with my continuing to hold a leadership position in the singles group. Finally, he spoke.

"I really disagree with you," he said. Then he added, "But I know you love the Lord, and I respect your Christian walk, and there's no reason why this should affect our fellowship." His charitable response made a lasting impact on me. He did not compromise his beliefs and he did not expect me to compromise mine. We were free to express disagreement with each other, while affirming that what we had in common was much more important than the issues on which we might differ.

I left the restaurant that afternoon feeling that I had learned something about Christian unity. It was not based on mentally assenting to a list of doctrinal statements. It was based on our mutual commitment to Christ and to his body, in spite of the fact that we might not agree on every detail of doctrine. In fact I felt more unified with Benjie than I did with some other people who shared my doctrinal beliefs but did not display his charitable spirit. Benjie and I continued to work together in the singles group until he and his wife Barbara left to become missionaries in Haiti. We never tried to change each other's minds; we worked together to make the singles group a place where people could find Christ and be strengthened in their relationship to him.

I do not mean to minimize how serious some disagreements can be. And I would never want to encourage people to compromise what they believe to be biblical. I realize that doctrinal differences may make it inappropriate for some Christians to participate together in certain activities. And I know that the church will not be totally unified until Christ comes again. Nevertheless, I can't help but wonder how many fractured friendships and churches could have remained intact if the parties involved had possessed the love and wisdom to say to each other, "I really disagree with you, but there's no reason why that should affect our fellowship"—and had meant it.

> I can't help but wonder how many fractured friendships and churches could have remained intact if the parties involved had possessed the love and wisdom to say to each other, "I really disagree with you, but there's no reason why that should affect our fellowship"—and had meant it.

In some ways our situation reminds me of when my brother and sister and I were kids. We are great friends now, but we had our share of squabbles as children. I think about the things we used to argue about. Who has to take the first bath? Whose turn is it to sit in the middle of the car's back seat? Who gets to open the garage door when we get home? I look back and can't believe that such things ever caused discord among us. But how important those things seemed at the time.

I can't help but wonder if a similar situation awaits us when we enter eternity. Will I be chagrined at some of the things that prevented me from being unified with some of my Christian brothers and sisters? There is a world of people who need to hear about Jesus. There is a body of believers that needs to be built up. What differences are so important that they can legitimately prevent us from working together to accomplish these tasks?

As Frederick Buechner points out, when we allow our differences to divide us, Christ's body is broken all over again:

> When Jesus took the bread and said, "This is my body which is broken for you" (1 Corinthians 11:24), it's hard to believe that even in his wildest dreams he foresaw the tragic and ludicrous brokenness of the Church as his body. There's no reason why everyone should be Christian in the same way and every reason to leave room for differences, but if all the competing factions of Christendom were to give as much of themselves to the high calling and holy hope that unites them as they do now to the relative inconsequentialities that divide them, the Church would look more like the Kingdom of God for a change and less like an ungodly mess.[4]

It strikes me that our differences may actually give us a unique opportunity to demonstrate Christian unity. It may be easy to cooperate with somebody who agrees with us on every point. But when Christians of different denominational and doctrinal stances work together despite such differences, it is obvious that our unity springs from a deeper source.

> Our differences may actually give us a unique opportunity to demonstrate Christian unity.

My friend Bill is an example of what can happen when different Christians work together, sharing their time and talents to build up the body of Christ. I met Bill years ago when he joined our singles Sunday school class. He was a new Christian when I met him. But he matured quickly, and he credits the body of Christ for his spiritual growth. He met his wife, Janet, through our class. Shortly before their wedding, before Bill and Janet moved on to a married couple class, he shared his testimony as he taught our class:

I want to talk to you today about this active, living part of the body of Christ and how it has nurtured and developed me. Before I accepted the gift of eternal life I was a foreigner in this church. I attended the service but had no personal contact with Christians, so I didn't know they were different from me. I enrolled in an adult training class on sign language and was surrounded by Christians! I became aware that they were different from me. I became friends with these people and they witnessed to me without knowing it. I could see and sense the Holy Spirit around them, even though I didn't know who the Holy Spirit was. I saw their faith and I saw them pray. It was here that I met David. In David, God gave me that crucial first Christian friend. I enjoyed his enthusiasm and his outgoing nature. I still do.

Bill went on to describe how after nine months of attending church and being involved with Christians, his heart softened and he received God's gift of eternal life. He then mentioned a series of class members, crediting them with helping him in his spiritual journey, including:

- John, who would call him regularly to see how he was doing and to ask if he had any prayer requests.
- Shelia, who sat next to him in church one evening, helped him find the Scripture passage the pastor was discussing, and offered some books she thought Bill might find helpful as a new Christian.
- Dave and Rosalie, the married couple who led the class and whom he considered to be his spiritual parents.
- Kathy, who teamed with Bill in the church's visitation program and who became a role model and inspiration to him.
- Terrell, who helped Bill through a difficult period when he was angered at being mistreated by someone.

Altogether Bill recognized ten people by name, in addition to his fiancé. He then concluded:

> My relationship with Janet is not like a bottle with a message in it that you throw into the ocean, and then walk away wondering what will happen to it. We want and need to continue the relationship we have with you. I have spoken of how many parts of the body have nurtured, supported, and loved me. I will continue to need that from you. I need it now more than ever. As Christ has loved me, so I love you.

I got a lump in my throat when I heard Bill speak these words. His testimony provides a counterpoint to my embarrassment over the imperfections in the body of Christ. Perhaps, like Buechner says, the church is in some ways an ungodly mess. But when God's people—imperfect though they are—use their gifts and work together to build up the body of believers, the church can make a profound difference in people's lives by helping them experience the *shalom* of the kingdom.

Evangelism

In addition to building up the body of believers, we who live in the overlap also have the mission of evangelizing unbelievers. I confess that evangelism has never been one of my favorite subjects. There's a shy streak in me that makes me feel awkward about approaching strangers for any reason, let alone discussing something that can be so touchy. I am not much more comfortable about approaching friends. I have squirmed through countless sermons that laid guilt trips on the congregation in an effort to motivate people to evangelize unbelievers. I have often seen evangelism as a huge, uncomfortable duty. I identify with Rebecca Manley Pippert's observation: "Christians and non-Christians have something in common. We're both uptight about evangelism."[5]

> I identify with Rebecca Manley Pippert's observation: "Christians and non-Christians have something in common. We're both uptight about evangelism."

But my understanding of the kingdom has started a reversal in my antipathy toward evangelism. I am coming to realize that it is the very opposite of a duty. As author and pastor Robert T. Henderson explains,

> I think immediately of the evening that the announcement came that the Second World War had ended. Our whole lives had been affected by that disaster for several years. I was working that evening in the public library. We had been told by the senior librarian that if the announcement came we could close the library in celebration. When the word came we closed the library and went onto the main street where thousands of people had gathered and were dancing for joy in the street, singing and shouting for sheer gratitude that it was all over. That's gospel. It thrills. It excites. It is full of gratitude and joy.
>
> The word *gospel* comes from a Greek word *euangelion* (meaning "joyous news or announcement"), which comes into English as *evangel*, and the verbal form *evangelism*, or *evangelization*. Given its origin, the word can hardly mean some body of doctrine served up like cold mashed potatoes. Nor can evangelization be properly conceived as some dutiful process of proselytizing done to keep the church rolls from showing a decrease in membership. Sadly, it has devolved into this too frequently. No! Evangelism is having such joyous news that it is spontaneously sloshed all over everybody.[6]

Thus, at its heart, evangelism is not a duty. To evangelize is to celebrate good news and to invite others to join in the celebration. The Evangelism Manifesto sums up this news about as well as I've ever heard it put:

> To proclaim "the kingdom of God has drawn near" is to herald those mighty events in which God's royal rule has invaded the earth in the coming of Jesus Christ and in the power of the Holy Spirit. It is to bring the thrilling news of God's victory in the death and resurrection of His Son over

all the dark powers that have enslaved mankind and make His good creation subject to bondage (Romans 8:19–25; Colossians 1:13, 14). It is to tell of what God has done to bring forgiveness to the guilty, help to the poor, release to the captives, sight to the blind, deliverance to the oppressed. It is to announce to the whole creation a divine reign of justice and peace (Luke 2:14; Acts 10:36; Ephesians 2:17).

Together with this grand announcement, the proclamation of the kingdom brings a summons. Hearers are called to renounce all sin, each false lord, every rival sovereignty, and to submit through repentance and faith to God's saving reign in Christ (Mark 6:12; Acts 17:30; 26:20). The proclamation demands commitment to God's lordship and obedience to His will in the world (Matthew 7:21). Although the decisive victory over the forces of evil has been won, the conflict still rages (Ephesians 6:11, 12). Christ is risen; the Spirit has been poured out upon the church; the powers of the coming age are at work in the world, but the end is not yet. Hosts of darkness resist God's sovereignty; rampant evils oppose His will. To repent and believe is to side with God's purpose in this conflict—assured of ultimate victory, while contending God's righteousness in every sphere of life (1 Corinthians 15:54–57; Acts 26:16–18). . . .

The same good news preached to the world must be constantly heard afresh in the church, for the call to repent and believe, to submit to God's gracious reign, is a call to growth as well as to conversion. The church lives by the gospel it proclaims (2 Corinthians 5:15).[7]

When I think about the awesome news of the kingdom of God, I am forced to an uncomfortable conclusion: if I am not motivated to proclaim the gospel, something is wrong with me. When World War II ended, the leaders of the Allied governments didn't have to meet and ask themselves, "How can we motivate people to spread the news that Hitler has been defeated?" When Jesus rose from the dead, the disciples didn't have to meet and ask themselves, "How can we motivate people to spread the news that Jesus has risen?" Nobody wagged a finger in the disciples' faces and laid a guilt trip on them to motivate them to evangelize. On the contrary, when the Sanhedrin tried to shut them up, their response was, "We cannot help speaking about what we have seen and heard" (Acts 4:20).

I remember when I was a new Christian. It was the most natural thing in the world to tell my friends about the difference Jesus was making in my life. Reading the Bible was exciting to me; I kept finding truths to help me in my daily life. Prayer was exciting to me; I would tell God all my concerns and I'd expect his help in living out my commitment to him. But somewhere along the line, things became routine. Somehow without realizing it, I had let my Christianity become stale. And much of my Christian life has vacillated between the meaningful times and the stale times.

Of one thing I am sure: if I really believe I've received good news, I do not need anyone to prod me into spreading it. Therefore if I don't feel like evangelizing, it must be that I've become numbed to how *good* the good news of the kingdom really is.

I've concluded that before I can evangelize others, I must sometimes *evangel*-ize myself; I must remind myself of the implications that the good news holds for me. I do not need more guilt trips. I do not need to learn new evangelism techniques. Instead, I need to remind myself of the present and future blessings that the kingdom has brought me.

> Before I can evangelize others, I must sometimes *evangel*-ize myself; I must remind myself of the implications that the good news holds for me.

These reminders take several forms. Sometimes I ponder the many benefits I enjoy as a citizen of the kingdom—forgiveness of sins, the empowering of the Spirit, assurance of eternal life, the armor of God, the body of Christ. Sometimes I do my own version of *It's a Wonderful Life*, and try to imagine what my life would be like if I had never entered the kingdom. Sometimes I listen to praise music that celebrates what God has done for us.

But there's one more thing I do to remind myself what the kingdom means for me. I go to church and open my eyes. And, I find reminder after reminder of the blessings of the kingdom. Friends like Bill remind me that when God's people work together as a body, the kingdom's power can turn lives around. Friends like J and Linda remind me that the power of the kingdom can break into this present age and bring physical healing in seemingly hopeless situations. Friends like Lois remind me that when healing does not come, we can face death knowing that it is the doorway to eternal life. Other friends, struggling with job pressures or divorce or raising a severely disabled child, remind me that the Holy Spirit can bring strength and comfort to those who face difficult situations. During times of praying and sharing and weeping together, my friends remind me of the support and encouragement of the body of Christ. In a million different ways my Christian friends remind me—their words and actions *proclaim* to me—that we presently experience a kaleidoscope of kingdom blessings, even as we wait for the kingdom to arrive in its fullness.

The Church's Mission and the Overlap

My friends' ministry to me has affected how I look at the mission of the church. I used to think of evangelizing unbelievers and building up the body of believers as two separate, largely unrelated tasks. I now see them as two sides of the same coin. How do we evangelize unbelievers? By proclaiming the kingdom of God in word and deed. How do we build up the body of believers? By proclaiming the kingdom of God in word and deed. The church's mission can be summed up as kingdom proclamation.

Our present experience of this kingdom is fragmentary. It may seem tenuous and fragile. But this will not always be the case. As George Eldon Ladd says,

> This is the mystery of the Kingdom: Before the day of harvest, before the end of the age, God has entered into history in the person of Christ to work among men, to bring to them the life and blessings of His Kingdom. It comes humbly, unobtrusively. It comes to men as a Galilean carpenter

went throughout the cities of Palestine preaching the Gospel of the Kingdom, delivering men from their bondage to the Devil. It comes to men as his disciples went throughout Galilean villages with the same message. It comes to men today as disciples of Jesus still take the Gospel of the Kingdom into all the world. It comes quietly, humbly, without fire from heaven, without a blaze of glory, without a rending of the mountains or a cleaving of the skies. It comes like seed sown in the earth. It can be rejected by hard hearts, it can be choked out, its life may sometimes seem to wither and die. But it *is* the Kingdom of God. It brings the miracle of the divine life among men. It introduces them into the blessings of the divine rule. It is to them the supernatural work of God's grace. And this same Kingdom, this same supernatural power of God will yet manifest itself at the end of the age, this time not quietly within the lives of those who receive it, but in power and great glory purging all sin and evil from the earth. Such is the Gospel of the Kingdom.[8]

Living in the overlap we have the privilege of following in the steps of those who have gone before us, and working together to announce this astonishing gospel. Though at present we only experience a fraction of the kingdom's blessings—foretastes, previews, fragments—how amazing that fraction is. What if we were to recapture the amazement Jesus' first disciples had in response to the news of the kingdom? What if, in the world's eyes, our lifestyles clearly marked us as belonging to a kingdom of righteousness, *shalom*, and joy? How different would our world be if the whole body of Christ recommitted itself to proclaiming Jesus' message of the kingdom?

PART THREE:
THE STORY BEHIND THE OVERLAP

One April night twenty centuries ago, Palestine's rulers rendered their verdict on Jesus' claim to be the inaugurator of the kingdom. Ironically, by rejecting his claim, they set into motion the events through which the kingdom's victory was won. Jesus' message of the kingdom has been revealed to us, not only through his teaching, but also through the story of his life and death. It's the story of how the long-anticipated age to come broke into this present age, creating the overlap. Jesus' teaching and his story are intertwined; I do not believe we can understand one without understanding the other. Therefore, I think it is fitting to conclude this book by exploring the story of how the kingdom dawned in the ministry of this roving Galilean rabbi, and how fishermen and Pharisees discovered that they could enter that kingdom here and now.

Part Three, then, tells the story of Jesus' impact on people like us, people confronted with a man who proclaimed the kingdom, people challenged to discover that kingdom for themselves.

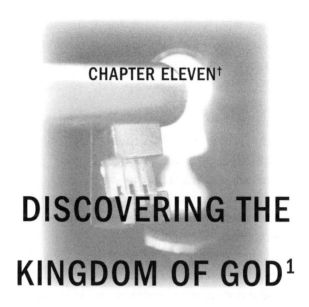

CHAPTER ELEVEN†

DISCOVERING THE

KINGDOM OF GOD¹

They were exasperating but he loved them anyway. The young rabbi² had invested so much time with his disciples, and they had been such slow learners. He had just warned them about events that would soon take place: "We will go up to Jerusalem where I will be betrayed to the authorities. They will sentence me to death and hand me over to the Gentiles to be mocked and whipped and crucified. Then on the third day I will be raised."³ What happened next revealed that they had utterly failed to comprehend his somber words.

His disciples James and John, along with their mother Salome, made a brazen request of the rabbi.⁴ They wanted him to guarantee that the two brothers would have the most prominent positions, sitting on his right and left, when he established his kingdom. Perhaps because they were related—the rabbi's mother Mary was Salome's sister⁵—they thought he owed this to them.

---

† In telling this story I have aimed to paint a picture that is consistent with mainstream evangelical scholarship. To preserve the flow of the story, I have chosen not to deal with conflicting scholarly viewpoints within the body of the chapter. At times the Endnotes section will give more information about a disputed matter. For the same reason, on a few occasions I have depicted a plausible incident as factual, without citing documentation within the chapter. However, I have also included this documentation in the Endnotes section.

"You don't know what you're asking for. Can you drink the cup I am about to drink?" It was a not-so-subtle reference to the fate he had just revealed to them. But its meaning fluttered over their heads like a wayward sparrow.

"Oh, yes, we can."

He fixed his gaze on them. "And so you will. But I can't grant your request to sit at my right and my left. Those places belong to the people for whom my Father has prepared them."

It did not take long for his ten other disciples to get wind of this episode, which incensed them. Once again he summoned them all together. The kingdom he had been proclaiming was not like other kingdoms, he explained.

"The rulers of the Gentiles lord it over them. But if you aspire to greatness, you must be a servant. And if you want to be first, you must be a slave. For I did not come to be served, but to serve, and to give my life as a ransom for many."

It wasn't just the disciples' selfish ambition that disturbed him. It was their inability to understand his message. Soon he would be gone and his message of the kingdom would be in their hands. When would they ever understand? *Would* they ever understand?

They were not alone in misinterpreting the nature of the kingdom he proclaimed. Friends and enemies alike fell into the same trap. Recently an enthusiastic but misguided crowd of admirers had sought to make him king by force. Yet on the other end of the spectrum, a powerful handful of religious and political authorities wanted him dead. All because of his proclamation of a kingdom.

> Recently an enthusiastic but misguided crowd of admirers had sought to make him king by force. Yet on the other end of the spectrum, a powerful handful of religious and political authorities wanted him dead. All because of his proclamation of a kingdom.

The very word conjured up images of a political monarchy. This was a natural assumption to make, given their country's situation. The Roman Empire ruled the world, and in 63 B.C it conquered tiny Palestine. Some of Palestine's residents, known as Zealots, plotted to violently overthrow the Romans. Others cooperated with Rome and were rewarded with prominent positions. The majority resigned themselves to peaceful coexistence.

Yet all the people looked forward to a time predicted by the prophets, a time when the kingdom of God—God's glorious reign—would arrive. It would be a time when God's power would defeat his enemies. It would be a time of liberation, when his people would be freed from their oppressors and ruled by the Messiah, the anointed descendant of King David. It would be a time of transformation, when the wilderness would bloom like Eden and swords would be beaten into plowshares. They prayed for the kingdom to come, and every new revolt brought hopes that the kingdom would soon be a reality.

In the decades that followed Palestine's defeat, a seemingly endless series of bloody uprisings against Rome resulted in the deaths of thousands. Varus, the Roman governor of Syria, burned the Galilean capital city of Sepphoris to the ground after Judas of Galilee had made it the headquarters for his rebellion. Varus also sold many of the rebels into slavery and crucified two thousand of their leaders.

A carpenter named Joseph found work rebuilding the city. Joseph lived in Nazareth, about four miles—or an hour's walk—away. His son apprenticed with him in Sepphoris.[6] The boy soon learned the fate that met those who had rebelled against Rome. He had even seen some of the rebels writhing on crosses in the Galilean countryside.[7] These public executions were his introduction to the horrors of crucifixion.

And now Joseph's grown son, a carpenter in his own right, was secretly claiming to be the Messiah.

Early in his ministry he revealed his identity to a most unlikely candidate.[8] She was drawing water from a well in Samaria, the province that separated Galilee from Judea. In the eyes of most rabbis, she had three strikes against her. She was a woman. She was a Samaritan. And she had a reputation—after having lost five husbands, she hadn't bothered to marry her current lover.

The rabbi asked her for a drink. Then he told her he could dispense living water that would sprout into a fountain of eternal life, the life of the age to come. But, not only did he strike up a conversation with her, he told her all her secrets and threw in one of his own. He revealed to her that he was the Messiah, a fact that he routinely kept hidden. It was safer to reveal this fact among the Samaritans than among the Jews in Galilee and Judea, who would expect the Messiah to follow in the footsteps of a political rebel like Judas of Galilee.

The woman hightailed it back to town so suddenly that she left her water jug behind. "There's a man at the well who told me everything I ever did," she announced to her neighbors. "Could he be the Messiah?"

Because of her testimony and the rabbi's subsequent teaching, many of the townspeople believed his claim. This teller of secrets, they concluded, was the Savior of the world.

He returned to Galilee with his disciples.[9] "Repent, for the kingdom of God is near!" he proclaimed. Such teaching was astonishing; God's reign, so long anticipated, was about to dawn. But accompanying the teaching were equally astonishing actions. He drove out evil spirits, prohibiting them from revealing his identity. He healed the sick, including his disciple Peter's mother-in-law, who had been bedridden with a fever. During his stay in the lakeside village of Capernaum, throngs gathered outside his house, seeking and finding healing from pain, seizures, and paralysis.

When he decided to move on, the townspeople pleaded with him to stay. He refused. "I must proclaim the good news of the kingdom of God to other towns, too. That's why I was sent." His remarkable ministry continued, and soon it was roundly condemned by certain authorities. He had a nasty habit (in their eyes) of healing on the Sabbath.[10] When they confronted him with the charge that such "work" violated the Sabbath observance, his response only escalated the conflict.

"My Father is always at work, and so am I."

The authorities were furious. By claiming such intimacy with his Father, this carpenter was making himself equal to God. This was a capital crime according to them. He became their target.

But all those who seek the righteousness of the kingdom had the potential to become such targets, the rabbi said. Standing on a mountain, like a new Moses giving a new law for citizens of a new kingdom, he announced, "Blessed are those who are persecuted because of righteousness. The kingdom belongs to them." [11]

Righteousness, he said, was not just a matter of complying with external rules, it was a matter of the heart. Harboring hate in your heart is like murdering your brother. Lusting is committing adultery in your heart. Righteousness means loving your enemies as well as your neighbor. And unless your righteousness exceeds that of the Pharisees, you will not enter the kingdom. God's kingdom and his righteousness must be your number-one priority in life, he said.

> God's kingdom and his righteousness must be your number-one priority in life, he said.

However, righteousness began with the receiving of forgiveness. This was plain the day a paralytic descended through a hole on the roof of the house where the carpenter was healing people. [12] Frustrated at their inability to enter the house, his friends had stationed themselves on the flat rooftop and lowered him on a mat fastened to ropes.

"Your sins are forgiven," the carpenter told the invalid. *This is blasphemy,* thought certain Pharisees and scribes who had come to watch the proceedings. *Only God can forgive sins.* The carpenter read their minds.

"Why do you harbor such thoughts? What is easier to say: 'Your sins are forgiven,' or 'Stand up and walk?' Here's proof that I have authority to forgive sins."

Turning to the paralytic, he said, "Stand up, take your mat, and go home." Before the astonished crowd, the man did just that, praising God the whole way home.

It was the kind of event that the carpenter pointed to when his cousin John the Baptist sent messengers to him. [13] Herod Antipas, who governed Galilee, had imprisoned John because John had spoken out against him for divorcing his wife to marry his brother's wife.

"John wants to know if you're the Messiah we've been waiting for, or if we should expect someone else," they said. Even John didn't understand. John, who had baptized him at the start of his ministry. John, who had called him the Lamb of God who takes away the world's sin.[14] John, who had told the crowds that this carpenter would baptize them with the Holy Spirit, the same Spirit who had anointed the carpenter for his own ministry.[15]

"Tell John what you are seeing and hearing. The blind see, the lame walk, lepers are cured, the deaf hear, the dead are raised, and the good news is preached to the poor."

As John's disciples returned to share this evidence with him, the carpenter turned to his own disciples.

"No one greater than John has ever been born. But the one who is least in the kingdom of God is greater than he." His comment revealed the greatness of the kingdom. The smallest child standing on a rooftop is in a more elevated position than the tallest man standing in the street. In the same way, the lowliest person in the kingdom is in a more exalted position than the greatest prophet who ministered before the coming of the kingdom. Throughout Israel's history the prophets had stood outside the kingdom, anticipating the day when it would come. And now that day was dawning.

> The smallest child standing on a rooftop is in a more elevated position than the tallest man standing in the street. In the same way, the lowliest person in the kingdom is in a more exalted position than the greatest prophet who ministered before the coming of the kingdom.

This was obvious from the incident in the synagogue at Nazareth.[16] The skeptical villagers there had heard about the miracles their hometown boy had worked in Capernaum, but they could not understand how this mere carpenter, the son of Joseph, could perform them. They crowded into the synagogue, where he stood to read from the scroll of Isaiah:

> "The Spirit of the Lord is on me,
> because he has anointed me
> to preach the good news to the poor.
> He has sent me to proclaim freedom for the prisoners
> and recovery of sight for the blind,
> to release the oppressed,
> to proclaim the year of the Lord's favor." [17]

Then he sat down, as rabbis did when they were about to teach. "Today this scripture is fulfilled in your hearing."

But if they were hoping to see miracles or even to hear an uplifting message, they were soon disappointed. He told them that he knew they just wanted him to prove himself by performing the kind of eye-popping miracles he had performed in Capernaum. But that was not going to happen.

Then he compared his situation with that of the prophets Elijah and Elisha. During a three-and-a-half year famine, Elijah did not minister among his own people, but he was sent to minister to a Gentile woman in Sidon. And though there were many lepers in Israel, the only leper healed through Elisha's ministry was the Gentile, Naaman. The implication was that their disbelief would disqualify them from experiencing the blessings he had just read about, but that believing Gentiles would experience them.

This was too much. They, not the detested Gentiles, were God's chosen people. The congregation became a lynch mob that tried to throw him off a cliff. But he freed himself from them and moved on to Capernaum.

If the people of Nazareth were overly zealous in their rejection of him, the crowds in Bethsaida erred in the opposite direction. After teaching about the kingdom and healing the sick among them, he fed the crowd by multiplying a boy's lunch: five loaves of bread and two fish. [18] After the people had eaten their fill, twelve full baskets of leftovers remained.

The astonished people saw a correlation between this and the miraculous provision of manna in the desert during the days of Moses. A prophet like Moses was among them, they concluded. The Galileans, all too ready to revolt against Rome again, decided to draft him as their leader and make him their king. But, the elusive rabbi managed to slip away from them.

It was in Caesarea Philippi, near the shrine of the pagan god Pan, that he discussed his true identity with his disciples.[19]

"Who do people say I am?" he asked them. Their response revealed that there was no shortage of opinions. Some saw him as a reincarnation of John the Baptist, whom Herod Antipas had recently executed. Others saw him as Elijah or Jeremiah or other prophets associated with the last days.

"But who do you say that I am?"

Peter, the impetuous spokesman of the group, exclaimed, "You are the Messiah, the Son of the living God."

The rabbi affirmed that this was true, but he warned them to keep it a secret. He was not the kind of Messiah the crowds had in mind. His kingdom was not the kind of kingdom they were expecting the Messiah to establish.

He explained that he would suffer and die, and then be raised to life. When Peter rebuked him for saying such things, he responded with a rebuke of his own: "Get behind me, Satan! You're not thinking of the things of God, but the things of men."

What did rising from the dead mean? About a week later his three closest disciples—Peter, James, and John—were still puzzling over this. They had accompanied him to a mountain top when suddenly his

> Moses and Elijah appeared and talked with him about the "exodus" he would accomplish in Jerusalem. Moses had led the Israelites on an exodus from bondage in Egypt; now this Galilean carpenter was to lead people on an exodus from bondage as well.

face and robe started shining like the sun, in a literal blaze of glory.[20] Moses and Elijah appeared and talked with him about the "exodus" he would accomplish in Jerusalem. Moses had led the Israelites on an exodus from bondage in Egypt; now this Galilean carpenter was to lead people on an exodus from bondage as well. Moses had led God's people to the brink of a promised land flowing with milk and honey, but this man would lead God's people into a promised kingdom of *shalom*.

A voice from heaven announced, "This is my beloved Son. Listen to him!" The disciples fell on their faces, terrified. Suddenly all was quiet and the disciples were alone with their master.

"Don't tell anyone about this until after I've risen from the dead," he told them. Privately, they discussed with each other what rising from the dead might mean. Yet, regardless of this confusing talk of death and resurrection, two things were certain: they had just glimpsed their master's supernatural glory, and God had commanded them to listen to him.

They also experienced his glory when they became part of the group of seventy-two believers, sent out on a mission by their master.[21] They were to pair up and proclaim the kingdom in the towns where he was about to minister. They returned joyfully, announcing that even the demons submitted to them when they ministered in his name.

Such events were evidence that the Evil One was suffering defeat, he said. "But don't rejoice that the spirits submit to you. Rejoice that your names are written in heaven."

Rejoicing was a major theme in their master's ministry. When certain Pharisees and scribes complained that he welcomed sinners and ate with them, he responded by telling a trio of parables.[22]

In the first, a shepherd leaves his ninety-nine sheep behind to seek his one lost sheep. Upon finding it, he calls his friends and neighbors to rejoice with him. "There's more rejoicing in heaven over one sinner who repents than over ninety-nine righteous people who do not need to repent."

In the second, a woman loses one of ten coins. She carefully searches for it, and after finding it she invites her friends and neighbors to celebrate with her. "There is joy in the presence of God's angels over one sinner who repents."

In the third parable, a son demands that his father give him his inheritance. Upon receiving it, he leaves home and squanders it on wild living. He is finally reduced to eating the food of the pigs he has been hired to feed. Realizing that he is worse off than his father's servants, he decides to return home and ask his father to treat him as a hired hand.

However, as he approaches home, his father spies him from a distance and runs to him. The father smothers him with hugs and kisses, and then commands his servants to prepare a celebration with feasting and dancing.

The older brother complains to the father that he has been a good son all his life and has never been honored with anything approaching this celebration. The father acknowledges this, adding that everything he has belongs to the older son. But he emphasizes that this occasion calls for a celebration; a dead brother has come back to life, and a lost son has been found.

Throughout the parables run the twin themes of repentance and joy. The former leads to the latter. The Pharisees and scribes got the point. Instead of condemning this rabbi for eating with sinners, they should be rejoicing that he was bringing them to repentance.

Other religious leaders—certain chief priests and elders whom he encountered in the temple—were the target of even harsher criticism: "Tax collectors and prostitutes are entering the kingdom of God ahead of you. John the Baptist came in the way of righteousness and you didn't believe him. But the tax collectors and prostitutes did. Yet even after you witnessed this, you refused to repent and believe." [23]

As Israel's elite, the religious leaders assumed that their place in the kingdom was assured. But this rabbi turned such elitism on its head. Only one class of people will enter the kingdom, he said: repentant sinners. And already they were entering it.

This illustrated an aspect of his teaching that people found so enigmatic. At times he spoke of the kingdom as a

> Only one class of people will enter the kingdom, he said: repentant sinners.

future event. He taught his disciples to pray for its coming.[24] He warned that the day of the Lord would come as unexpectedly as a thief in the night, and he warned them to be ready.[25] Yet at other times he spoke as if the kingdom were a present reality. Tax collectors and sinners were already entering it. He told certain Pharisees that the kingdom was already within their grasp.[26] And his healings and exorcisms seemed to indicate that the power of the kingdom was present.

If his message of the kingdom was enigmatic, so was the man himself. Crowds who heard his teaching in the temple courts wondered how he became so learned without formal rabbinic training. Some saw him as the Messiah but others insisted that he was a deceiver.

Certain chief priests and Pharisees were among the latter. He had made himself equal with God, and he was attracting a huge following. Deciding he had to be stopped, they sent solders from the temple guard to arrest him when he was in Jerusalem.[27] But—transfixed by his teaching and afraid of his throngs of supporters—the guards returned empty-handed.

"Why didn't you arrest him?" the authorities demanded.

"No one ever spoke like this man," was the only reply the soldiers could manage.

Jerusalem—in fact, the whole southern province of Judea—became a dangerous place for the rabbi. When he made another visit to Jerusalem, his enemies tried to stone him.[28] He withdrew to the other side of the Jordan River. It was there that he received tragic news—his friend Lazarus was seriously ill. [29] After waiting two days, he told his surprised disciples that they were going back to Judea.

"They just tried to stone you there," the disciples protested.

"Lazarus has fallen asleep and I have to wake him up."

"But if you let him sleep, he'll get better." Once again they had missed his meaning.

"Lazarus is dead."

The wary but loyal disciples resigned themselves to making the trip with their master. As Thomas said, "Let us go too, so we can die with him."

After the rabbi arrived at the funeral, Lazarus' sister Martha laid a guilt trip on him. "If you had been here, Lazarus wouldn't have died."

"He will rise again."

"I know he will, in the resurrection on the last day." Martha didn't get it. But Lazarus did. After the rabbi commanded, "Lazarus, come out!" the man who had been dead four days had no choice but to obey. Stunned mourners saw the dead man shuffle out of the grave, restricted by his mummy-like linen grave clothes.

This marked a turning point. Many eyewitnesses became followers of this miracle-working carpenter from Galilee. Word of Lazarus' resurrection soon spread, reaching the ears of Joseph Caiaphas.

As high priest, Caiaphas presided over Palestine's supreme court, the Sanhedrin. The position was supposed to be hereditary, passed from generation to generation like a prized heirloom. But since Rome had conquered Palestine, the Roman government had been appointing the high priests. Rather than choosing them for their piety, Rome chose them for their willingness and ability to keep the empire happy. Sometimes bribery also played a role.

Caiaphas had honed his ability to play the political game with Rome. He did not take his position for granted. The Galilean carpenter now posed a threat to it. This carpenter had been stirring up crowds all over Palestine, proclaiming that the kingdom of God was at hand. Many saw him as the Messiah, who would free Palestine from Rome and set up his own kingdom. The nation now appeared to be teetering on the edge of another bloody conflict. If this man were to lead a revolt, Rome would certainly crush it, decimating the country in the process.

Caiaphas hastily convened a meeting of the Sanhedrin. [30] Agitation was in the air.

"This man keeps performing miracles," one man clamored. "If we let him go on, soon everyone will believe in him. Then the Romans will take away our temple and our nation."

There was little doubt about what had to be done. "It's better that one man should die for the people than that the whole nation should perish," Caiaphas said, prophesying better than he realized. The others agreed.

Shortly afterward, the rabbi surfaced in Jericho. The crowds surrounding him were so massive that the tax collector Zacchaeus couldn't catch a glimpse of him.[31] The rich man, short in height and shorter on ethics, resorted to the undignified strategy of climbing a sycamore tree to get a look.

"Come down right now, Zacchaeus!" the rabbi called. "I must go to your house to visit with you."

It was hard to tell who was more shocked, Zacchaeus or the crowd. Zacchaeus was not only considered a traitor to his country, collecting taxes for the Roman government, he also gouged his countrymen by forcing them to pay more than they owed. Didn't this rabbi know that Zacchaeus was a sinner?

But like a character in one of his own parables, the rabbi found something that had been lost. During their visit Zacchaeus made the U-turn called repentance: "I'll give half my possessions to the poor, and to anyone I've cheated I'll repay four times what I took from them."

"Salvation has come to this house today," said the rabbi. "For I have come to seek and to save what was lost."

Salvation has come. It was a familiar theme to his disciples, a theme that reverberated every time someone received his message. A woman with a past became a woman with a future who introduced her Samaritan village to the Jewish Messiah. A lame man stood and walked, carrying his mat with him and leaving his sins behind him. A crooked little tax collector straightened out to become a big man who lost his wealth and found salvation. Salvation—wholeness, *shalom*, the life of the age to come—came in the most unlikely places to the most undeserving people when they responded to the rabbi's call.

> Salvation—wholeness, *shalom*, the life of the age to come—came in the most unlikely places to the most undeserving people when they responded to the rabbi's call.

In the meantime, his enemies waited for an opportune time to set their trap. They thought they might be able to strike when the Feast of the Passover rolled around.[32] During this celebration Jerusalem's population of fifty thousand swelled to several times that as pilgrims swarmed into the holy city. The carpenter would probably be among them though he could conceivably make himself inconspicuous in the crowds. The authorities ordered anyone who discovered his whereabouts to notify them immediately.

They need not have bothered. His return wound up being as inconspicuous as Joshua's military parade around the walls of Jericho. Crowds lined the roads that Sunday, cheering as he sat atop a donkey that trotted down a major thoroughfare into Jerusalem.[33] "Hosanna!" they shouted, which means, "Save now!" They waved palm branches and cast their cloaks on the road before him as if to celebrate the arrival of a king. This was no outlaw sneaking into town. This was practically a coronation.

He was even more brazen the next day in the temple.[34] Like a human earthquake, he toppled tables and benches, hurled coins, and scared sheep and money changers into stampeding. You'd have thought he owned the place. The priests had allowed concessions in the outer court—the Court of the Gentiles—to service pilgrims who needed to buy sheep or doves to offer as sacrifices. Money changers converted the currency of foreigners who had to buy animals or pay the half-shekel temple tax. Gentiles were thus deprived of the one area in the temple where they could gather to worship Israel's God.

"Isn't it written, 'My house will be called a house of prayer for all nations?'" spewed the carpenter, erupting against them like Vesuvius. "But you have turned it into a den of robbers!"

The authorities were more convinced than ever that he had to be killed. But, if they took action now, his hordes of adherents could cause a riot.[35] They decided not to arrest him until after the Feast. Then an astonishing opportunity knocked on their door. One of his disciples, disillusioned with him, offered to deliver him into their hands at night while he was away from the crowds.[36] If the authorities tried him immediately after the arrest, they could convict him before his followers even knew what was happening. They paid the traitor thirty silver coins and considered it a bargain.

The rabbi knew his time was short. During his last meal with his men, he gave them a final object lesson. Rising from the table, he wrapped a towel around his waist, poured water into a large bowl, knelt by each of his disciples, and washed their feet.[37] It was a task usually reserved for the lowliest servant.

"You call me 'Teacher' and 'Lord,' and that is what I am. But just as I, your Lord and Teacher have washed your feet, you also should wash each other's feet. I have given you an example to follow. No servant is greater than his master."

Servanthood—it was a lesson he had taught, and a lifestyle he had modeled, throughout his ministry. Yet, the disciples had no idea of the depth of their master's servanthood.

The prophet Isaiah had spoken about a figure known as the suffering Servant of God.[38] It was a multifaceted image. At times the Servant referred to a group—either the people of Israel or a faithful remnant within Israel. But on another level the Servant appeared as an enigmatic individual with a mission. Thus Isaiah brought this word from God:

> It is too small a thing that you should be my servant to restore the tribes of Jacob and bring back those of Israel I have kept. I will also make you a light for the Gentiles, that you may bring my salvation to the ends of the earth.[39]

Therefore, the Servant would be greater than Moses—not only leading Israel out of bondage, but also bringing salvation to all nations of the world. The God of Israel invited all people to experience the salvation of his kingdom. And how would this salvation be won? Not through military might, but through the Servant's suffering and death. Like a sacrificial lamb he would become a guilt offering, bearing the sins of his people, healing them with his wounds, becoming a covenant on their behalf. The rabbi understood this all too well.

He picked up a loaf of bread and broke it.[40] "This is my body. Take this and eat it." His physical body would soon be broken. But he would leave behind a body of believers who would inherit the Servant's task. They too would be called to sacrificial service, being a light to all nations, bringing to all people the good news of salvation.[41]

The rabbi held up a cup of wine. "This is my blood of the covenant, poured out for many for the forgiveness of sins. I will not drink again from the fruit of the vine from

> His physical body would soon be broken. But he would leave behind a body of believers who would inherit the Servant's task.

now on until that day when I drink it anew with you in, my Father's kingdom." Obeying but not comprehending, his disciples ate and drank.

Later that night, amid the olive trees in the garden called Gethsemane, he watched as the pinpoints of light from the approaching soldiers' torches and lanterns grew bigger and brighter. Two hundred soldiers[42] crossed the Kidron Valley to arrest the unarmed carpenter who was accompanied only by three drowsy disciples: Peter, James, and John.[43] Oddly enough, when the soldiers arrived, the carpenter was the one who took control of the situation.

He asked them who they were looking for, and confirmed that he was the one they had been sent to arrest. Something about his response startled them, causing the soldiers closest to him to step backwards and fall all over themselves, sprawling on the ground.

With typical rashness, Peter attacked Caiaphas' servant Malchus with a sword and lopped off his right ear. The last miracle the Galilean carpenter performed before his death was to heal this servant who was ushering him to his trial and execution.

"Put your sword away, Peter," he said. "Shall I not drink the cup the Father has given me?"

The soldiers allowed the disciples to flee. Their sole mission was to deliver the carpenter to the authorities so proceedings could begin.

The soldiers took the prisoner to the house of Annas, a former high priest. Though no longer in office—he had held the position from A.D. 6 to A.D. 15—he was the powerful patriarch of the current high priestly dynasty. Five of his sons and one of his grandsons became high priest. His son-in-law, Caiaphas, would have to conduct the official hearing before the Sanhedrin. But out of deference to his position, the Sanhedrin allowed Annas to conduct a preliminary investigation.[44]

"Tell me about your teachings and who your disciples are," he ordered the prisoner.

"Everything I've taught is public knowledge," he said. "I taught openly in the synagogue and the temple. Ask those who heard me." The reply, though absolutely valid, was unexpected. Most defendants approached the judge with deference and fear, hoping for mercy.

A nearby official struck him in the face and demanded, "Is this how you answer the high priest?" (Annas retained that title after leaving office.) But the prisoner was curiously unrepentant.

"If I said something wrong, tell me. But if I spoke the truth, why did you strike me?"

It seemed useless for Annas to continue questioning the uncooperative defendant. Besides, the sooner he appeared before the Sanhedrin the sooner he would be convicted. So Annas sent him, shackled, to Caiaphas.[45]

Caiaphas felt triumphant at the sight of the lone troublemaker, abandoned by his closest disciples, standing helpless before him. Technically it was illegal for Caiaphas and the Sanhedrin to try a capital case at this late hour. But time was of the essence. They could consider this meeting an informal hearing to establish a charge against him. At daybreak—about five o'clock—they could reconvene to pronounce an official verdict, thus complying with the letter of the law.

Almost immediately a string of witnesses began testifying against the prisoner. But what should have been a victorious interlude for Caiaphas soon turned nightmarish. The law of Moses plainly stated that two or three witnesses had to agree on a charge before a man could be convicted.[46] Yet these "witnesses" were not agreeing with each other. In their haste to get the carpenter arrested and tried, Caiaphas and his associates had neglected to find credible witnesses. Without them, he'd have to let the prisoner go. Not only would he and his comrades look incompetent, but the carpenter, apparently vindicated by the Sanhedrin, could become more popular—and dangerous—than ever.

Finally two witnesses came forward to testify, "He threatened to destroy the temple of God and rebuild it in three days." But upon closer examination even their testimonies did not agree. In spite of his dramatic conduct in the temple on Monday, they could not establish that he intended to demolish the building. In fact they could not establish anything at all.

Caiaphas tried some dramatics of his own. "Aren't you going to answer?" he demanded. "What about the testimony these men are bringing against you?" Actually no charges had officially been brought against him. There was nothing to reply to, so the prisoner remained silent. Desperate, Caiaphas tried one last ploy. If he couldn't find witnesses to incriminate him, he'd get the prisoner to incriminate himself. The judges themselves would become witnesses.

"I charge you under oath by the living God. Tell me if you are the Messiah, the Son of God." A person charged under this oath was legally bound to answer.[47]

"I am. And you will see me sitting at the right hand of the mighty God, and coming on the clouds of heaven."

Caiaphas had what he wanted. With more relief than rage, he ripped his robe—the symbolic gesture that one had heard blasphemy—and exclaimed, "What further need do we have for witnesses? He has blasphemed! You've heard it yourselves! What is your verdict?"

"He deserves death!" the judges answered.

After the authorities pronounced their verdict, they turned the prisoner over to the guards until sunrise. They beat him, spit on him, slapped him, and taunted him. "Who hit you? Prophesy to us!" they jeered, finding it hard to believe that this pitiful figure had caused Caiaphas to fear for the future of the nation.

At daybreak the Sanhedrin reconvened.[48] Caiaphas asked the judges, sitting in a semicircle, to render their verdicts. Starting with the youngest and working up to the oldest (so the younger members would not be influenced by their elders) each cast his vote. Caiaphas voted last.

"He deserves death." The phrase echoed as each judge stood and gave his verdict.[49]

Having pronounced the prisoner guilty, the Sanhedrin would ordinarily have executed him by stoning, if Palestine had been independent and Jewish law had been followed. But Rome forbade the Sanhedrin to carry out a death sentence. So the Sanhedrin had to ask the Roman prefect of Judea, Pontius Pilate, to order a Roman execution. Rome executed by crucifixion. Pilate lived in Caesarea on the Mediterranean coast. But the Feast of the Passover had brought the governor to his Jerusalem residence, the Praetorium. Hundreds of people had been trampled in riots at previous celebrations, and he was supervising the increased security designed to prevent any unrest.

The early hour was not a problem. Officials like Pilate customarily began meeting with their subjects at sunrise. This morning Pilate moved his judgment seat outside the Praetorium, since going inside would make the Jews ceremonially unclean. The prosecution had rounded up a large crowd of its supporters, including some of the thousands of temple workers they employed. They all assembled around the judgment seat.[50]

There was a "fly in the ointment" as far as Caiaphas and the Sanhedrin were concerned. They had convicted the prisoner on the religious charge of blasphemy, a serious enough charge in the Jewish faith, but nothing that a Roman governor would consider a crime.

"What charge do you bring against him?" asked Pilate.

"If he weren't a criminal we would not have handed him over to you," several Sanhedrin spokesmen said, hoping Pilate would just confirm their verdict without wading into the specifics of the charges.

"Then take him and judge him according to your own law."

"But we have no right to carry out the death penalty."

To execute someone would require formidable allegations. Therefore, they were ready with three accusations that a Roman prefect would have to take seriously.

"He corrupts our nation, he opposes paying taxes to Caesar, and he claims to be a Messiah, a king."

Since the prisoner had no one representing him, Pilate ordered him inside the palace to question him away from his accusers. These were grave charges, but Pilate soon concluded that they were groundless. Yes, the carpenter was popular with the masses, but he was not inciting them to revolt or withhold their taxes. And yes, he claimed to be a king but his kingdom was "not of this world" and he did not seem to pose a threat to Rome. This was apparently a religious squabble.

Pilate returned outside and told the accusers, "I find no basis for a charge against him." But they would not demur, and Pilate realized he could have a battle on his hands.

"But he stirs up people all over Judea with his teachings. He started up in Galilee and worked his way down here."

Galilee? This pricked up Pilate's ears.

"Is he a Galilean?" Pilate saw a potential solution to what threatened to become a crisis. A sword of Damocles hung over his head. He knew it and so did the carpenter's accusers. Pilate's career was on the line. Three times since taking office in A.D. 26 he had undermined his governorship by exercising abysmal judgment. He could not afford another incident.

First was the affair of the standards.[51] These poles topped with busts of the emperor were carried by the Roman soldiers stationed at Caesarea. Because of the Jewish Scriptures' ban on "graven images," however, previous governors prohibited them from taking the standards into the holy city of Jerusalem. Pilate chose not to show such deference. Under his command, one night soldiers brought the standards into Jerusalem with them. The next morning pious Jews were outraged that images of the emperor—who was considered a pagan deity—were desecrating Jerusalem.

> Pilate's career was on the line. Three times since taking office in A.D. 26 he had undermined his governorship by exercising abysmal judgment. He could not afford another incident.

They rushed to Caesarea and for six days pleaded with Pilate to remove the standards. He feared such an action would insult the emperor, so he refused. Finally Pilate granted them an audience in the stadium, where they continued to plead. Pilate, intent on showing them who was in control, ordered his soldiers to surround them. He then commanded them to stop protesting, under penalty of death.

But then the unthinkable happened. The people bared their necks and said, "We will die rather than see our holy city violated." Amazed and chagrined, Pilate backed down and removed the standards.

Next came the affair of the aqueduct.[52] Pilate built an aqueduct to bring water into Jerusalem, but paid for it with funds from the temple treasury. The people were outraged that temple funds were diverted for the project. They protested when he visited Jerusalem. On Pilate's orders, the Roman troops infiltrated the crowd dressed in plain clothes. He signaled them to club some of the more extreme agitators, intending just to rough them up and cause the crowd to disperse. But the violence got out of hand. By day's end, many people had been either clubbed or trampled to death.

Finally came the affair of the gold shields.[53] Pilate displayed these votive shields in King Herod's former, Jerusalem palace. This time there were no graven images, just inscriptions dedicating them to the emperor, Tiberius Caesar. But the people protested, again. Graven images or not, they were still dedicated to a pagan god. A delegation of political leaders, including Herod Antipas, lobbied Pilate to remove them. When he refused, they wrote a letter of protest to the emperor.

Immediately after receiving the letter, a livid Tiberius fired off a threatening reply to Pilate, reproaching him for his audacity and commanding him to take down the shields without delay. Pilate could not afford another episode like this. The message was clear. He would have to keep his subjects placated and uphold their laws.

And now his subjects said their laws demanded the execution of this prisoner. Yet, as far as Pilate could determine, he had done nothing to deserve death. But, if the prisoner were a Galilean, Pilate might have an escape hatch.

"Yes, he's from Galilee," the accusers said, realizing this could help their case. Everyone knew that Galileans were prone to rebellion.

"Then Herod Antipas can judge him."

Legally, the accused could be tried either by the authorities in the location where the alleged crime took place or by the authorities of his home province.[54] And Herod Antipas, the tetrarch of Galilee, just happened to be in Jerusalem for the Feast. By letting Antipas decide the prisoner's fate, Pilate could remove himself from this delicate situation.

Caiaphas and his allies had mixed feelings about this. On the one hand they would have preferred that Pilate simply approve their verdict and get on with the execution. On the other hand, Antipas might be more sympathetic to their cause. After all, he had executed the prisoner's cousin, John the Baptist.

Herod Antipas was the son of Herod the Great, that legendary builder of buildings and killer of men. Herod the Great had ruled Palestine from about 37 B.C to 4 B.C. Among his notable achievements was the construction of the Jerusalem temple. Among his notorious atrocities were the murders of his wife, mother-in-law, and three sons. Augustus had said it was safer to be Herod's pig than his son since, being half-Jewish, Herod might presumably refrain from eating pork. Near the end of his reign Herod also slaughtered young boys around Bethlehem to eliminate a rival "king of the Jews" who was reported to have been born there. His intended victim escaped. But decades later Herod's son would have the chance to accomplish what his father had failed to achieve.

After Herod the Great's death, his sons Archelaus and Antipas each struggled to succeed him as king. This resulted in the realm being divided. Archelaus became ethnarch—a princely title—over Judea and Samaria, about half the realm. Antipas became tetrarch of Galilee and Perea. ("Tetrarch" literally means "ruler of a quarter," but it also came to refer to a minor ruler one grade below ethnarch.) A third brother, Herod Philip II, became tetrarch of Iturea and Trachonitis. In A.D. 6 Rome deposed and exiled Archelaus because of his brutality and incompetence. A series of Roman governors replaced him, Pilate being the latest.

Herod Antipas was glad to see the prisoner brought before him.[55] Antipas had heard about his miracles and hoped to witness some. Antipas didn't want to conduct a hearing. He wanted to see a magic show.

The prisoner disappointed him. Not only did the carpenter refuse to perform; he even refused to speak. Antipas assailed him with questions, and the priests and teachers of the law recited a litany of charges against him, but he stayed silent. Yet Antipas was less interested in the charges than in gaining some entertainment value from him. So the man who had failed to become king put a robe on the man who claimed to be king and, along with his soldiers, made a joke out of the prisoner. When the show was over Antipas sent him back to Pilate.

> Antipas didn't want to conduct a hearing. He wanted to see a magic show.

After having made a martyr out of one popular "prophet," Antipas had no desire to create another. Yet, he didn't want to infuriate the priestly aristocracy by releasing the prisoner. He recognized that whoever rendered judgment in this case was in a "no win" situation, and was all too happy to have the matter removed from his courtroom.

Pilate gained one benefit from sending the prisoner to Antipas. His gesture of deferring to Antipas' expertise healed their previously hostile relationship. However, Pilate's goal, to escape from judging the prisoner, was unrealized. The accusers reassembled before Pilate's judgment seat and their spokesmen hurled charge after charge against the accused. When Pilate asked him to answer the charges, he refused to speak.

"Aren't you going to defend yourself? Don't you see how many charges they're bringing against you?" Pilate demanded. The only response was silence, and Pilate was amazed. Throughout his public life this carpenter's words and actions had shocked the nation, but now his silence and lack of action were as shocking as anything that had gone before.

Pilate saw an opportunity to placate the crowd without having to execute the prisoner. It was the custom to release a criminal at Passover. He would let them choose between the carpenter and a murderous revolutionary named Barabbas. Without being forced to admit his innocence, presumably the crowd would agree to release the carpenter. Given the choice between a real insurrectionist and an alleged one, Pilate reasoned, how could they do otherwise? But this backfired.

"Give us Barabbas!" they shouted.

"What should I do with the one you call the king of the Jews?"

"Crucify him!"

"Why? What has he done?"

"Crucify him!"

In a desperate attempt to forestall a crucifixion, Pilate reasoned, "If we

> Throughout his public life this carpenter's words and actions had shocked the nation, but now his silence and lack of action were as shocking as anything that had gone before.

beat him brutally enough, maybe the crowd will take pity on him and drop their demand."

Such beatings involved tying the victims to a post and scourging them with leather straps tipped with sharp bones, spikes, or pieces of lead that ripped strips of flesh off their bare backs.[56] In the more severe cases it exposed their bones or internal organs, reducing the victims to a bloody pulp. The number of lashes was unlimited (unlike the Jews' thirty-nine lashes). Many men died from the beatings. This savagery served a practical purpose. It shortened the length of time the victim would endure the agonies of the cross.

In addition to flogging the prisoner, the soldiers dressed him in a kingly purple robe and a crown of thorns. They spit on him, mocked him, struck him in the face, and beat the crown into his head with a staff, shouting, "Hail, king of the Jews!" When the soldiers were finished with him, Pilate paraded him before the mob. This prisoner seemed stronger than most, Pilate noted. The halting, lacerated figure remained conscious and coherent—even if the gashes and bruises on his blood-streaked face had rendered him almost unrecognizable. Surely the crowd would take pity on him now.

"Look at him!" Pilate exclaimed to the crowd.

"Crucify him!" the crowd shouted.

"You crucify him! There's no basis for a charge against him!"

"According to our law he must die, because he claimed to be the Son of God!"

This terrified Pilate. It was a common belief that the gods could appear in human likeness. And this "king" said his kingdom was not from this world. Might he actually be more than a human being? Was this why his wife had warned him, because of a dream, not to have anything to do with "that innocent man"? He hastened back inside for another private talk with the prisoner.

"Where are you from?"

Silence.

Fear and fury welled up in Pilate. Any other prisoner would be frantically defending himself. This one seemed intent on thwarting all attempts to exonerate him. It looked to Pilate as if—for some unexplainable reason—the prisoner was as determined as the mob that this crucifixion would take place.

"Don't you know I have the power either to free you or execute you?"

"You would have no power over me at all unless it had been given to you from above."

Nothing Pilate could say would persuade him to defend himself. But Pilate tried one last time to persuade the crowd to free him. Then they delivered the *coup de grâce*.

"If you set him free, you are no friend of Caesar. Anyone who makes himself out to be a king opposes Caesar."

It was a death blow. If word got back to Caesar that Pilate had freed this self-proclaimed "king," Pilate could be found guilty of treason, and

> It looked to Pilate as if—for some unexplainable reason—the prisoner was as determined as the mob that this crucifixion would take place.

he would be dealt with accordingly. What would his fate be? Removal from office? Exile? Compulsory suicide? All were viable options.

What had earlier seemed like a parochial religious squabble had snowballed into a threat that could cost him his career and quite possibly his life.[57] The choice was clear. Pilate had to decide between two kings, and the wrong decision could cost him everything. He weighed the alternatives. Then the governor who literally tried to wash his hands of the whole affair announced his verdict.

"Take the prisoner away and crucify him."

Crucifixion was designed to torture the victim to death. It was reserved for slaves, insurrectionists, murderers, and other despised outcasts. The victim was stripped naked[58] and fastened to a horizontal crossbeam, either with ropes, or by hammering seven-inch-long spikes through his wrists. The crossbeam was then attached to a vertical post that already stood at the crucifixion site. Sometimes the victim hung for several agonizing days before dying.

When the carpenter arrived at the execution site, he was offered wine mixed with myrrh to dull the pain.[59] He refused it. Then, the soldiers started their grisly task. They expected this man, like many of their previous victims, to hurl curses and obscenities at them. But as other soldiers had observed earlier, no one ever spoke like this man. And the first words he screamed out[60] after they hammered the spikes through his nerves[61] were, "Father, forgive them—they don't know what they're doing!"

Death came quickly, only hours later. "It has been accomplished!" the prisoner gasped.[62] "Father, I commit my spirit into your hands." His body slumped and his breathing stopped. The soldiers looked at each other with perplexed amusement. Such strange last words. *What* had been accomplished? With his final breath, this victim had seen himself as some sort of victor.

After making sure he was dead, they removed his body from the cross. They also removed the sign that had hung above his head. It read: "Jesus of Nazareth, King of the Jews."

They laid the corpse in a tomb, which was like a shallow cave sealed with a huge stone, and then it was all over. A new day dawned, then another. Behind closed doors the carpenter's enemies breathed a sigh of relief, confident that they could resume business as usual now that the noisy Galilean had been silenced.

In a village just outside the city,[63] behind humbler doors, a broken and bewildered group of disciples wondered how they could have been so deceived. They now feared for their own lives. But safely behind those closed doors none of them were in a position to observe something happening outside, in a garden, as a massive boulder started rolling away from a grave. And when it rolled, it turned this planet upside down.[64]

It wasn't until after this last event that the disciples began to realize what his ministry had been about. That he had come to free them, not from the chains of Rome, but from the sin that separated them from their creator. That he had come to inaugurate, not the political rule of Palestine, but the redemptive rule of a loving God in a world twisted by death and despair.

Yes, his people still looked forward to the coming of the kingdom of God. But they realized that in a sense the kingdom had already arrived in the person of a Galilean carpenter; softly, inconspicuously, like a tiny seed sprouting unseen in the dirt, or a pinch of yeast working its magic throughout the whole loaf. One day God's kingdom would come in all its glory. One day the power of God would liberate the world from the effects of sin and transform it into a new heaven and earth. But they recognized that right now in this present age, ordinary men and women who surrendered to the king could begin to taste something of the power and liberation and transformation that the coming kingdom would one day bring in all its fullness. And it dawned on them that in some mysterious way the crucifixion was the instrument through which all of this had been accomplished.

So, convinced that their master had actually conquered the grave,

But safely behind those closed doors none of them were in a position to observe something happening outside, in a garden, as a massive boulder started rolling away from a grave. And when it rolled, it turned this planet upside down.

his disciples no longer feared it. And, stepping out of the shadows, they proclaimed his message and met with his fate—arrest, torture, execution. But nothing could silence them. Their voices echo down the halls of history. And we still hear them today proclaiming that we too can discover God's kingdom, that his Spirit can empower us, that our chains can be broken and our wounds healed, and that we can know that we have the life of the age to come, because a carpenter was hammered onto a cross.

The kingdom is coming. The kingdom has come. The king calls us, we who live in this present age, to inherit the life of the next. He calls us to follow in his footsteps, on a mission of sacrificial service to God and to each other. He calls us to experience, and to proclaim, the blessings of God's redemptive reign. He calls us to spend a lifetime—and beyond—discovering the kingdom of God.

ENDNOTES

Chapter 1: The Overlap—Old Testament Predictions

1. Carl F. H. Henry, *The Uneasy Conscience of Modern Fundamentalism* (Grand Rapids: William B. Eerdmans Publishing Company, 1947), 46–47.
2. Craig L. Blomberg, *Making Sense of the New Testament* (Grand Rapids: Baker Academic, 2004), 89.
3. Psalm 47:7; Psalm 99:1–4.
4. Isaiah 43:15; 44:6.
5. Daniel 2:44; 7:13–14, 27; Obadiah 1:21; Zechariah 14:9.
6. The vast majority of evangelical scholars maintain that the kingdom of heaven (a phrase not found in any Gospel but Matthew's) is synonymous with the kingdom of God. But some scholars make a distinction between the two. The kingdom of heaven is seen by these scholars to refer to Christ's earthly messianic rule, whereas the kingdom of God is seen to refer to God's cosmic, eternal rule. The main reason for this is that only Matthew tells the parables of the tares (Matthew 13:24–29) and the dragnet (Matthew 13:47–50), both parables describing a mixture of good and evil, and both

referring to the kingdom of heaven. Thus the kingdom of heaven is said to refer to Christ's earthly messianic rule, where there will be a mixture of good and evil men; the kingdom of God is said to refer to his eternal rule, which ultimately only those who follow him will enjoy (though there is said to be a certain fluidity in the use of the term "kingdom of God" because it is subsumed by the kingdom of heaven). See John F. Walvoord, "Biblical Kingdoms Compared and Contrasted," *Issues in Dispensationalism*, eds. Wesley R. Willis and John R. Master, (Chicago: Moody Press, 1994), 76–79.

Though I respect those who hold this view, I believe it is incorrect to make such a distinction. Repeatedly, when discussing the same event, Matthew uses "the kingdom of heaven" whereas Mark or Luke (or both) use "the kingdom of God." (For example, compare Matthew 19:14 with Mark 10:14–15 and Luke 18:16–17.) And even Matthew treats the two as synonyms in Matthew 19:23–24. (Compare with Mark 10:24–25 and Luke 18:24–25.) It seems to me that the more natural reading of Scripture is to see the two terms as referring to the same reality. Therefore, I agree with those scholars who believe that Matthew—apparently with Jewish readers in mind—tended to follow the ancient Jewish practice of substituting "heaven" to avoid the direct use of God's name. See Robert H. Stein, *The Method and Message of Jesus' Teaching* (Louisville: Westminster John Knox Press, 1994), 60–65.

7. Those who read Greek are in a better position to appreciate the New Testament's two-age orientation than those who must rely on English translations. A concordance can provide English readers with many references to the two ages (such as Matthew 12:32, Mark 10:29–30, and Ephesians 1:21). But English Bibles sometimes mask the two-age theme when they use a different word (such as "life" or "world") to translate "age" (as in Mark 4:19 and Romans 12:2). In addition, sometimes the Greek for "unto the ages" or "unto the ages of the ages" is translated "forever" or "forever and ever" (as in John 6:51 and Hebrews 13:21).

8. As New Testament scholar I. H. Marshall says, "During this period Jesus spoke about the arrival of the kingdom of God (Mark 1:14–15), which is to be understood as the future realm of justice and peace

announced by the prophets (rather than simply the eternal heavenly rule of God over the whole world)." I. H. Marshall, "Jesus Christ," eds. T. Desmond Alexander, Brian S. Rosner, D. A. Carson, Graeme Goldsworthy, *New Dictionary of Biblical Theology* (Downers Grove: InterVarsity Press, 2000), 596.

9. Joel 1:15; 2:1–2, 30–31; Zephaniah 1:14–18; Isaiah 13:6–13; 66:15–16. Sometimes the term "that day" includes not only the day of judgment and redemption, but also the age to come. See, for example, Isaiah 4:2–6; Hosea 2:16–23. Though the term "day of the Lord" ultimately applies to the eschatological event that will precede the age to come, the term can also describe times of God's intervention to bring judgment or salvation within history. For example, Isaiah 13:6 describes God's future judgment upon Babylon as the day of the Lord, and Lamentations 2:1–10 describes the fall of Judah (an event already in the past when Jeremiah wrote about it) in similar terms. These lesser days of the Lord are previews of the ultimate eschatological day of the Lord.

10. Isaiah 9:6–7; 11:1–5; 42:1; Jeremiah 23:5–6; 30:9; 33:15–16; Ezekiel 34:23; 37:24–25; Daniel 9:25; Micah 5:2–5; Zechariah 9:9–10. Oddly enough, the simple title "the Messiah" never appears in the Old Testament when referring to the coming king. As New Testament scholar George Eldon Ladd points out, "The word always has a qualifying genitive or suffix such as 'the messiah of Jehovah,' or 'my messiah.' . . . In most of the prophecies looking forward to the final Davidic King, 'messiah' is not applied to him. There are, however, a number of important prophecies that look forward to the rule of a Davidic King." George Eldon Ladd, *A Theology of the New Testament*, ed. Donald Hagner (Grand Rapids: William B. Eerdmans Publishing Company, 1974, revised 1993), 134–135.

11. 1 Samuel 13:14.

12. Isaiah 9:6–7; 16:5; 28:17; 32:1, 16; 33:5; 42:1–4; Jeremiah 23:5; 33:15; Hosea 2:19.

13. Isaiah 13:9–11; 24:21–22; 27:1; 66:16; Haggai 2:21–22; Malachi 4:1–3.

14. Isaiah 16:5; 54:10; Hosea 2:19; 12:6; 14:4; Zephaniah 3:17.

15. Genesis 15:1–21; 17:1–22.

16. Exodus 19–24.

17. 2 Samuel 7:4–16; 1 Chronicles 17:3–14.

18. Isaiah 61:8; Jeremiah 31:31–34; Ezekiel 37:26.

19. Jeremiah 31:33–34; Hosea 2:18–20. Though some may see it as an argument from silence, certain scholars see significance in the fact that most Old Testament believers are not said to know the Lord. For example, Michael Green argues, "In the Old Testament days the majority of Israel would never have professed to know the Lord. A few of the great ones, such as David and Isaiah, of course did. But not ordinary Israelites. They would go to consult God through prophet or priest." Michael Green, *The Message of Matthew* (Downers Grove: InterVarsity Press, 1988, 2000), 275. And Leon Morris says, "Not many people in the Old Testament are said to have actually known the Lord. In those days it was rather an aspiration, something that people might greatly long for, but which they felt they were not likely to attain." Leon Morris, *The Atonement*, (Leicester: InterVarsity Press, 1983), 29.

20. Leviticus 16:1–34; Hebrews 9:7.

21. O. Palmer Robertson, *The Christ of the Covenants* (Phillipsburg, New Jersey: P&R Publishing, 1988), 293–294.

22. Isaiah 33:24; 44:22; Jeremiah 31:34; Micah 7:19; Zechariah 13:1.

23. William J. Dumbrell, *The Faith of Israel* (Grand Rapids: Baker Academic, 2002), 146.

24. Isaiah 43:19; 62:2; 65:17; 66:22; Jeremiah 31:31; Ezekiel 11:19; 18:31; 36:26.

25. Isaiah 32:14–15; 44:3; Ezekiel 36:27; 37:14; Joel 2:28–31.

26. James M. Hamilton, Jr., *God's Indwelling Presence* (Nashville: B&H Academic, 2006), 25–26. Emphasis Hamilton's. For a concise look at the work of the Holy Spirit in Old Testament times, see also J. Rodman Williams, *Renewal Theology*, vol. 2 (Grand Rapids: Zondervan, 1990, 1996), 155–161.

27. 1 Samuel 11:6; 16:14.

28. Numbers 11:16–29.

29. Isaiah 2:2–3; 11:10; 56:3–7; Zechariah 8:20–23.

30. Ezekiel 37:26–28; 43:9; 48:35.

31. Isaiah 40:5; 60:1–3; 66:18; Ezekiel 39:21; 43:1–5; Haggai 2:7.

32. Isaiah 2:4; 9:6; 11:6–9; 32:17; 65:25; Ezekiel 34:25; 37:26; Micah 5:4–5; Haggai 2:7–9; Zechariah 9:9–10.

33. Isaiah 30:23–26; 33:24; 35:5–7.

34. Isaiah 11:6–9; 35:9; Ezekiel 34:28; Hosea 2:18.

35. Along with the subsequent references quoted from Isaiah and Daniel, see Hosea 13:14.

36. Isaiah 41:17–20; 49:9b–10; Jeremiah 31:12–14; Ezekiel 34:26–29; 36:11; Joel 3:18; Amos 9:13; Zechariah 8:12.

37. Isaiah 35:1–2, 9–10; 61:7; Zechariah 10:7.

38. John N. Oswalt, *The Book of Isaiah, Chapters 1–39*, The New International Commentary on the Old Testament (Grand Rapids: William B. Eerdmans Publishing Company, 1986), 626.

39. Though Malachi is commonly regarded as the latest of the Old Testament prophets, some scholars believe that Joel might actually be the latest.

Chapter 2: The Overlap—New Testament Fulfillment

1. Matthew 3:1–12.

2. Luke 13:18–20.

3. Matthew 6:10; Mark 9:1.

4. See Luke 11:20 and Matthew 21:31. Though the kingdom of God is an end-time reality, the New Testament generally refers to its present nature. As author and professor D. Brent Sandy reveals: "The primary designation of a future time of blessing is the 'kingdom of God.' Yet out of 160 occurrences of *kingdom* in the New Testament, the majority refer to the kingdom in the present sense. Only twenty-three occurrences include the idea of nearness or of a kingdom that is yet coming, while five other verses refer to the future restoration. Very few images of this future kingdom are actually given. The Son will rule it. All other kingdoms will have been destroyed. The righteous will be welcomed into it and will shine. Eating and drinking will have special significance. We know that the kingdom will be great, but its greatness is beyond our comprehension." (D. Brent Sandy, *Plowshares and Pruning Hooks* [Downers Grove: InterVarsity Press, 2002], 181. Emphasis Sandy's.)

5. For a brief explanation of the kingdom, see Gordon D. Fee & Douglas Stuart, *How to Read the Bible for All Its Worth* (Grand Rapids: Zondervan Publishing House, 1982, 1993), 131–134. This book is an invaluable guide to understanding the Bible. For another excellent yet concise introduction, see Herman Ridderbos, "Kingdom of God, Kingdom of Heaven," *The Illustrated Bible Dictionary*, ed. J. D. Douglas, et al., vol. 2 (Wheaton: Tyndale House Publishers, 1962, 1980), 853. Likewise, Darrell L. Bock's *Jesus according to Scripture* (Grand Rapids: Baker Academic, 2002), 565–593, gives a more comprehensive survey of the kingdom and its implications. George Eldon Ladd's *The Gospel of the Kingdom* (Grand Rapids: Wm. B. Eerdmans Publishing Company, 1959) provides a more lengthy introduction to the kingdom, though some readers may take issue with Ladd's nondispensational premillennial viewpoint. Two other helpful scholarly introductions are Mortimer Arias, *Announcing the Reign of God* (Philadelphia: Fortress Press, 1984), and John Bright, *The Kingdom of God* (Nashville: Abingdon Press, 1953, 1981.) Though in some details the last two books stand outside the mainstream of evangelical thought, these books are still illuminating. For a readable retelling of the entire biblical story stressing the kingdom theme, see Craig G. Bartholomew and Michael W. Goheen, *The Drama of Scripture* (Grand Rapids: Baker Academic, 2004). A valuable introduction for lay readers and based on solid scholarship.

6. As the *Dictionary of Biblical Prophecy and End Times* observes, discussing the day of the Lord, "The New Testament writers pick up this term from the Old Testament and use it frequently to refer specifically to the second coming of Christ (1 Corinthians 5:5; 1 Thessalonians 5:2; 2 Thessalonians 2:2; 2 Peter 3:10, 12). As in the Old Testament, the New Testament apparently also uses associated terms such as 'that day,' 'those days,' 'the great day,' or 'the day of our Lord Jesus' in a sense synonymous to 'the day of the Lord,' referring to the time of Christ's return (Mark 13:24; 1 Corinthians 1:8; Revelation 6:17; 16:14)." (J. Daniel Hays, J. Scott Duvall, and C. Marvin Pate, *Dictionary of Biblical Prophecy and End Times* [Grand Rapids: Zondervan, 2007], 110.

7. *What about the millennium?* Some readers may wonder about the relationship between the kingdom of God and the millennium. The millennium is the thousand-year period described in Revelation 20:1–10 where Christ reigns with his people and Satan is bound. There are three major views concerning the millennium.

    Premillennialists believe that Christ will return *before* the millennium. They interpret the millennium as a time when Christ and his people will literally reign over the earth. They see this literal rule of Christ as another phase of God's kingdom program that precedes the consummated kingdom. The consummated kingdom—sometimes called the eternal state—will be realized after Satan's ultimate destruction. Premillennialism is divided into two categories: dispensational premillennialism and historic premillennialism.

    Dispensational premillennialism holds that a new temple will be rebuilt, with priests offering sacrifices during the millennium as occurred during Old Testament times. This view also tends to see the millennium as lasting a literal 1000 years.

    Historic premillennialism denies that there will be a return to the temple and Old Testament sacrificial system during the millennium, holding that Jesus' once-and-for-all sacrifice precludes this. Thus they see predictions such as Ezekiel's vision of the eschatological temple (Ezekiel 40–47) as symbolic. Historic premillennialism also tends to see the 1000 years as a symbolic number that represents an extended period of time.

    Postmillennialists believe that Christ will return *after* the millennium. They interpret the millennium less literally than premillennialists—as a period of peace and prosperity (resulting from the acceptance of the gospel throughout the world) that precedes Christ's return and the consummation of the kingdom.

    Amillennialists interpret the millennium as a symbol for a present reality, not as a literal period of time. Some see it as representing the new life in Christ experienced by Christians on earth. Others see it as representing the idea that the souls of believers who have died are presently reigning with Christ in heaven while they await the resurrection. Like postmillennialists, amillennialists see the consummated kingdom arriving after the millennium, without the intermediate literal earthly rule of Christ envisioned by the premillennialists.

The millennium has been defined as "a thousand years of peace that theologians like to fight about"—Judy Culbertson and Patti Bard, *Games Christians Play* (New York: Harper & Row, 1967), 116. For nonviolent explorations of the various viewpoints concerning the millennium see Stanley J. Grenz, *The Millennial Maze* (Downers Grove: InterVarsity Press, 1992); Millard J. Erickson, *A Basic Guide to Eschatology* (Grand Rapids: Baker Academic, 1999); and Robert G. Clouse, ed., *The Meaning of the Millennium: Four Views* (Downers Grove: InterVarsity Press, 1977). It's important to note that all the above millennial viewpoints have advocates whose commitment to Scripture is beyond question. As pastor Scotty Smith says after discussing the three major millennial views:

"Once again let me acknowledge that each of these positions has been held and is currently championed by Christians who hold the Scriptures to be the inspired Word of God, inerrant, and fully authoritative as the only rule of faith and life that God has given His people. Our decision is not a matter of choosing between conservative and liberal theological schools of biblical interpretation. This cannot be emphasized too much. . . . Even those Christians in our fellowship who have come from the most hardened and dogmatic millennial backgrounds conceded that mutual respect and humility are called for as we discuss this important part of biblical revelation with one another. What matters most today is not what position we take in the ongoing millennial debates. What matters is for each of us to ponder how our position is affecting the way we live life to the glory of God. If any one of these understandings of the millennium is taken seriously, then all of life will be noticeably altered and redirected for the purposes of eternity." Scotty Smith and Michael Card, *Unveiled Hope* (Nashville: Thomas Nelson, Inc., 1997), 198, 201–202.

The already/not-yet view of the kingdom (which theologians sometimes call "inaugurated eschatology") is compatible with all the above millennial viewpoints. Some dispensational premillennialists, though, equate the kingdom of God with the future earthly millennium and would therefore not speak of a present (or inaugurated) aspect of the kingdom. (Classical dispensationalism holds that the messianic kingdom would have come in all its fullness during Jesus' first coming, but it was postponed because Israel rejected Jesus' offer of the kingdom.)

But other dispensational premillennialists affirm an "already" (or inaugurated) aspect to the eschatological kingdom. For example, dispensationalist scholar Herman A. Hoyt says, "I am in perfect agreement that these days constitute an inaugurated eschatology while at the same time remembering a final consummation lies ahead called 'the last day.' . . . This means that believers are tasting the blessings of the future such as the 'first fruits of the Spirit.'" Herman A. Hoyt, "A Dispensational Premillennial Response," in Robert G. Clouse, ed., *The Meaning of the Millennium*, 196–197. See also his discussion "Dispensational Premillennenialism," in Clouse, 63–92.

And dispensationalist scholar J. Carl Laney says, "The kingdom order has been inaugurated. . . . There is a sense of tension concerning the kingdom reflected in the phrase 'already, but not yet.' Because the king has come, the glorious, redeeming, recreating reign of God has commenced. Because the King is still to come, the kingdom is not yet in the form it will exist in when Christ returns. . . . The kingdom of God already inaugurated, but not yet consummated. It is a present developing reality to be fully realized at the return of Christ—the King. Then the literal throne, dynasty and kingdom (Luke 1:32–33) will be consummated and continue throughout all eternity." J. Carl Laney, *God's Plan for the Ages*, www.westernseminary.edu/Papers/Index.htm.

The already/not-yet view of the kingdom is the view of the overwhelming majority of evangelical scholars. As theology professor Richard B. Gaffin, Jr. says, "Briefly, one of the most important developments in biblical studies in this century has been the rediscovery of the already/not yet structure of New Testament eschatology. This broadened understanding of eschatology, which has now virtually reached the status of consensus, has brought a growing recognition that for the New Testament writers (most clearly Paul), the present work of the Spirit in the church and within believers is inherently eschatological." Richard B. Gaffin, Jr., "A Cessationalist View," in Wayne A. Grudem, ed., *Are Miraculous Gifts for Today?* (Grand Rapids: Zondervan Publishing House, 1996), 29.

8. Raymond E. Brown, *The Gospel According to John, I–XII, vol. 29,* The Anchor Bible (New York: Doubleday, 1966), 507–508.

9. R. G. V. Tasker, *The Gospel According to St. John,* The Tyndale New Testament Commentaries (Grand Rapids: William B. Eerdmans Publishing Company, 1960, 1994), 72. Emphasis Tasker's.

10. For example, pastor and evangelist John Stott says, "The Bible divides history into two ages or eons. From the Old Testament perspective they were called 'the present age' (which was evil) and 'the age to come' (which would be the time of the Messiah). The Bible also teaches that Jesus Christ is that long-awaited Messiah, and that therefore the new age began when he came. At the same time, the old age has not yet come to an end. So for the time being, the two ages overlap. Unbelievers belong to the old age and are still in the darkness. But those who belong to Jesus Christ have been transferred into the new age, into the light. Only when Christ comes in glory will the present overlap end. The old age will finally vanish and the new age will be consummated." John Stott with Dale and Sandy Larsen, 1 & 2 Thessalonians, *Living in the End Times* (Downers Grove: InterVarsity Press, 1998), 36.

Likewise, in his discussion of Hebrews 6:5, scholar and pastor Eli Landrum explains: "The gospel is the announcement of salvation and eternal life available to people who will trust Christ. The people who had tasted the powers of the coming age had experienced Christ's enabling power. The coming age is the messianic age Jesus initiated; it overlaps this age and will be fulfilled in His return. The power He demonstrated in His earthly ministry continues to be operative." "Determine to Mature," *Explore the Bible Adult Leader Guide*, 11, no. 1, (2006), 68–69. Emphasis Landrum's.

And in his analysis of Paul's eschatological views, New Testament scholar Richard B. Hays similarly reasons: "The old age is passing away (1 Corinthians 7:31b), the new age has appeared in Christ, and the church stands at the juncture between them. . . . Thus Paul thinks of the present time as an anomalous interval in which the 'already' and the 'not yet' of redemption exist simultaneously in dialectical tension. The ends of the ages have overlapped." *The Moral Vision of the New Testament* (San Francisco: HarperSanFrancisco, 1996), 20–21.

New Testament scholar N. T. Wright discusses the change in Paul's pre-Christian and Christian views of the end-time resurrection: "Many Jews, and no doubt Paul himself, had believed that when the Messiah came he would usher in a new age at once. There would be no overlap period. The Messiah would establish the kingdom of God, raise the dead, make everything new, all overnight. What has happened instead, as Paul grasps, is that God's purposes are being fulfilled in a two-stage process, rather than a single act." *Reflecting the Glory* (Minneapolis: Augsburg Books, 1998), 153–154.

Bible professor C. Marvin Pate also discusses the difference between Jewish and Christian end-time views in Paul's day: "At this point a distinction between Jewish apocalypticism and Christian eschatology surfaces: Early Christians believed that the age to come had already dawned in the life, death, and resurrection of Jesus. That is, apocalyptic end-time events had occurred within, but without replacing, human history. So, in effect, Christian eschatology refers to the overlapping of the two ages in Christ." *The End of the Age Has Come* (Grand Rapids: Zondervan Publishing House, 1995), 30.

Biblical scholar and author Daniel J. Lewis adds: "This paradoxical overlapping of the present and the future, sometimes called 'the already, not yet' tension, demonstrates that the earliest Christians in fact did not view eschatological categories to be irrelevant to themselves. For them, the last days had already dawned in the coming of Jesus. Jesus was the Messiah anticipated by the prophets. The wonderful benefits of the new age, such as salvation and acquittal, the gift of the Spirit, the enthronement of God's people, the dethronement of the worldly powers of evil, the gift of eternal life, and the inauguration of the kingdom of God, were already the present experience of Christians. With the ascension of the Lord to the Father's right hand, the messianic reign had begun

(Romans 5:17, 21; 1 Corinthians 15:25; Ephesians 1:20–21; Philippians 2:9)! Still the old age had not yet reached its consummation, nor would it until the return of the Lord. Between the enthronement of Christ at the Father's right hand and the Lord's second coming, believers experience eschatology, and at the same time they anticipate eschatology. They live in both the present and the future. Already they are in the last days, yet the day of the Lord is still to come." *3 Crucial Questions about the Last Days* (Grand Rapids: Baker Books, 1998), 66–67.

And pastor and author David Prior, discussing alternative interpretations of 1 Corinthians 10:11, says: "Paul's own contemporaries were living in an uniquely privileged generation, one upon whom the end of the ages has come (11). These 'ages' could be a combination of 'this present age or world-order' and 'the age to come' (heralded by the first coming and to be consummated by the second coming of Christ). On this explanation, every person in Christ is living in crucial days 'between the ages' (what theologians often call 'living in the overlap'), with each extra day a bonus." *The Message of 1 Corinthians, The Bible Speaks Today* (Downers Grove: InterVarsity Press, 1985), 169. Emphasis Prior's.

11. Can we pinpoint a time or event during which Jesus inaugurated the kingdom? Some theologians speak of the kingdom being inaugurated through Jesus' crucifixion and resurrection. But, though these are momentous events in the coming of the kingdom, we can't overlook the presence of the kingdom before these events, in Jesus' earthly ministry.

Other theologians see the kingdom being inaugurated during Jesus' baptism, when the eschatological Spirit anointed him for ministry. But we can't overlook the activity of the eschatological Spirit in the king's miraculous conception. Perhaps it's best to see multiple phases of the kingdom's inauguration:

1. Jesus' conception (by the Holy Spirit), and birth
2. Jesus' baptism (with the anointing of the Holy Spirit)
3. Jesus' public ministry (demonstrating the kingdom's arrival)

4. Jesus' crucifixion (when the kingdom's victory was won) and resurrection (to the new life of the eschatological kingdom)
5. Jesus' ascension to reign at God's right hand (his enthronement), and the resultant outpouring of the Spirit on the Day of Pentecost

However, as John Stott points out, it may be misguided to focus extensively on the time of the kingdom's inauguration: "The controversy has been unnecessarily complicated by a tendency to forget that in the New Testament as a whole the conception of the Kingdom is not a static one. There was no one moment in the triumphant progress of our saving Lord from His cradle in Bethlehem to His final glory at the Father's right hand, at which it may be said 'the Kingdom came or will come then.' The Kingdom was coming all the time." Quoted in Donald English, *The Message of Mark, The Bible Speaks Today* (Downers Grove: InterVarsity Press, 1992), 50.

12. Oscar Cullmann, *Christ and Time* (Philadelphia: The Westminster Press, 1964), 84.
13. John 2:1–11; Luke 5:4–11; Mark 6:30–44.
14. Craig Blomberg, *The Historical Reliability of the Gospels* (Downers Grove: InterVarsity Press, 1987), 93, 96.
15. John 10:10.
16. Revelation 21:21.
17. See also Isaiah 61:1–2.
18. Graham H. Twelftree, *Jesus the Exorcist* (Peabody: Hendrickson Publishers, 1993), 119.
19. Romans 8:23; Philippians 3:21.
20. Revelation 20:10–15. For the development of the viewpoint of Satan's destruction see Graham H. Twelftree, *Jesus the Exorcist*, 66, 219–220. See also Graham H. Twelftree, *Jesus the Miracle Worker* (Downers Grove: InterVarsity Press: 1999), 270, 389n73.
21. John 3:16; 10:28–29; 1 John 5:18; Jude 24; Revelation 21:4.
22. Peter T. O'Brien, *The Letter to the Ephesians*, The Pillar New Testament Commentaries (Grand Rapids: William B. Eerdmans Publishing Company, 1999), 458–459.

23. Galatians 1:4; Ephesians 1:7; Colossians 1:13–14; 1 Timothy 2:5; Hebrews 9:26–27; 10:12;
24. Luke 22:20; Hebrews 8:6–13; 9:1–18; 10:15–18; 12:24.
25. N. T. Wright, *The Challenge of Jesus* (Downers Grove: InterVarsity Press, 1999), 45, 70. Emphasis Wright's.
26. Matthew 12:18; Romans 3:21–26; 6:13; 10:4; 14:17; Ephesians 4:24; Philippians 1:11; 3:9.
27. C. Marvin Pate, *The End of the Age Has Come* (Grand Rapids: Zondervan, 1995), 82. Emphasis Pate's. But as Rabbi David Rosen clarifies, Jewish scholars commonly believed that a person had to be bad indeed to miss out on the blessings of the age to come: "Rabbinic Judaism as the heir of Pharisaic Judaism believes emphatically in the concept of the afterlife or continuity of the soul and the reward (i.e., the consequence of our good actions) that the soul enjoys accordingly. . . . Judaism teaches that righteous Gentiles, as righteous Jews, have their portion (reward) in the world to come. Moreover, in keeping with Judaic teaching regarding infinite compassion, great Jewish thinkers like Maimonides have believed that it takes an inordinately evil individual to destroy any goodness in his or her divine soul and thus of any reward/continuity." See "Letter 7," R. T. Kendall and David Rosen, *The Christian and the Pharisee* (New York: Faith Words, 2006), 64.

Furthermore, not all those of the Jewish faith in Jesus' day or our own would affirm the existence of an afterlife. The Sadducees of Jesus' day disbelieved in a resurrection and afterlife. And in our own day, Rabbi Harold Kushner represents an alternative Jewish viewpoint. Discussing the promise of immortality in a World to Come, he says: "I confess I have problems with that promise. First, I have to wonder how much of it is wishful thinking. The fact is, I don't know what happens to us after we die and neither does anyone else. Beyond that, much as I might want to live longer and regain the companionship of people I have loved and lost, an eternity which would be a lot like this life but would never end might be a little hard to take. . . . God cannot redeem me from death, no matter how good a person I am, but He redeems me from the fear of death so that I don't have to clutch frantically at this life as if it were all there is. He lights my path through 'the valley of the shadow of death' by assuring me that the words I have written and spoken, the hearts I have touched, the hands I have reached out to, the child I leave behind, will gain me all the immortality I need. More than that, I am assured that even when the last person who ever knew me dies, and the last copy of my book has been removed from the library shelf, the essential me, the nonphysical me, will still live on in the mind of God, where no act of goodness or kindness is ever forgotten." *Who Needs God* (New York: Pocket Books, 1989), 169, 173.

28. 1 Corinthians 15:20–58; Philippians 3:21; 2 Timothy 1:10; Revelation 21:4.

29. Mark 5:22–24; 35–42; Luke 7:11–15; John 11:1–44.

30. 2 Corinthians 5:17; Ephesians 4:22–24; 2 Peter 3:13; Revelation 2:17; 5:9; 14:3; 21:1,4–5.

31. Stephen Travis, *I Believe in the Second Coming of Jesus* (Grand Rapids: William B. Eerdmans Publishing Company, 1982), 212. Emphasis Travis's.

32. Acts 2:1–21; 1 Corinthians 3:16, 6:19; 2 Corinthians 6:16.

33. 2 Corinthians 1:22; 5:5; Ephesians 1:13–14.

34. O. Palmer Robertson, *The Israel of God* (Phillipsburg: P&R Publishing, 2000), 134.

35. Matthew 28:20; Hebrews 13:5; Revelation 21:3.

36. Galatians 3:8–9, 26–29; Ephesians 3:6; Revelation 5:9; 21:24–26.

37. Acts 10:36; Romans 5:1; 14:17; Galatians 5:22; Ephesians 2:14; 6:15; Philippians 4:7; Colossians 1:20; 3:15.

38. Andrew T. Lincoln, *Ephesians*, vol. 42, Word Biblical Commentary (Nashville: Nelson Reference & Electronic, 1990), 449.

39. Acts 2:31–36; 1 Corinthians 15:24–26; Ephesians 5:5; Philippians 2:9–11; Colossians 1:13; 1 Timothy 1:17; Hebrews 1:3, 8; 2:7–9; Revelation 11:15; 12:10.

40. George H. Guthrie, *Hebrews*, The NIV Application Commentary (Grand Rapids: Zondervan, 1998), 99.

41. Romans 8:14–19; Galatians 4:6; Hebrews 8:10–12; 1 John 2:3–14; 4:7; Revelation 19:7–9; 22:4.

42. Hebrews 4:16; 10:19–22.

43. Romans 5:5–8; 8:39; 1 Corinthians 13; 16:14; 2 Corinthians 5:14; Galatians 5:22; Ephesians 5:2; Colossians 3:14.

44. Tom Wright, *1 Corinthians*, Paul for Everyone (Louisville: Westminster John Knox Press, 2003, 2004), 177.

45. Luke 15; Galatians 5:22; Hebrews 12:2; 1 Peter 1:8–9; Revelation 12:11–12.

46. S. S. Smalley, "Joy," *New Dictionary of Biblical Theology*, eds. T. Desmond Alexander, Brian S. Rosner, D. A. Carson, Graeme Goldsworthy (Downers Grove: InterVarsity Press, 2000), 610.

47. Luke 9:32; John 1:14; 2:11; 11:4; Colossians 3:4; 1 Peter 4:13; 5:10; Revelation 21:11, 23, 26.

48. P. E. Enns, "Exodus," *New Dictionary of Biblical Theology*, eds. T. Desmond Alexander, Brian S. Rosner, D. A. Carson, Graeme Goldsworthy (Downers Grove: InterVarsity Press, 2000), 150.

49. Richard N. Longenecker, "The Return of Christ," *A Guide to Biblical Prophecy*, eds. Carl E. Armerding, W. Ward Gasque (Eugene: Wipf and Stock, 1977, 1989), 161.

50. Luke 9:23.

51. Luke 14:28–33.

52. Matthew 13:44–46.

53. I am indebted to my friend Scott Presson for the insight that Jed exemplifies our already/not-yet status in the overlap.

54. James Robert Ross, "Living Between Two Ages," *A Guide to Biblical Prophecy*, eds. Carl E. Armerding, W. Ward Gasque (Eugene, Wipf and Stock, 1977, 1989), 233.

Chapter Three: Living in the Light of the Kingdom

1. See George Eldon Ladd's helpful discussion on how Scripture describes people's activity with respect to the kingdom. George Eldon Ladd, *A Theology of the New Testament*, ed. Donald Hagner (Grand Rapids: William B. Eerdmans Publishing Company, 1974, revised 1993), 101–102.

2. Peter Kusmic, "History and Eschatology: Evangelical Views," *In Word and Deed*, ed. Bruce Nicholls (Grand Rapids: Wm. B. Eerdmans Publishing Company, 1985), 147–148. Emphasis Kusmic's.

3. Mortimer Arias, *Announcing the Reign of God* (Philadelphia: Fortress Press, 1984), xv.

4. Howard A. Snyder, *A Kingdom Manifesto* (Downers Grove: InterVarsity Press, 1985), 9, 12.

5. Gordon D. Fee & Douglas Stuart, *How to Read the Bible for All Its Worth* (Grand Rapids: Zondervan Publishing House, 1981, 1993), 133–134. Emphasis Fee's.

6. Titus 2:12–13; Philippians 1:6; Galatians 1:3–4; Romans 8:18; 1 Timothy 6:18–19.

7. I am indebted to Mortimer Arias for the insights concerning why the term "kingdom" becomes less prominent in the epistles. See Mortimer Arias, *Announcing the Reign of God* (Philadelphia: Fortress Press, 1984), 57–58, 62.

8. Lesslie Newbigin, *The Open Secret* (Grand Rapids: William B. Eerdmans Publishing Company, 1978, 1995), 40. I first encountered this quote in Arias, *Announcing*, 58.

9. Greg K. Beale: "The Eschatological Conception of New Testament Theology" in *Eschatology in Bible & Theology*, ed. Kent E. Brower and Mark W. Elliott (Downers Grove: InterVarsity Press, 1997), 18. Emphasis Beale's.

10. Ladd, *A Theology of the New Testament*, 522, 525. Ladd quotes Johannes Behm, *Theological Dictionary of the New Testament*, ed. Gerhard Kittel, trans. Geoffrey W. Bromiley, vol. 3 (Grand Rapids: Wm. B. Eerdmans Publishing Company, 1965), 449.

11. Some scholars argue that this verse is more properly translated as, "If anyone is in Christ, there is new creation." The new creation would thus refer not to the individual Christian but to the eschatological new creation (the new heaven and earth) which was predicted by Isaiah, and inaugurated by Jesus. See, for example David E. Garland, *2 Corinthians*, The New American Commentary (Nashville: Broadman & Holman, 1999), 286–288. My point—that we are not just readers of the story but characters in it—remains valid regardless of which interpretation is taken.

12. 1 Corinthians 15:6.

13. Russell D. Moore, *The Kingdom of Christ* (Wheaton: Crossway Books, 2004), 12.

14. George R. Beasley-Murray, *The Coming of God* (Exeter: The Paternoster Press, 1983), 16.
15. See Hartmut Beck and Colin Brown, "Peace," *Dictionary of New Testament Theology*, ed. Colin Brown, vol. 2 (Grand Rapids: Zondervan Publishing House, 1967, 1969, 1971), 777.
16. J. D. Douglas, ed., *Proclaim Christ Until He Comes* (Minneapolis: World Wide Publications, 1990), 30.
17. M. Scott Peck, *People of the Lie* (New York: Simon and Schuster, 1983), 182, 183.
18. 1 Peter 5:8; 2 Corinthians 4:4; John 8:44; 2 Corinthians 11:14.
19. Calvin Miller, *Disarming the Darkness* (Grand Rapids: Zondervan Publishing House, 1998), 79. Emphasis Miller's.
20. Clinton E. Arnold, *3 Crucial Questions about Spiritual Warfare*, (Grand Rapids: Baker Books, 1997), 32.
21. Arnold, *3 Crucial Questions*, 42–43.
22. Attributed to David Claydon, ed. J. D. Douglas, "Theology Implications of Radical Discipleship," *Let the Earth Hear His Voice*, 1974 Lausanne Congress (Minneapolis: World Wide Publications, 1975), 1294–1295. Emphasis Claydon's.
23. For a helpful way to develop a global perspective, see Patrick Johnstone, Jason Mandrick, and Robyn Johnstone, *Operation World* (Carlisle: Authentic Lifestyle, 2005). This daily guide to praying for the world gives information about the state of the gospel in virtually every nation. In addition to providing background information (about the economy, politics, etc.) of each country, it lists items for praise and prayer.

Chapter Four: Praying for Healing

1. Acts 19:11–12.
2. Philippians 2:25–28.
3. 2 Timothy 4:20.
4. Galatians 4:13–14.
5. Matthew 4:23; 9:35.
6. Mortimer Arias, *Announcing the Reign of God* (Philadelphia: Fortress Press, 1984), 3, 75.

7. Michael Green, *The Message of Matthew* (Downers Grove: InterVarsity Press, 1988, 2000), 86–87.

8. The atonement is the reconciliation of God and humankind brought about by Christ's death.

9. Charles Farah Jr., *From the Pinnacle of the Temple* (Plainfield: Logos International, n.d.), 35–36. Evangelist and scholar R. A. Torrey had a similar view. He said that those who see physical healing in the atonement are making a "fair inference" from Scripture. But he also argued that we cannot thereby claim physical healing from every infirmity in this life, because the full fruits of the atonement become ours only when Christ comes again. Yet he maintained, "We do get in many, many, many cases physical healing through the atoning death of Jesus Christ even in the life that now is." R. A. Torrey, *Divine Healing* (Grand Rapids: Baker Book House, 1924), 46–47.

10. An ancient Greek translation of the Old Testament.

11. Ancient Aramaic translations or paraphrases of the Old Testament.

12. Gordon D. Fee, *The Disease of the Health & Wealth Gospels* (Vancouver: Regent College Publishing, 1985, 2006), 23–25. Emphasis Fee's. This helpful booklet does an effective job of exposing the fallacies behind prosperity theology.

13. Matthew 8:14–15. For a helpful analysis of this passage and its implications for present day healings see D. A. Carson, *Jesus' Sermon on the Mount and His Confrontation with the World* (Grand Rapids: Baker Books, 1978, 1987), 168–172.

14. *Matthew*, 116–117.

15. Francis Schaeffer, *True Spirituality* (Wheaton: Tyndale House Publishers, 1971), 64. This highly recommended book is a lucid study of how the finished work of Christ on the cross brings us freedom.

16. I am indebted to Fee for the insight on James and Peter. See *Disease*, 24.

17. Fee, *Disease*, 34–35. Emphasis Fee's.

Chapter Five: Being Used by God

1. Exodus 3.

2. Joshua 6.

3. Acts 16:6–10.
4. Genesis 24.
5. Esther 2:21–23.
6. 1 Samuel 17.
7. I do not mean to minimize the importance of seeking God's guidance; seeking and expecting such guidance is paramount. But Scripture reveals more than one model for this situation. We see this in the life of Paul. At times God gave Paul specific instructions about where he should and should not minister (such as Acts 16:7–10), and Paul obeyed. Yet at other times, in the absence of a direct word from the Lord, Paul felt free to make a wise decision (such as Acts 20:2–3). There is no indication that these latter actions were less valid than those resulting from following God's overt instructions.

   The example of Luke is also instructive. We know that all writers of Scripture were inspired by the Holy Spirit (2 Peter 1:21; 2 Timothy 3:16). However, when Luke explained what motivated him to write his Gospel, he expressed no awareness of such inspiration. Instead he said he wrote the Gospel because it "seemed good" to write an orderly account of his subject matter.

   Thus it seems that following the Holy Spirit's inspiration and following our sanctified common sense are not necessarily mutually exclusive options; rather, at times they can be two sides of the same coin. God has a way of using godly people even when they are not conscious of his guidance.
8. Leighton Ford, *The Power of Story* (Colorado Springs: NavPress, 1994), 85. Emphasis Ford's.
9. Matthew 25:14–30.
10. Genesis 12, 20.
11. Genesis 26.
12. Joshua 2:1.
13. Exodus 2:11–12.
14. Genesis 9:20–27.
15. Genesis 27.
16. Judges 16.
17. 2 Samuel 11.

18. Oswald Chambers, *My Utmost for His Highest* (New York: Dodd, Mead & Company, Inc., 1935), 139.
19. Ron Lee Davis, *Gold in the Making* (Nashville: Thomas Nelson Publishers, 1984), 101–102. Emphasis Davis's.

Chapter Six: Loving Others

1. Michael Green, *The Message of Matthew* (Downers Grove: InterVarsity Press, 1988), 42.
2. George Eldon Ladd, *A Theology of the New Testament,* ed. Donald Hagner (Grand Rapids: William. B. Eerdmans Publishing Company, 1974, revised 1993), 130.
3. Luke 6:27–36.
4. It is true that the four Greek words had a wider range of meaning than popular contemporary usage generally recognizes. For example, *erōs* could refer to the passion of patriotism; *storgē* could refer to the devotion of people to their ruler; and both *philia* and *agapē* could refer to physical love. The Septuagint—a Greek translation of the Hebrew Scriptures, begun in the third century B.C.—even used *agapē* to refer to the "love" that drove Amnon to rape his half-sister Tamar (2 Samuel 13:1–21).

   It is also true that in New Testament times, in both biblical and nonbiblical literature, there was a substantial overlap of meaning between *philia* and *agapē* (which appear in the New Testament more often in their cognate verb forms *phileō* and *agapaō*). Thus a few New Testament passages use *phileō* to describe a higher love (God's love for his people, as well as Christians' love for God and for each other). This is seen in Revelation 3:19, 1 Corinthians 16:22, Titus 3:15, and John 16:27.

   Conversely, other New Testament passages use *agapaō* to depict less noble love. This is seen in 2 Timothy 4:10 (where Paul writes, "Demas, because he loved this world, has deserted me"), 2 Peter 2:15 (where Peter describes Balaam as one who "loved the wages of wickedness"), and John 3:19 where Jesus says, "men loved darkness instead of light"). Many, if not most, scholars see *phileō* and *agapaō* as synonyms in the New Testament.

Such considerations are especially pertinent when interpreting John 21:15–17. In this passage, Jesus asks Peter three times (twice using *agapaō* and once using *phileō*) if Peter loves him. All three times Peter replies affirmatively, using *phileō*. Scholars debate whether or not the two words are used synonymously here.

Because of these considerations—and the fact that the New Testament doesn't even use *erōs* or *storgē*—some scholars discourage using the four Greek words in a discussion of Christian love. But, since in contemporary usage the Greek words represent four major categories of love, I see merit in using them in this discussion.

For more information on love in the New Testament, see William Barclay, *New Testament Words* (Philadelphia: The Westminster Press, 1964, 1974), 17–21; also L. H. Marshall, *The Challenge of New Testament Ethics* (New York: St. Martin's Press, 1947, 1948, 1950, 1956), 104–107; Victor Paul Furnish, *The Love Command in the New Testament* (London: Abingdon Press/ SCM Press Ltd, 1972), especially 200–202, 219–231; Colin Brown, Walther Gunther, Hans-Georg Link, "Love," *The New International Dictionary of New Testament Theology*, ed. Colin Brown, et al., vol. 2 (Grand Rapids: Zondervan Publishing House, 1967, 1969, 1971, 1976), 538–551; and D. A. Carson, *Exegetical Fallacies* (Grand Rapids: Baker Books, 1996), 28–32, 51–53.

5. Though *erōs* does not appear in the New Testament, it does appear in the Septuagint (an ancient Greek translation of the Old Testament) in Proverbs 7:18; 30:16, and, in verb form, in Esther 2:17.

6. Though *storgē* itself does not appear in the New Testament, two compound words derived from it do appear. *Astorgos* ("without natural affection") appears in Romans 1:31 and 2 Timothy 3:3. *Philostorgos* ("loving dearly") appears in Romans 12:10.

7. William Barclay, 21–22. Emphasis Barclay's.

8. Keith Miller, *A Second Touch* (Waco: Word Books, 1967), 84–85. Emphasis Miller's.

9. Paul Ramsey, *Basic Christian Ethics* (New York: Charles Scribner's Sons, 1950), 99–100. Emphasis Ramsey's.

10. C. S. Lewis, *The Four Loves* (New York: Harcourt Brace Jovanovich, 1960), 135.

11. Tom Sine, *The Mustard Seed Conspiracy* (Waco: Word Books, 1981), 188.
12. Roger Mohrlang, "Love," *Dictionary of Paul and his Letters*, ed. Gerald F. Hawthorn and Ralph P. Martin (Downers Grove: InterVarsity Press, 1993), 578.
13. Leon Morris, *Testaments of Love* (Grand Rapids: William B. Eerdmans Publishing Company, 1981), 174–175.
14. Catherine Marshall, *Something More* (New York: Avon Books, 1974), 208–209.
15. D. L. Dykes, Jr., *The Power of Love* (Nashville: Abingdon Press, 1988), 18–19.

Chapter Seven: Keeping Our Focus

1. I have changed certain details, including his name, in order to disguise my friend's identity.
2. Matthew 6:25–33.
3. John 4.
4. Acts 2, 3, 10, 13.
5. For a clear presentation of this issue see C. S. Lewis, "Man or Rabbit?" *God in the Dock* (Grand Rapids: William B. Eerdmans Publishing Company, 1970), 108–113.
6. The Christian recognizes that other religions contain much that is admirable, and that many of their teachings are true. But ultimately, the Christian must insist on the uniqueness of Jesus. Some people try to minimize the differences between Christianity and other religions, arguing that all major religions are equally valid. A popular analogy says that religions are like different paths up the same mountain, all leading to God. However, this viewpoint is illogical and it devalues truth.

   It overlooks the fact that different religions give radically different—and often contradictory—explanations about such crucial things as the nature of God (or the gods), the universe, our responsibilities as human beings, the afterlife, sin, salvation, and the need for a Savior.

   A better analogy is that of a hospital emergency room. Suppose I am rushed to the hospital with extreme stomach pains. After a preliminary examination, one doctor says, "You have appendicitis. We need to perform an appendectomy or you will die." A second doctor says, "There's nothing wrong with your appendix. You've been poisoned. We have to pump out your stomach or you will die." A third doctor says, "Both of the other doctors are wrong. You just have a bad case of indigestion. We'll give you some antacid and send you home." It would be foolish for me to say, "It doesn't matter which of these options I choose. They're all equally valid paths up the same mountain of health." Instead, I would need to take more tests to find out the true cause of my condition, then take action to address that true cause.

Different religions offer different diagnoses of what is wrong with us, and different prescriptions for correcting it. They can't all be equally valid. If Religion A gives the true diagnosis, then Religions B, C, and D are true only insofar as they agree with Religion A; they are false insofar as they contradict Religion A. We owe it to ourselves and our creator to discover—and commit ourselves to—the religion that gives the true diagnosis.

Christianity makes the uncompromising diagnosis that, although God loves everyone and desires to have an intimate relationship with everyone, we have all sinned and our sin separates us from him. It also offers the prescription that salvation can be found through the Savior whom God has provided for everyone—Jesus Christ, who is the only way to God (John 3:16–18, 36; John 14:6; Acts 4:12; 1 Timothy 2:3–5; 1 John 5:11–12). If this is true, then everyone should accept it. If this is false, then everyone should reject it.

Some may object that such a view is "intolerant." But does tolerance require us to abandon our commitment to the truth? Suppose you tell a couple of friends that two plus two equals four, but one friend responds, "No, two plus two equals twelve," and the other friend responds, "No, two plus two equals six thousand." Does tolerance require you to affirm that all three views are equally valid? Or can you be a tolerant person while affirming that if X is true, anything that contradicts X must be false?

7. For a congenial look at evidence for Christianity, see Timothy Keller, *The Reason for God* (New York: Dutton, 2008). With a

respectful, skeptic-friendly approach Keller begins by discussing objections to Christianity (in chapters with titles such as "There Can't Be Just One True Religion," "How Could a Good God Allow Suffering?" and "Science Has Disproved Christianity"). Then he discusses reasons for faith in Christ. A thought-provoking work for both seekers and believers.

For another helpful work, see Dr. Gregory A. Boyd and Edward K. Boyd, *Letters from a Skeptic* (Colorado Springs: David C. Cook, 1994, 2008). It consists of a series of real-life letters exchanged between a skeptical father and his Christian son. They deal with a multitude of questions about the validity of the Christian faith. Through this correspondence the father forsook his agnosticism and became a Christian.

Also see Lee Strobel, *The Case for Christ* (Grand Rapids: Zondervan Publishing House, 1988). Strobel, former legal affairs editor of the *Chicago Tribune*, was an atheist who investigated the evidence that Jesus is the Son of God. In this book he presents his findings, which led him to become a Christian.

8. Wilbur E. Rees, *$3.00 Worth of God* (Valley Forge, PA: Judson Press, 1971), 5.
9. Adrian Plass & Paul McCusker, *You Say Tomato* (London: Marshall Pickering, 1995), 94.
10. Luke 14:28–32.
11. J. D. G. Dunn, "Repentance," *The Illustrated Bible Dictionary*, ed. J. D. Douglas, et al., vol. 3 (Wheaton: Tyndale House Publishers, 1962, 1980), 1327.
12. I. H. Marshall, "Disciple," *The Illustrated Bible Dictionary*, ed. J. D. Douglas, et al., vol. 1 (Wheaton: Tyndale House Publishers, 1962, 1980), 389.
13. Dallas Willard, *The Spirit of the Disciplines*, Harper & Row Publishers, 1988), 262–263, 265. I first encountered this quote in *Devotional Classics,* ed. Richard J. Foster and James Bryan Smith (San Francisco: HarperSanFrancisco, 1990, 1991, 1993), 16.
14. Matthew 13:44–46.
15. Matthew 19:24; Mark 10:25; Luke 18:25.

Chapter Eight: Building Fences

1. For an excellent overview of the Pharisees, see D. A. Hagner, "Pharisees," *Zondervan Pictorial Encyclopedia of the Bible*, ed. Merrill C. Tenney, et al, vol. 4 (Grand Rapids: Zondervan Publishing House, 1975, 1976), 745–752.
2. "Whitewashed tombs," etc.: Matthew 23.
3. Mark 3:6.
4. Christian sources are not alone in painting a mixed picture of Pharisees; the Jewish Talmud does the same. As Rabbi Yechiel Eckstein says, "This would correspond to the talmudic statement that classified the Pharisees into seven groups, six of which were regarded as self-righteous hypocrites, and the seventh, the most important one, being the 'Pharisees of love' of whom it is said, 'And none of them is beloved by God except the loving Pharisee, who is like Abraham.'" Yechiel Eckstein, *What You Should Know About Jews and Judaism* (Waco: Word Books, 1984), 257.
5. John 3:1–21; 7:45–52; 19:38–42.
6. As biblical scholar Stephen Westerholm says, "Since the scribe who admired Jesus' reply to the Sadducees was probably a Pharisee, the passage suggests that there were Pharisees whose views of what is fundamental overlapped substantially with those of Jesus." S. Westerholm, "Pharisees," *Dictionary of Jesus and the Gospels*, ed. Joel B. Green, Scot McKnight, I. Howard Marshall (Downers Grove: InterVarsity Press, 1992), 613.
7. Matthew 27:57–60; Mark 15:42–47; Luke 23:50–56; John 19:38–42. Joseph was a member of the Sanhedrin, the Jewish Supreme Court, which was primarily composed of Sadducees and Pharisees. It's more likely that Joseph was a Pharisee since they were theologically closer to Jesus than the Sadducees. (The Pharisees believed in angels and the resurrection of the dead, both of which the Sadducees denied.) Plus his association with the Pharisee Nicodemus would make it more likely that he was a Pharisee too.
8. Acts 5:33–40. Author's paraphrase.
9. Acts 15:5.
10. Acts 23:9.

11. James A. Brooks, *Mark*, The New American Commentary, (Nashville: Broadman Press, 1991), 198.

12. Matthew 23:37.

13. Matthew 12:39.

14. Matthew 17:17.

15. Scripture paints a complex picture of Jesus' relationship to the Pharisees. In his account of Jesus healing a blind man, John emphasizes that—rather than being united against Jesus—the Pharisees were divided in their response to him (John 9:16). Furthermore, Luke quotes some Pharisees warning Jesus to leave the area because Herod wanted to kill him (Luke 13:31). Some scholars see this as a ploy to scare Jesus into Galilee, where the Pharisees had more power. But others see it as a sincere effort to save Jesus' life.

16. R. V. G. Tasker, *The Gospel According to St. Matthew*, The Tyndale New Testament Commentaries (Grand Rapids: William B. Eerdmans Publishing Company, 1961), 215.

17. The image of making a fence around the Torah comes from the Mishnah (*Abot* 1.1), a code of rules formulated toward the end of the second century A.D. by Jewish sages, but representing oral tradition that came before.

18. Mishnah, *Shabbath* 7:2.

19. Babylonian Talmud, *Shabbath* 11a.

20. Babylonian Talmud, *Shabbath* 11a–11b.

21. Babylonian Talmud, *Shabbath* 149a.

22. Paul E. Little, *How to Give Away Your Faith* (Chicago: InterVarsity Press, 1966), 100–101.

23. F. F. Bruce, *The Letter of Paul to the Romans*, The Tyndale New Testament Commentaries (Grand Rapids: William B. Eerdmans Publishing Company, 1963, 1985), 230.

24. J. H. Hertz, Foreword to *The Babylonian Talmud*, vol. 1 (London: The Soncino Press, 1938). xv.

25. R. Kittel quoted in J. H. Hertz, Foreword to *The Babylonian Talmud*, vol. 1, xv. Emphasis Kittel's.

Chapter Nine: Walking by Faith

1. Matthew 21:21; Mark 11:22–23.

2. For example, Matthew 8:26; Matthew 16:8; Luke 12:28.

3. George Eldon Ladd, *A Theology of the New Testament*, ed. Donald Hagner (Grand Rapids: William B. Eerdmans Company, 1974, revised 1993), 631.

4. John 1:43–51.

5. Matthew 11:1–19.

6. Isaiah 35:5–6a; 61:1–2.

7. John 20:24–29.

8. I am indebted to my former pastor, Dr. Ken Hemphill, for the insight about this passage's possible relationship to Thomas.

9. John 11:16.

10. George MacDonald, *Unspoken Sermons*, Second Series, "The Voice of Job," quoted in *George MacDonald: An Anthology*, ed. C. S. Lewis (New York: Macmillan Publishing Company, Inc., 1947, 1974), 67.

11. Frederick Buechner, *Wishful Thinking: A Thinker's ABC* (San Francisco: HarperSanFrancisco, 1973, 1993), 23, 30.

12. Matthew 12:38; Mark 8:12.

13. John 3:19.

14. Luke 16:31.

15. Matthew 15:21–28.

16. Luke 17:11–19.

17. Luke 7:1–10; Matthew 8:5–13.

18. Luke 10:17.

19. Mark 4:36–41.

20. Matthew 14:22–34.

21. Matthew 17:14–23; Mark 9:14–29

22. Mark 9:24, NASB.

23. John 14:8–9.

24. Matthew 21:22.

25. John 15:7.

26. Joshua 24.

27. Nehemiah 9.

28. Two events in particular—Jesus' resurrection and the empowering of the Holy Spirit—go a long way in explaining the disciples' transformation.

29. Sheldon Vanauken, *A Severe Mercy* (San Francisco: Harper & Row, 1977), 98–99. Emphasis Vanauken's.
30. Acts 12:1–17.
31. 1 Corinthians 13:9–10, 12–13a, Scripture from THE MESSAGE. Copyright 1993, 1994, 1995, 1996, 2000, 2001, 2002. Used by permission of NavPress Publishing Group.
32. Leaps of faith and battles with doubt: See Philip Yancey, *Disappointment With God* (Grand Rapids: Zondervan Publishing House, 1988). This modern classic explores Christian faith through the eyes of those who doubt. With honesty and sensitivity, Yancey deals with three questions: Is God unfair? Is God silent? Is God hidden? A thought-provoking and enriching work. Also see the works by Keller, the Boyds, and Strobel recommended in the notes on chapter seven.

Chapter Ten: Working Together as a Body

1. For surveys of different evangelical viewpoints concerning this topic see Bonnidell Clouse & Robert G. Clouse, eds., *Women in Ministry: Four Views* (Downers Grove: InterVarsity Press, 1989) and James R. Beck, ed. *Two Views on Women in Ministry* (Grand Rapids: Zondervan, 2001, revised 2005).
2. Darrell L. Bock, "The Reign of the Lord Christ," *Dispensationalism, Israel and the Church*, Craig A. Blaising and Darrell L. Bock, eds. (Grand Rapids: Zondervan Publishing House, 1992), 65–66.
3. I'm speaking here of our mission toward other people. Additionally, as the *Westminster Shorter Catechism* says, "Man's chief end is to glorify God and to enjoy him forever" (A. 1.)
4. Frederick Buechner, *Whistling in the Dark* (San Francisco: Harper-SanFrancisco, 1998, 1993), 37–38.
5. Rebecca Manley Pippert, *Out of the Salt Shaker & into the World* (Downers Grove: InterVarsity Press, 1979), 15.
6. Robert T. Henderson, *Joy to the World* (Grand Rapids: Zondervan Publishing House, 1980, 1991), 27. Emphasis Henderson's.
7. "Evangelism Manifesto" of the Christian Reformed Church and Reformed Churches in America, Acts of Synod 1997, 1975, 639–640. I first encountered this document in Henderson, 38–39.

8. George Eldon Ladd, *The Gospel of the Kingdom* (Grand Rapids: Wm. B. Eerdmans Publishing Company, 1959), 64–65. Emphasis Ladd's.

Chapter Eleven: Discovering the Kingdom of God

1. All quotes in this chapter are the author's paraphrase, unless otherwise noted. This chapter combines details from all four Gospels, generally following the chronology of Donald Guthrie, *Jesus the Messiah* (Grand Rapids: Zondervan Publishing House, 1972). Guthrie's book is an excellent overview of the life of Jesus.

   Readers interested in background information about the story of Jesus may want to consult Craig S. Keener, *The IVP Bible Background Commentary: New Testament* (Downers Grove: InterVarsity Press, 1993. This unique commentary gives the cultural, social, and historical background for every passage in the New Testament.

   Historian Paul L. Maier has also produced several helpful books:

   In the Fullness of Time (Grand Rapids: Kregel Publications, 1991), looks at Jesus' birth and death, and the story of the early church, from the standpoint of conservative Christian scholarship. It's fascinating and exceedingly readable.

   Josephus: The Essential Works (Grand Rapids: Kregel Publications, 1988, 1994), is an easy-to-read translation and condensation of Josephus' *Antiquities* and *The Jewish War*, important ancient sources for shedding light on historical events chronicled in the Bible.

   The biographical novel *Pontius Pilate* (Grand Rapids: Kregel Publications, 1968, 1995) is a historically accurate and gripping portrayal of Pilate. This and *In the Fullness of Time* were especially helpful sources for the section in this chapter dealing with Jesus' trials.

2. Though Jesus did not have formal rabbinical training, he was considered a rabbi because of his teaching. *Rabbi* is a term of great respect for a teacher. See John 1:38.

3. Matthew 20:17–19.

4. Matthew 20:20–28.

5. Salome's identity as Jesus' aunt is deduced from Gospel accounts of the women at the foot of the cross. Apparently the same woman is identified as the mother of Zebedee's sons (Matthew 27:56), Salome (Mark 15:40), and Jesus' mother's sister (John 19:25). Since James and John were the sons of Zebedee, she would be their mother. However, not all scholars agree that these passages refer to the same person.

6. Although Scripture does not say that Joseph and Jesus worked in Sepphoris, it is a plausible assumption. See Richard A. Batey, *Jesus & the Forgotten City* (Grand Rapids: Baker Book House, 1991), 20, 70–76.

7. It is plausible that Jesus would have witnessed some of these crucifixions, though Scripture does not mention it. See William Barclay, *The Mind of Jesus* (New York: Harper & Row Publishers, 1960, 1961), 245.

8. John 4:1–42.

9. Galilee ministry: Mark 1:21–45; Luke 4:31–44; Matthew 4:23–25; 8:14–17.

10. John 5:16–18. For other instances of Sabbath healings see Matthew 12:9–14; Mark 3:1–6; Luke 6:6–11; 13:10–17; 14:1–6; John 9:1–34.

11. Matthew 5:10.

12. Luke 5:17–26.

13. Matthew 11:2–11; Luke 7:18–28.

14. John 1:29.

15. Matthew 3:11; Mark 1:7; Luke 3:16; John 1:33.

16. Luke 4:14–28; Matthew 13:53–58; Mark 6:1–6.

17. Luke 4:18–19 (NIV), rendering Isaiah 61:1–2a.

18. John 6:1–14; Luke 9:10–17.

19. Matthew 16:13–23.

20. Luke 9:28–36; Mark 9:2–10. Luke 9:31 refers to Jesus' "exodus," sometimes translated as "decease" or "departure." Luke's word choice is significant. As Leon Morris says, "The use of the word *exodos* for death is unusual and we should probably discern some Exodus typology. The Exodus had delivered Israel from bondage. Jesus by His 'exodus' would deliver his people from a far worse

bondage." Leon Morris, *The Gospel According to St. Luke*, The Tyndale New Testament Commentaries (Grand Rapids: Wm. B. Eerdmans Publishing Company, 1974), 172.

21. Luke 10:1–20. Some manuscripts put the number at seventy.

22. Luke 15.

23. Matthew 21:31–32.

24. Matthew 6:9.

25. Matthew 24:36–44.

26. Luke 17:21. I agree with those scholars who believe that Jesus was telling the Pharisees the kingdom was within their reach rather than "within them" (which would be an odd thing for Jesus to tell the Pharisees). See, for example, G. R. Beasley-Murray, *The Coming of God* (Exeter: The Paternoster Press, 1983), 30.

27. John 7:32, 45–46.

28. John 10:31–39.

29. John 11:1–45.

30. John 11:46–53. We must stress that this was not a case of "the Jews against Jesus." Unfortunately, sometimes certain Christians—unthinkingly and with no malice intended—may talk about "the Jews" doing this and that, as if the entire Jewish nation united against Jesus. We may need to remind ourselves that this is not the case, and that we owe an unpayable debt to the Jewish heritage. God chose the Jews as his beloved people. Through them we received our Scriptures and our Savior. Though the Gospels maintain that certain Jewish leaders helped engineer the death of Jesus, they are equally explicit in maintaining that many other Jews were ardent followers. In fact, the whole reason for a hasty night trial was to get a quick conviction before Jesus' many supporters—Jewish supporters—could discover what was happening and intervene. As Rabbi Samuel Sandmel says (while maintaining that "we Jews have been made to pay for what Romans did"): "Perhaps we might be willing to say to ourselves that it is not at all impossible that some Jews, even leading Jews, recommended the death of Jesus to Pilate. We are averse to saying this to ourselves, for so total has the charge been against us that we have been constrained to make a total denial. Yet if we admit—admit, not confess!—that some Jews were

involved, then why blame us all, both then and now? And since Jesus was a Jew, is it not reasonable to say that *people* killed Jesus, than to put the statement as though Jesus were not a Jew, but his opponents were? Is it not equally unfair to say the Americans killed Lincoln and Kennedy?" Samuel Sandmel, *We Jews and Jesus* (New York: Oxford University Press, 1965, 1973), 140, 141. Emphasis Sandmel's.

It is true that in his Gospel, John often uses the phrase "the Jews" in negative ways, but it's obvious to the careful reader that he's referring to certain hostile Jewish leaders, not to Jews in general. He also uses the phrase in positive ways. For example, he uses it when he refers to certain Jews—who were not yet believers in Jesus—mourning Lazarus' death (John 11:33, 45). Again, he quotes Jesus telling the woman at the well that "salvation is from the Jews" (John 4:22). We must choose our words carefully. We will never know the depths of tragedy sparked by Christians sweepingly—and erroneously—blaming "the Jews" for Jesus' death. It is not only historically inaccurate; it's theologically inaccurate as well. Theologically speaking, you and I played as much a role as anyone; Jesus died for our sins.

31. Luke 19:1–9.
32. John 11:55–57.
33. John 12:12–19; Matthew 21:1–11.
34. Mark 11:12–18.
35. Matthew 26:3–5.
36. Matthew 26:14–16.
37. John 13:1–17.
38. Isaiah 41:8–10; 42:1–9; 18–20; 43:10–13; 44:21–23; 45:4–7; 49:1–13; 50:4–11; 52:13–53:12. In discussing the Servant, I am indebted to John Bright, *The Kingdom of God* (Nashville: Abingdon Press, 1953, 1981), 146–155, 208–214.
39. Isaiah 49:6.
40. Matthew 26:26–29; Mark 14:22–25.
41. Acts 13:46–47.
42. It could have been more. John 18:12 uses a term that usually means a cohort of six hundred troops, but can mean a smaller band of

two hundred troops. Scholars debate whether this refers to the Jewish temple guard or to Roman troops. The number of soldiers sent to arrest Jesus is unclear. F. F. Bruce observes, "We need not suppose that every member of the cohort was called out on the present occasion, but evidently a sufficiently large detachment was sent to warrant the presence of the officer commanding the whole garrison." F. F. Bruce, *The Gospel of John* (Grand Rapids: Wm. B. Eerdmans Publishing Company, 1983), 340.

43. Matthew 26:36–56; Mark 14:32–51; Luke 22:39–53; John 18:1–11.

44. John 18:12–24.

45. Matthew 26:57–68; Mark 14:53–65; 15:1; Luke 22:54–71. The Gospel accounts of the trial before the Sanhedrin have sparked a controversy among scholars. Our information about the Sanhedrin's rules comes from the Mishnah. The Mishnah—a written outline of an oral law code—was completed about A.D. 200. There are a host of differences between the Sanhedrin's procedures as mandated in the Mishnah and as described in the Gospels. According to the Mishnah, the Sanhedrin could meet officially only in the Chamber of Hewn Stone. Capital cases could not be tried at night. In capital cases, the conviction could not be pronounced until the following day, so that after a night's thought and prayer the judges could reconsider the verdict. The court's procedures were designed to preserve the interests of the person on trial. The case began with arguments in favor of the person's acquittal. The accused's testimony could not be used to convict him. Death sentences were to be rare. It was said that a Sanhedrin that condemns one man to death in seven years was destructive. Rabbi Eliezer ben Azariah would have amended that to seventy years (Babylonian Talmud, *Yoma* 8b.).

These differences have led some scholars to allege that the trial as described in the Gospels could never have occurred. Others defend the accuracy of the Gospels and maintain that the trial was, therefore, illegal from top to bottom. But we should note several things with respect to this controversy.

First, many scholars argue that the Mishnah deals principally (or at least frequently) with a later Sanhedrin, and that we cannot be certain about which of its rules apply to the Sanhedrin of Caiaphas' day. There were two Sanhedrins: the old one that existed before Rome destroyed Jerusalem in A.D. 70, and a new one that developed afterwards in the city of Jamnia. The Gospels deal with the old one, and the Mishnah was compiled generations after the old one ceased to exist.

Thus, the German scholar Josef Blinzler says, "When the Mishna speaks of the Sanhedrin, it has in mind primarily or, at least, often this later institution, which definitely was not identical with the Old Sanhedrin." *The Trial of Jesus*, trans. Isabel and Florence McHugh (Westminster, MD: The Newman Press, 1959), 142. We should also note Raymond E. Brown's observation: "As for the Mishna's claim that the scholarly Beth-Din [Sanhedrin] it describes is an ancient institution, the Mishna is very often anachronistic in its assumptions, indeed even in the most basic assumption claiming great antiquity for the oral law stemming from Moses himself. The work of many recent Jewish scholars shows how hard it is to establish authentic pre-[A.D.] 70 situations from the Mishna. . . . The burden of proof is made much more heavy when 1st-cent. witnesses, both Christian and Jewish, describe a situation different from that envisaged by the Mishna." Raymond E. Brown, *The Death of the Messiah*, vol. 1 (New York: Doubleday, 1994), 346.

Scholars offer two major reasons for the differences between the procedures of the old and new Sanhedrins. First, it is argued that the old Sanhedrin was dominated by Saducean rules, whereas the new one was dominated by Pharisaic rules. Second, it is argued that the new Sanhedrin was reduced to being more of an academic institution than a fully functioning court.

Second, certain scholars argue that some of the Mishnah's rules represent an ideal to aim at, rather than a description of actual procedures. Therefore, religion professor George Foot Moore says, "These rules of procedure [making conviction of a capital offense nearly impossible] impress us as purely academic. . . . It cannot be imagined that any government charged with the maintenance of public order and security ever devised and put into practice a code of procedure the effect and intent of which was to make the conviction of criminals impossible. . . . The unreal character of the procedure should not, however, lead us to ignore the idea which inspired it." *Judaism*, vol. 2 (New York: Schocken Books, 1927, 1946), 187.

Third, even if the old Sanhedrin were bound by the Mishnah's rules, it would not seem out of character for Annas and Caiaphas to set them aside in this exceptional situation. The Gospels are not alone in painting an unflattering picture of their clan. "Woe to the house of Annas! Woe to their serpentlike hisses!" laments a Talmudic passage that characterizes certain high priestly dynasties as corrupt enemies of the people. Babylonian Talmud, *Pesachim* 57a, as translated in Maier, *In the Fullness of Time*, 139.

Fourth, even the more moderate members of the Sanhedrin may have believed that the end justified the means in this case. As New Testament scholar Raymond E. Brown says, "While there may well have been corruption among the high priests, much of this misses the point that if genuinely religious men decided that the law of God demanded the death of someone like Jesus, they would not have been villainous in finding the surest way to accomplish that." Raymond E. Brown, *The Death of the Messiah*, vol. 1, 422.

46. Deuteronomy 17:6.

47. Some scholars see this oath as a standard courtroom oath. But others see an applicable reference to a passage in the Mishnah (*Shebu'ot* 4:13), which says that a person is compelled to comply with an oath that uses the name of God. I believe the latter view better explains Jesus' initial silence, followed by his climactic confession (see Matthew 26:62–66).

48. Only Luke reports this (22:66–71). Darrell L. Bock points out, "There is some debate whether the Lukan scene is exactly the same as that in Matthew and Mark, since Luke alludes to a morning trial and Matthew and Mark describe a night examination. However, one of two things is happening here. Either Luke is relating the end of the trial before the council, whose decisive moments took place at daybreak, or the separate Lukan morning session was nothing more than a replay of what had occurred earlier that evening." Darrell L. Bock, "The Words of Jesus in the Gospels: Live, Jive,

or Memorex?" *Jesus Under Fire*, ed. Michael J. Wilkins and J. P. Moreland (Grand Rapids: Zondervan Publishing House, 1995), 87. Luke's language, together with Matthew and Mark's account of the early morning verdict (Matthew 27:1; Mark 15:1), seems to me to indicate a separate hearing. Therefore I have followed those scholars who see two hearings before the Sanhedrin.

49. What about Joseph of Aramathea and Nicodemus, judges who were sympathetic to Jesus? Luke says Joseph had not consented to the Sanhedrin's decision, implying either that he was not present or did not cast a guilty verdict (Luke 23:50–51). Some theorize that they must have abstained from voting. But other Scriptures indicate that the whole Sanhedrin—or at least all the members present—condemned Jesus (Matthew 26:59; Mark 14:53, 64; Luke 23:1). Perhaps the best explanation is that Caiaphas failed to summon judges who might be sympathetic to Jesus.

50. Matthew 27:11–31; Mark 15:1–20; Luke 23:1–25; John 18:28–19:16.

51. Josephus, *Antiquities* 18:55–59, *The Jewish War* 2:169–174.

52. Josephus, *Antiquities* 18:62, *The Jewish War* 2:175–177.

53. Philo, "On the Embassy to Gaius," xxxviii, 299–305. Scholars are uncertain whether the shields' incident took place before or after the crucifixion. The date of the shields' affair is unknown, and the two most plausible dates for the crucifixion are A.D. 30 and A.D. 33. But a strong case can be made that the shields' incident preceded the crucifixion, especially if we accept the later date for the crucifixion. The argument for a crucifixion date of A.D. 33 is supported by the fact that Lucius Aelius Sejanus was removed from power and executed in a.d. 31. Sejanus, a Roman noble who had virtually become co-ruler of the empire, and who Philo portrays as anti-Semitic, may have been Pilate's patron. This would help explain the lack of support Pilate could expect from Rome. Yet even if the crucifixion took place before the shields incident, Pilate was still in a precarious position. We should also note that some scholars believe Philo's account is biased against Pilate.

54. Some scholars believe that the procedure of having the defendant tried by the authorities of his home province was not an option

until after the time of Jesus. If this is correct, presumably Pilate sent Jesus to Antipas to get Antipas' unofficial opinion on the situation before Pilate would render a final verdict. Since Pilate's initial investigation led him to believe Jesus was innocent, he was giving Antipas an opportunity to produce evidence of his guilt. Thus he was still looking for Antipas to provide a way out of his dilemma. See Raymond E. Brown, *The Death of the Messiah*, vol. 1, 764–768.

55. Luke 23:8–12.

56. The Romans had three degrees of beatings: the *fustigatio*, which was the least severe and often accompanied by a warning; the *flagellatio*, which was more severe; and the *verberatio*, which was most severe and always combined with other punishments including crucifixion. See George R. Beasley-Murray, *John*, Word Biblical Commentary, vol. 36, (Nashville: Thomas Nelson Publishers, 1999), 335–336. Scholars debate which degree of punishment Pilate's men administered in this case. But as F. F. Bruce says, "any beating carried out by Roman soldiers was brutal enough." F. F. Bruce, *The Gospel of John* (Grand Rapids: Wm. B. Eerdmans Publishing Company, 1983), 358. And in Jesus' case it had to be vicious enough to turn the mob around.

57. The Jewish historian Josephus reports two subsequent events that shed light on the potential consequences of Pilate's decision. First, in A.D. 35 a pseudo-messiah tried to assemble a multitude of armed followers on Mount Gerizim in Samaria, announcing that he would dig up sacred vessels Moses had allegedly buried there. But Pilate's soldiers blocked their access to the site. They battled, resulting in civilian deaths. The leaders of the revolt were executed. The Samaritan council protested to Pilate's superior, Vitellius the governor of Syria. He replaced Pilate with another prefect and ordered him to return to Rome to defend himself before Tiberius Caesar. However, before Pilate arrived, Tiberius died. Pilate then faded from history. We don't know what happened to him after that. Despite the tradition that Pilate committed suicide (and a host of legends alleging various other consequences), there are no historical records of Pilate's life after returning to Rome. Yet we

should note that he lost his position precisely because the people he governed protested to his superior about Pilate's handling of an inflammatory situation. (Josephus, *Antiquities*, 18:87–89.)

The second event took place after Gaius succeeded Tiberius as emperor. He appointed Petronius to replace Vitellius, and ordered Petronius to erect a statue of Gaius in the Jerusalem temple. Thousands of Jews protested, and Petronius capitulated to them. He wrote Gaius a letter, advising him that unless he wanted to tear the country apart he should rescind the order. The letter infuriated Gaius and he ordered Petronius to commit suicide. Fortunately for Petronius, bad weather delayed the ship carrying Gaius' message. Before it arrived, another ship had brought news that Gaius had been assassinated. Thus only by a hair's breadth did Petronius escape the compulsory suicide ordered by an irate emperor. If Pilate had displeased Caesar, he could have faced a similar fate. (*Antiquities*, 18:257, *The Jewish War*, 2:184.)

58. Though the victims were usually naked, some scholars think it possible that in Palestine Rome may have made a concession to Jewish religious scruples against nudity and allowed victims to wear loincloths.

59. Matthew 27:32–56; Mark 15:21–41; Luke 23:20–49; John 19:17–37.

60. These are the first words as recorded by Luke (23:34), and they appear first in many harmonies of the crucifixion accounts.

61. Though the accounts of the crucifixion do not tell us how Jesus was anchored to the cross, his post-resurrection appearances indicate that both his hands (or wrists) and feet had been nailed. See Luke 24:39 and John 20:25–27. See also Psalm 22:16, which prefigures Jesus' crucifixion.

62. The frequent rendering, "It is finished" dilutes the meaning of the single Greek word John uses (John 19:30). As George R. Beasley-Murray points out, the verb "fundamentally denotes 'to carry out' the will of somebody, whether of oneself or another, and so to fulfill obligations or carry out religious acts. 'It is *accomplished!*' renders that aspect of the word." George R. Beasley-Murray, *John*, Word Biblical Commentary, ed. David A. Hubbard and

Glenn W. Barker, vol. 36 (Nashville: Thomas Nelson Publishing, 1999), 352. Emphasis Beasley-Murray's.

63. I am following Dorothy L. Sayers in supposing the disciples stayed in Bethany. See Dorothy L. Sayers, *The Man Born to be King* (London: Victor Gollancz Ltd., 1944), 317.

64. Matthew 27:57–28:20; Mark 15:42–16:20; Luke 23:44–24:53; John 19:38–20:31.

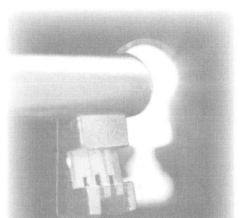

RECOMMENDED READING

New Testament Studies:

George Eldon Ladd. *A Theology of the New Testament*. Grand Rapids: Wm. B. Eerdmans Publishing Co., 1974, revised 1993. This classic work, updated under the supervision of editor Donald A. Hagner, provides an outstanding introduction to the already/not-yet orientation of the New Testament. The average reader can skip the scholarly Introduction (chapter one), which deals with the history of New Testament theology and with Biblical theology in general. However, I know of no better guide to the inaugurated eschatology of the New Testament than this lucid survey.

Tom Wright. *". . . for Everyone"* New Testament series. Louisville: Westminster John Knox Press, 2001+. British theologian N. T. "Tom" Wright's series of guides (such as *Matthew for Everyone*) are geared toward the lay person and deal sensitively with the New Testament's already/not-yet viewpoint.

John R. W. Stott, editor. *The Bible Speaks Today* New Testament series. Downers Grove: InterVarsity Press. There's considerable variety in the authorship and format of each volume in this series (all of which are entitled with the introductory phrase, "The Message of . . ." such as *The Message of Matthew* by Michael Green). But despite this variety, many of the volumes effectively highlight the already/not-yet orientation of the books they survey.

Biblical Interpretation:

Gordon D. Fee and Douglas Stuart. *How to Read the Bible for All Its Worth.* Grand Rapids: Zondervan, 1981, 1993, 2003. I consider this book to be "must reading" for every Christian, especially Christian workers such as Bible study leaders and Sunday school teachers. Fee and Stuart discuss the various genres of literature that appear in Scripture and they offer solid principles for interpreting each genre. Chapter seven offers a clear, concise explanation of the Gospels' already/not-yet foundation.

D. Brent Sandy. *Plowshares and Pruning Hooks.* Downers Grove: InterVarsity Press, 2002. Though it doesn't deal with Scripture's already/not-yet viewpoint to the extent of the other works listed here, this book is a valuable resource for anyone interested in understanding the enigmatic language of prophetic literature.

End Times Studies:

Daniel J. Lewis, *3 Crucial Questions about the End Times.* Grand Rapids: Baker Books, 1998. Grounded in the New Testament's teaching about the overlap of the ages, this helpful book examines what Scripture teaches about the last days and Christ's return. At a time when scripturally irresponsible teaching abounds on this subject, Lewis's perceptive and balanced book deserves a wide audience.

Spiritual Warfare:

Clinton E. Arnold. *3 Crucial Questions about Spiritual Warfare.* Grand Rapids: Baker Books, 1997. Based upon the New Testament's teaching about the overlap, this book provides a solid foundation for understanding spiritual warfare. Practical and wise counsel from one of evangelicalism's foremost scholars on this subject.

Healing and Prosperity:

Gordon D. Fee, *The Disease of the Health and Wealth Gospels*. Vancouver: Regent College Publishing, 1985, 2006. In three brief chapters ("The 'Gospel' of Prosperity," "The 'Gospel' of Perfect Health," and "The New Testament View of Wealth and Possessions") this eminent scholar refutes the unbiblical teaching that God guarantees financial prosperity and perfect health to those who claim them in faith. His refutation rests on the biblical reality of the already/not-yet kingdom.

Biblical Introduction:

Craig G. Bartholomew and Michael W. Goheen, *The Drama of Scripture*. Grand Rapids: Baker Academic, 2004. A retelling of the biblical story from Genesis to Revelation, highlighting Scripture's emphasis on the kingdom of God. A first-rate, succinct, and reader-friendly introduction to the Bible and its already/not-yet kingdom theme.